The Anatomist

The Anatomist

The autobiography of
Anthony Sampson

POLITICO'S

First published in Great Britain 2008 by
Politico's Publishing, an imprint of
Methuen Publishing Ltd
8 Artillery Row
London
SW1P 1RZ

10 9 8 7 6 5 4 3 2 1

A CIP catalogue record for this book is available from the British Library.

ISBN 978-1-84275-227-2

Set in Baskerville by SX Composing DTP, Rayleigh, Essex
Printed and bound in Great Britain by The Cromwell Press, Trowbridge, Wiltshire

To Nadine Gordimer

Contents

	List of illustrations	ix
	Foreword by Peter Hennessy	xi
	Preface by Sally Sampson	xv
1	Englishness	1
2	Drum	17
3	Observer	43
4	Anatomy	69
5	The other Africa	86
6	'Only connect'	109
7	Young Europeans	117
8	The boss from Hell	135
9	Nixon's America	147
10	The power of oil	159
11	New merchants of death	170
12	Saving the world?	182
13	Breaking the mould	193
14	Money kings	207
15	Revolutionaries and capitalists	220
16	Mandela	235
17	The fire and the rose	256
	Notes	261
	Bibliography	267
	Index	269

List of illustrations

First section
1. AS's father, Michael Sampson, as a young man.
2. AS's mother, Phyllis Seward, as a nurse during the First World War.
3. AS's parents' wedding, 17 March 1923.
4. With his parents, 1926.
5. In front of Downing College, Cambridge, *c*.1928, where his grandfather was master.
6. With his sister, Dorothy, and his brother, John, on holiday at Swanage, 1936.
7. On holiday in Suffolk with his mother and sister, *c*.1938.
8. In a school production of *Henry IV, Part 2* as the Archbishop of York, 1943.
9. Oliver Tambo and Nelson Mandela, ambitious young lawyers in the 1950s.
10. Jim Bailey, co-founder of *Drum*, at his desk in the magazine's office.
11. The editor of *Drum* at his desk.
12. Henry Nxumalo.
13. Jürgen Schadeberg.
14. Can Themba.
15. Todd Matshikiza.
16. The *Drum* office in Johannesburg.
17. Father Trevor Huddleston, a close friend of *Drum*.
18. David Astor, proprietor and editor of the *Observer*.
19. Promoting *The New Anatomy of Britain* in 1965 at a Hodder & Stoughton sales conference, with Robin Denniston, AS's publisher and friend since schooldays.

20. Norland Cottages, Walberswick. AS wrote his first Anatomy at No. 8, his mother's cottage.
21. In the garden of Valley Farm, Walberswick, early 1970s.

Second section

22. 'The Listener': with Sally and Louisa Lasdun.
23. In the study in Ladbroke Grove, 1991.
24. Lecturing on the British press at Vincennes.
25. With Sheikh Yamani after publication of *The Seven Sisters*, 1975.
26. With his Brandt commission colleague Kay Graham.
27. Willy Brandt.
28. AS and Sally at the Oriental Hotel, Bangkok.
29. David Owen, Shirley Williams and Bill Rodgers at the 1984 SDP annual conference in Buxton.
30. With David Owen and Oliver Tambo, 1985.
31. Nelson Mandela and Oliver Tambo meet for the first time in more than 28 years, Stockholm, March 1990.
32. Oliver Tambo's handwritten note that accompanied the photograph above.
33. AS and Mandela meet at the Dorchester Hotel, July 1996.
34. AS and Trevor Huddleston. They remained friends for life.
35. Celebrating Jim Bailey's CBE, May 1996.
36. With Katie, Ladbroke Grove, *c.*1991.
37. With his granddaughter, Anna, on his 75th birthday, 2001.
38. Aboard his grandfather's caravan, *Esmeralda*, which he had restored, 1991.

Foreword

Of few journalists and authors can it be said that they shaped the mind of a generation. Anthony Sampson did. Mine. For the young, ambitious meritocrats – children of Rab Butler's 1944 Education Act – who filled the sixth forms in the 1960s, Anthony's first two Anatomies of Britain were the keys which opened our minds to how our country operated, and, in some cases, they became an aid to deciding which profession we wished to pursue. For Anthony, too, was a natural social anthropologist. He penetrated, uncovered and explained the then ruling tribes in Britain with such brilliance that we, Rab's children, who had never met a Cabinet minister, a permanent secretary or a top industrialist or banker, when we finished our first Anatomy actually sensed that we knew them, or, at least, would recognise members of these tribes when we eventually met them. Anthony passed the Zadie Smith test – that a writer can't just *know*, he or she has to *feel* – with distinction.

Anthony Sampson was the epitome of an old English courtesy, modesty and understatement that has now almost entirely disappeared from a public life saturated with celebritocracy rather than meritocracy (in which he powerfully believed) and peopled, largely if not wholly, by what Antony Jay, co-author of *Yes, Minister*, calls 'non-ebrities'. Yet, for all the self-doubt revealed in this remarkable book, every subject to which Anthony applied himself he passed with flying colours. And his range was enormous – not just his own country but South Africa (which one feels was his second country), the global reach of multinationals, the oil and arms trades, and the Europe of the Six in the years just before the UK joined. He was also an ace biographer – of Harold Macmillan, his 'study in ambiguity', on a small scale, and his friend Nelson Mandela on a huge one.

Anthony was, as he says on page 259, 'driven by curiosities in every direction'. And his curiosity was contagious, which is why he was, and will remain for a long time, such a marvellous example to aspiring or tyro journalists. He stands four square against the trash-laden tide of lifestyle and celebrity journalism. But what were the key ingredients of the Sampson tradecraft?

First, he was the master of the slow-burn, long-haul approach. He went for real kills as opposed to quick kills. Like I. F. Stone in Washington (whom he much admired), Anthony read everything – and then started digging. As Neal Ascherson said at Anthony's memorial service,

> I never knew such an artist at questioning. Anthony was the most skilful, relentless listener in the world. Sometimes I watched him at it. He hardly seemed to speak himself: just the odd interrogative mutter. And the subject would grow trusting. And do the talking. 'Yerss,' Anthony would murmur, and nod in apparent sympathy. But he always kept that direct gaze trained into the other's eyes. Irresistible!

Anthony never underestimated the importance of people but always knew, too, the indispensability of understanding institutions, systems and processes – of how revealing sloggy routine could be for those determined to understand how things actually worked. He also felt the pull of the past, tradition as shaper, especially in an ancient polity like the UK.

On first acquaintance, Anthony was the incarnation of the quiet courtesy of old-style British rulership – the very model of the highest-minded district commissioner of Empire days. Yet he was very uneasy about all of that. It was Anthony's living on the rim of insiderdom/outsiderdom which gave him a real edge as an observer of his own country. But that gentlemanly, modest and slightly self-ironic style of his made Anthony especially effective. Curiosity + courtesy = confidences; that was his secret equation. And people *did* confide in him – in droves, over decades.

Anthony did not preach or proselytise, but there was no finer mentor if you sought his advice. When I was setting out on my first big book, *Whitehall*, in the 1980s (for which the Anatomies had been a direct inspiration), we had lunch together. 'Tell me the pitfalls,' I said. 'Well,' said Anthony, 'it's like transatlantic oarsmanship. The bad time will come when you're 1,500 miles out of Falmouth and there's still 1,500 miles to go to Newfoundland.' He was absolutely right. I don't think he ever fully realised how much he meant to fellow-journalists or authors. Those who knew him will hear the special Anthony once more in the pages which follow. Those who did not will realise why he meant so much to his contemporaries and why no serious treatment of the history of Britain in the second half of the twentieth century can ever be complete without a full appreciation of the Sampson style and Sampsonian insights. For Anthony was not just *the* anatomist; he was an artist, a painter of people, mood and episode. A truly distinctive and special man.

Peter Hennessy
Attlee Professor of Contemporary British History
Queen Mary, University of London
June 2008

Preface

'Why don't you write your memoirs?' Anthony's friends and colleagues would constantly nag. 'You've had such an interesting life.' As a reporter who hated recent 'look at me' tendencies in journalism, writing in the first person did not come easily to him. But finally in 1998 he sat down at his computer and started a first draft, which he put aside in order to write his polemic against Blairism and the Iraq War, *Who Runs This Place?*, published early in 2004. Between then and his unexpected death from a heart attack in December of that year, Anthony returned to his memoirs, and began trying to bring a more personal touch to the story of how he came to be a writer after an outwardly conventional upbringing in Hampstead and education at Westminster and Oxford. There is some candid self-revelation, but essentially it is a record of an extraordinarily varied and exciting working, rather than private, life. Although he loved parties and the company of family and friends, Anthony was a reserved man.

As a writer and journalist, Anthony was driven not so much by ambition as by a determination to find out the truth and tell it in a way that everyone could understand. As one of his researchers put it, 'he made journalism exciting, important and fun. He knew all about the fickle attention of readers, and showed us ways to hook them in.' (Many of those researchers went on to be successful journalists in their own right.) Whether he was writing a gossipy paragraph about bishops for Pendennis in the *Observer* or the Brandt report about the stark divide between the northern and southern hemispheres, Anthony was always clear and readable, and he got to the point fast. Because of his Cambridge family background, he occasionally felt guilty about not being more scholarly; but his skills in communication were extraordinary. He cultivated the art of quiet, persistent listening, and people confided in him freely. His friend and mentor, the American lawyer Jerry

Levinson, wrote to me: 'If there is a single word to sum him up, I would say it is trust. You just knew that he would treat information with discretion . . . He had a gift for taking otherwise dry and academic material and bringing it to life.'

Anthony's productivity was enormous, partly thanks to self-discipline and total professionalism: in forty years of marriage, I never saw him miss a deadline, whether for an op-ed piece on the arms trade for the *Daily Mail* ('by lunchtime at the latest, please!') or for a biography of Nelson Mandela. Every day, more often than not including weekends, he would be in his study at his typewriter or computer by 9 a.m. (5.30 a.m. in the last months of his life), where he would light up a large Havana cigar, his only major extravagance; he did not emerge until lunchtime, when he would usually head for his delightfully eccentric club, the Beefsteak, up a staircase just off Leicester Square, where he would pick up the latest political gossip and chat with old friends like the historians Hugh Thomas and Thomas Pakenham or the wine wizard Tom Jago. In later years, he would stroll across Piccadilly to the London Library for an afternoon browse on a comfortable leather sofa, then home for a couple of hours' writing or seeing callers who came to pick his brains. He was always very happy to give advice, especially to young people starting a career in journalism: 'The vital thing is to have curiosity,' he would say. He would emerge from his study at around 6 p.m., to watch the news on television and catch up on the children's activities or my ups and downs at work over a glass of wine before dinner. Friends from abroad constantly came and went, bringing news from a wider world: informed gossip was part of Anthony's bloodstream, and vital to his writing.

We would often spend the school holidays travelling with the children in Europe or America, but by the early 1980s Anthony seemed to be perpetually in the air, jetting to and from Tokyo or New York or Riyadh. This took its toll on family life, but also on Anthony's health: at his sixtieth birthday party in 1986 he looked tired and pale, and complained about approaching old age. Two years later he had a major heart attack, followed by a quadruple bypass at New York Hospital, described in Chapter 17. This gave him new priorities in life, though it did not prevent him from writing major books, including the authorised biography of Nelson Mandela, which took us on an exciting quest for information in South Africa and involved tireless, patient research. In a more personal vein, he wrote *The Scholar Gypsy*, an affectionate portrait of his bohemian grandfather John Sampson, lexicographer of the Romani language, bigamist and friend of Augustus John. Anthony also found time to chair the Society of Authors from 1992 to 1994 and joined the Independent Newspapers International Advisory Board. He mellowed, and rejoiced in the birth of his grandchildren, but at the same time became more radical with old age, marching with our daughter Katie against the Iraq War and writing articles attacking the government's gradual erosion of civil liberties. His final Anatomy of Britain, *Who Runs This Place?*, is an angry book of which Simon Jenkins wrote in his review: 'He has stood back from the trees and given us a view of the wood. He is right to find it rotten.'

But the moral linchpin of Anthony's life was his involvement with South Africa, which began in 1951 when, summoned by telegram by his eccentric Oxford friend Jim Bailey, he set sail for Cape Town to become editor of *Drum* magazine. As he makes clear in these memoirs, *Drum* transformed his life from grey to glorious Technicolour, and left him with a lifelong gratitude and commitment to his friends in South Africa and to the ANC, to which, as this book shows, he gave his unstinting support while it was in exile. ANC friends flowed into our house in Ladbroke Grove, and made contact with important British politicians and businessmen through Anthony's broker-age. In his speech about Anthony at a memorial event at the Nelson Mandela Foundation in Johannesburg our son Paul recalled watching a football Cup Final on television in our sitting-room with Thabo Mbeki, a fellow-fan of the game. At that same memorial, Mandela himself remembered reading *Anatomy of Britain* while in prison and described Anthony as 'in many ways so English and in so many ways so African'. He also told Paul: 'You chose a very good father.'

In April 2006, Anthony was awarded a posthumous Order of the Companions of O. R. Tambo in Silver for his 'excellent contribution to South African journalism and fighting for the ideals of freedom and justice'. Katie and I were flown out to Pretoria to receive the award (a silver medal, a ceremonial wooden staff and a scroll) at a magnificent, very African ceremony. The official booklet that accompanied the ceremony contains the following words:

Sampson proved that the unity of humanity is not defined by the place of one's birth. He came to South Africa from England with a mission to contribute to the liberation of humanity. His bold and principled writing stirred the consciousness of many, increasing an awareness of apartheid among many white South Africans.

Anthony wrote all the chapters in the book himself; many of them had been completed, but some were still in draft form. Several of the chapters had been rewritten and there was also extra material for which it was not always clear in which chapter it belonged. I worked on the text and helped to revise the book.

The first draft was delivered to Politico's, where Alan Gordon Walker and Jonathan Wadman began detailed work on the structure of the book. The essential process ran to several months as the text took its final shape, with attention to the order and completion of the chapters themselves, followed by the essential editing process and the selection of the illustrations. I am most grateful for all their work and the final result is a book of which I am sure Anthony would have been proud. It was his expressed wish that his autobiography should be published.

I would also like to thank Peter James for his help and advice to Anthony at the first stage, Graham Greene and Peter Hennessy, who made this book possible, Nadine Gordimer for permission to quote from her letters to Anthony, and Anne Chisholm for her wise advice. But above all, my thanks go to Katie and Paul Sampson and Anthony's sister, Dorothy Meade, for all their help and support.

The royalties from this autobiography will be paid to the Anthony Sampson Foundation in South Africa, set up with the aim of encouraging good investigative reporting by Africans in a country which was his second home.

Sally Sampson
July 2008

1

Englishness

Childhood

It had seemed a quite conventional, secure childhood. We lived in a big house in Hampstead, with a cook and sometimes a nanny or a governess, and a garden where I played with my elder sister and younger brother, rolling down the sloping lawn and climbing up to the tree-top house. My mother, a loving and anxious person with a talent for watercolours, came from an academic, artistic background. She had been brought up in the self-enclosed world of Cambridge academics before 1914, where her father, Sir Albert Seward, was a professor of geology and later master of Downing College and vice-chancellor of the university. Sometimes we would spend holidays with him in the master's lodge, whose grand staircase was out of bounds to children; so we ran around behind the green baize door and up the back stairs, welcomed by the fat cook and the thin maid. There was a huge-seeming garden with a loveable stone lion called Leo, and my grandfather would take us round the Botanic Garden, which was his kingdom, showing us magical plants including one with petals which folded to capture insects.

We spent our happiest holidays at the seaside village of Walberswick in Suffolk, a children's paradise where we could hunt for agates and cornelians along the wide beach, and cross the river on the rattling steam ferry to Southwold, with its lighthouse, tea shops and a pier full of games. Walberswick, where my grandmother had owned a house, had been a favourite retreat for artists and also the families of Cambridge professors, who arrived by a little train that chuffed from Halesworth to Southwold across the common. The railway had closed down; but we could still bicycle along the track and across the bridges, and the deserted stations still had sheds housing the old railway carriages and engines with tall funnels, which we climbed over. The village still evoked the lost world of artists like Philip Wilson Steer or Charles Rennie Mackintosh, who had painted in the black huts which still stand along the river. (Behind my desk I have a small but magical watercolour by Steer of children sitting on the dunes.)

My mother was always nostalgic for the world of Cambridge and Walberswick and her old artist friends from the Slade, where she studied painting under Professor Henry Tonks, or the families of professors from the intellectual and scientific aristocracy – Darwins, Huxleys, Barlows or Keyneses. But she was abruptly removed from this sequestered life when she married my father, a research scientist from Liverpool whom she met at Cambridge. She often recalled the shock of moving from the Downing College master's lodge to the small, bleak company house at 1 Mill Lane in the new ICI ammonia town of Billingham-on-Tees, where I was born. (I still have the watercolour she painted of a steam roller preparing a new road in the forsaken landscape with factory chimneys in the background.) In Billingham she was soon surrounded by inarticulate scientists and brash corporate managers, who had no time for art or academia. They were engrossed in building up the great chemical works, which then seemed – to Aldous Huxley among others – the forerunner of a rational new universe of imperial science. My parents moved to Hampstead soon afterwards, where my mother found artistic friends like the Carringtons; but my father was still immersed in the world of ICI and science. I was always conscious of the rival pulls of those two magnetic fields, of individual art and corporate science, and remained half-fascinated by the benign empire of ICI. I always remember visiting my father in the imposing new ICI palace on the Thames at Millbank, with its great nickel doors decorated with images of industry. Inside I found my father in an awesome office protected by a secretary with a chattering teleprinter, in an atmosphere of grandeur and authority which he never enjoyed at home.

I was always daunted by my father, a tall handsome man with an intimidating nose and chin but gentle blue eyes, who seemed imprisoned in himself. In Hampstead he retreated into his study, where he made models of molecules with Meccano and listened to Brahms and Mahler. He was a chain-smoker, always coughing, and had a cigarette machine installed in the hall. He was aloof from his three children, never touching or kissing them. He distrusted all emotion, and enveloped himself in silences which cast a pall over the family: I tried telling jokes from Christmas crackers but he took them very literally. I was amazed to come across other families where the parents were always talking and laughing. My father was always pessimistic, exasperating my mother because he would not look forward to anything: when I once asked him about happiness he quoted Solon: 'Call no man happy until he is dead.'

He had reason to be gloomy about the world: he had been wounded and gassed in the First World War, when he won the Military Cross on the Somme, and his brother had been killed in the Royal Flying Corps. Memories of the war haunted our parents' friends: 'Why do people keep on talking about the war?' I asked my mother. And by the mid-1930s my father was talking about another.

I felt different from other boys. I was shy and awkward, clumsy with bats and balls, very conscious of being left-handed with all it meant: gauche, maladroit and sinister. I was easily rebuffed and retreated into long sulks: I was much less nice than my elder sister, Dorothy, or my young brother, John. I was afraid of the dark: our house had a cavernous cellar, and in bed at night I was terrified of dark shapes that came up from it. I was briefly scared about death until I resolved never to think about it again. I was curious about God, partly no doubt because I had been brought up as an atheist, which made me more interested in religion. When I was seven Dorothy told me about God, who had a white beard like Father Christmas and lived in the sky, but I could not get the hang of him. I felt I was missing out on something. One day at school the French master asked me to translate the word *parrain*: when he told me it meant 'godfather' I had no idea what that meant, and when I realised that other boys had godfathers I felt deprived, for what could be more formidable than someone who was both god and father?

I felt there was something odd about the whole family. When I was quite young my father's father, John Sampson, came down to stay from Liverpool. He seemed a magical old man, with a big bald head and large chin: he told us stories, gave us a board game he had invented and taught us to make cat's cradles with string. He died when I was five but I remained fascinated by him because my father never talked about him, but my mother later mentioned him with some dread: she told us about his wild drinking, his ferocious temper and his dangerous friends, including the painter Augustus John. And

I saw intriguing clues about the house, including a lascivious drawing of carousing gypsies by John, a dictionary of the Romani language by my grandfather, and some thrilling press cuttings about his funeral on a Welsh mountain, where gypsy mourners scattered his ashes and John gave the funeral address. They all conjured up a world far away from our conventional Hampstead existence.

The mystery deepened when a new aunt called Mary Arnold came briefly to stay with us, soon after my grandfather died. Mary was quite unlike our other sociable aunts: she was a gauche schoolmarm, heavy and awkward with big eyes behind pebble glasses. She was obviously distressed, and my sister heard her weeping in her room. Later she came on holidays with us: she demoralised our mother by talking about ancient Greece and Latin verse, and my father kept away, but we children were fond of her: she played board games, took us on adventurous walks across the hills, and taught me how to play chess and let me win. When I asked my mother about Mary she promised to tell me when I was older, which only made me more curious. We soon guessed the truth, that she was my grandfather's illegitimate daughter: for she looked like him with her big head and jaw. Later I went to see her in Edinburgh, where she taught at a girls' school and lived alone in a cold tenement flat full of classical books. She would sometimes talk about her father, whom she had adored, but never about her mother. I was all the more intrigued by my grandfather's secret life. My father remained silent, retreating into the certainties of science and corporate life. But my grandfather became a romantic legend for me, as he never could for my father.

I very early felt an itch to write: I would sit alone in a tent in our garden, scribbling in different coloured inks. It was not until much later that I discovered that the Romans had a phrase for it: *insanabile cacoethes scribendi*: the incurable mania for writing. I had nothing much to write about: I put down lists, and facts and stories, like little encyclopaedias – anything to escape from family tensions.

But I still wanted to conform, and I was glad that I was English, that all my family were English, because England was the best: London was the biggest city in the world, the Royal Navy had the most powerful fleet, the *Flying Scotsman* was the fastest train, Rolls-Royce the best car. The British Empire had put red spaces all over the map, run by fair and dedicated

Englishmen, and peopled by grateful natives. Englishmen did not swank, like Americans, because we didn't need to: we made self-deprecating jokes about ourselves. We exchanged jokes about the mean Scots, the hopeless Irish, the emotional French and humourless Germans; while we were the strong silent men, who quietly got on with the job, supported by wives who were absolute bricks. England was the centre of the world, and all our books, plays and poems revolved around it. My favourite stories were mostly about English heroes outwitting wicked or unreliable foreigners: Buchan's Richard Hannay tracked down unspeakable Huns; Sherlock Holmes outwitted the wicked foreigner Moriarty; Bertie Wooster made fun of vulgar Americans. I loved Arthur Ransome's books about the typical English children, the Swallows and Amazons who sailed and skated in the Lake District. It was not until years later that I realised that Hannay was Scottish, that the Swallows and Amazons were based on a part-Armenian family, and that many stereotypes of Englishness had been invented by foreigners and outsiders.

My sense of Englishness was reinforced by my experience of schools. At six I was sent to the Hall School near Swiss Cottage, the forcing ground for children of ambitious Hampstead parents, as it still is today. It was dominated by its founder-headmaster, G. A. Wathen, who was a veteran of the Indian civil service; he was a friend of E. M. Forster and was said to be the model for Fielding in *A Passage to India*. He appeared thoroughly conventional: one day he summoned a group of seniors to complain with a shudder that he had heard a boy utter a terrible swear word, *bloody*. He cultivated favourite boys who came to special lunches, for 'macaroni wallahs'. But while I was at school we were told that he was taking a year's leave, although it was not until later that we learnt he had gone to jail for the usual prep school reason.

The Hall had another reason to want to be very English, for in the late 1930s it was taking in a large number of Jewish boys, including many sons of refugees. Among them were the Freud boys, the grandsons of Sigmund, who arrived speaking comic German-English: the youngest and cockiest, Clement, was in my class. The refugees provoked the more anti-Semitic masters, and the Freuds were double targets, for their surname in those days implied sex, the great taboo. Yet the Jewish boys had a self-confidence and drive which the Gentiles lacked, and later they excelled in many different fields. Clement Freud became a Liberal MP, television celebrity and caterer, while his eldest brother, Lucian, became Britain's leading artist. The precocious Paul Hamlyn turned into a millionaire publisher and philanthropist, while his intellectual brother, Michael Hamburger, became a distinguished poet. I envied these confident Jewish boys and briefly wondered if I might not be Jewish myself, with my long nose and sense of separateness.

It was from the Jewish boys at school that I heard more about the mad dictator Hitler, who was looming in the late 1930s. My father too was full of foreboding and told me to read *Mein Kampf*, in order to understand that this man wanted to dominate the world; I listened to his ranting speeches on the radio, but I couldn't take seriously the hysterical German with his comic moustache, and most Englishmen seemed to regard him as a figure of fun: the cartoonist Low depicted Hitler and Mussolini as two mischievous puppies, Hit and Muss. Gradually the danger looked more serious: the news films showed aircraft dropping bombs in Spain, and the history master drew a map showing the menacing shape of Germany, looking like a wolf's head with jaws closing on little Czechoslovakia. At the time of the Munich conference in 1938 the school evacuated for a few days, expecting war. But it proved a false alarm when the kindly prime minister, Neville Chamberlain, told us he had secured peace in our time. I knew that England was invincible, thanks to the Royal Navy: I collected cigarette cards of warships, and the school organised an excursion to the Isle of Wight, to watch the great naval review at Spithead, where our launch steamed between the rows of great battleships with shining guns, which were obviously far more powerful than the Germans'.

At first I was thought quite clever myself, particularly in mathematics: I was excited by differential calculus when I was twelve, and my parents were convinced I had inherited brainy genes. I was bored by sport, particularly by cricket, which I never understood, and was happier with books. But after puberty with all its turmoil, I lost my concentration and confidence in my brain; and I was surprised to win a scholarship to Westminster School.

I looked forward to being in the heart of imperial London, tucked between Westminster Abbey and the Houses of Parliament. But then the war broke out, my father was called up, and the school was evacuated. The most metropolitan school became the most rural, dispersed in decaying country houses in Herefordshire between which we bicycled 12 miles a day. The great abbey shrank into the village church; the library became a few bookshelves; and the sports fields gave way to a garden where we dug for victory. But the exile liberated the school, turning little prigs in starched collars into country pioneers in corduroy shorts and open necks, who could take less for granted.

We were still conscious of being 'King's Scholars' and managed to generate our own precocious hothouse in the small Herefordshire village of Whitbourne, defying the conformity of wartime. We lapped up the new *Four Quartets* of T. S. Eliot, which were just appearing, listened to Beethoven's late quartets on a gramophone in the stables, and performed Shakespeare plays in the village hall, where I played Prospero in *The Tempest*. We created our own microcosm in this remote village, which still holds magical memories with its church bells, its music and plays.

It was a hothouse too of intimate relationships and sexual desires and frustrations. I remained virginal and rather prudish, embarrassed by dirty talk in the dormitory. But I made close friends – more easily than ever afterwards – which lasted a lifetime. Robin Denniston, who would become my most creative publisher and editor, went on to be publisher at Oxford University Press and vicar of Great Tew. I joined a pretentious trio of rebels, 'Les Trois Cyniques', with Pierre Young, a half-French mathematician whose parents were communists, and John Robinson, a provocative troublemaker: we debunked all institutions and mocked the militarists in the army training corps. (Pierre went on to design the Concorde engine for Rolls-Royce, but refused to disown his communist past; John became a diplomat and helped to mastermind Britain's entry into Europe.) I was always amazed when my contemporaries achieved worldly success: when the Honourable A. N. Wedgwood Benn (whose flow of talk made his classmates groan 'Oh, Benn!') became the left-wing Cabinet minister Tony Benn; when M. R. O. Havers became Lord Chancellor; or when my cocky little fag, C. C. C. Tickell, became Sir Crispin, ambassador to the United Nations.

I had little confidence in my own future. I studied science, encouraged by my father, but I could never quite believe in gravity, organic compounds or electrons, and felt oppressed by the lack of human contact: I looked with envy at the subjects called 'the humanities'. I vaguely wanted to be a writer, but when I sat for one examination I was told: 'His English essay was particularly unsatisfactory.'

And the whole of Britain was feeling much less optimistic as the war went on. By the time I left school in 1944 the Allies were clearly winning, and the school was preparing to move back to London; but the call-up continued and the future looked bleak. It was clear that England had been impoverished by the war, that we were losing our power over the world, and that the Americans were now dominant. What had happened to that secure pre-war country, and where if anywhere did I belong in it?

Royal Navy

I had had a brief and disillusioning experience of Britain's role abroad in a two-year stint as a conscript in the Royal Navy, which soon dispelled my schoolboy romanticism. I had begun, like all recruits, on the lower deck, which gave me a crash course in four-letter words and the workings of rigid hierarchies. Elderly petty officers drilled the clumsy recruits with despair: I was always adrift, as a left-hander turning port instead of starboard. The training-course provided a lesson in irrelevant rigmarole: on a lavatory wall I first saw the crucial motto 'BULLSHIT BAFFLES BRAINS'. We were sent to a training-cruiser, HMS *Dauntless*, which steamed round Britain packed with ordinary seamen trying to show 'officer-like qualities'. One day we were polishing Oerlikon guns when we heard the news that an atom bomb had been dropped on Japan; and a few days afterwards the world war ended. But the training continued with its own momentum, and nothing seemed to change after the Labour victory in the general election of July 1945.

Eventually, to my surprise, I was transformed first into a midshipman then into a sub-lieutenant, with wavy gold rings round my sleeves. But I never really felt like an officer, and never seemed to fit properly into the uniform – or into any suit. And the navy was now much diminished and still being run down. I was posted to a minesweeper, which never left its jetty near Sheerness, alongside a row of mouldering ships which bumped against each other as the tide rose and fell; and then to an ancient monitor with two big guns, designed to bombard foreign natives, which likewise never moved. Most warships were now 'in mothballs' rusting on jetties or in estuaries, theoretically kept in readiness for another war. The vast dockyard at Portsmouth was grotesquely overmanned, kept busy with elaborate rituals and class distinctions: there were separate lavatories for each rank, down to chief petty officers, petty officers and ratings. The Mothball Navy provided a caricature of bureaucracy, presided over by scores of shore-based admirals with few seagoing ships to command – a system which years later inspired Parkinson's law: 'Work expands so as to fill the time available for its completion.'

My final posting was more interesting but more depressing, to Germany, which gave me a still more macabre view of post-war confusion. I sailed from Hull to Cuxhaven at the end of February 1947 – in the coldest winter of the century – to join a small motor launch which was frozen into the harbour: my cabin could only be kept warm in an airless fug. The Baltic Sea was iced over, so that refugees could walk all the way from Kiel to Copenhagen. Germany was desperately short of fuel and much of the continent had frozen to a halt. It was not until much later that I understood the global consequences of that historic freeze-up: it brought about a fuel crisis which crippled Britain's Labour government and hastened its retreat from empire.[1] All I knew at the time was that Germany was devastated.

I would never forget my first sight of post-war Hamburg. I saw the railway marshalling-yards which had so often featured in the BBC news as the targets for British bombing-raids. Now (I wrote home) they were 'a vast expanse of twisted frameworks of coaches and trucks, with engines lying on their sides and bits of track all over the place. No-one, it seems, had attempted to do anything about it.' I hardly realised that I was in a city at all, as we passed streets of low rubble, from which shivering families clambered out. The shattered buildings round the Alster lake looked uninhabitable, while in the middle of them the Hotel Atlantic, reserved for British officers, stood almost untouched. Inside it was more comfortable than anything in England, and hard-drinking officers were lined up along the Long Bar. From my overheated bedroom with a luxurious bathroom I looked out on the rubble which was Hamburg. Yet I could still find an improvised opera house which produced an entrancing German performance of *The Magic Flute*. It was my first glimpse of the resilience of the German spirit.

The hardship of that winter was visible everywhere. When I took German lessons with a pedantic Dr Sommer in a tiny cold flat in Cuxhaven I had to bring my own candle to read by, while his family sat in darkness in the kitchen. I was shocked by the contrast with the British families who had commandeered mansions with several servants and cars with unlimited petrol, and who could buy luxuries cheaply in the special officers' shops. 'Utterly disgraceful,' I wrote home. 'Again and again one hears the two opposite points of view: whether or not the German people really are enemies. Most people seem to feel some degree of compassion.' But the British government was still continuing its 'de-Nazification': one day Dr Sommer had disappeared; he had been taken away for questioning about his Nazi connections. I was surprised, both then and later when I often revisited Germany, that my German friends did not show bitterness towards the devastation and misery caused by the British bombing. But there was a very long time lag before the resentment began to surface. It was not until sixty years later, after reading W. G. Sebald's book *On the Natural History of Destruction*, that I realised the extent of the collective amnesia which had buried the humiliation and traumas: 'The darkest aspects of the final act of destruction, as experienced by the great majority of the German population, remained under a kind of taboo like a shameful family secret.'[2]

The British forces were forbidden to fraternise with the 'Krauts', and Cuxhaven's restaurants and bars were strictly 'non-frat'. British officers officially encountered Germans only as servants in the officers' club, where they behaved as a master race, rather as the Germans would have, I imagined, if they had occupied Britain. In the spotless dining-room the German band endlessly played 'Lili Marlene' or 'Ach, du liebe Augustin' while obedient German waiters served British officers who got drunker and drunker and occasionally lurched round the dance floor with each other's wives, or provoked arguments with the waiters in joke-German: '*Warum? Warum nicht?*' As more officers were demobilised the club became emptier and more forsaken, but the barmen still had to wait until the small hours: they were kept there by one irremovable officer, the 'Mad Major', who went on shouting 'Fritz!' and got drunk every night while his nymphomaniac wife searched for handsome young officers.

But there was plenty of discreet fraternising in the bedrooms. Most British officers had 'parties', as they called their German girlfriends. Many of the army officers in Cuxhaven were based in the comfortable main hotel which they had taken over, but when I stayed there briefly I was puzzled to notice that it was quite empty at night: then in the morning I woke up early and saw a small procession of officers walking back to their hotel with their little suitcases, just in time to rumple their sheets and appear at breakfast.

Many of the 'parties' were married, and their husbands connived in their adultery for the sake of cigarettes, the precious currency which had replaced the devalued marks: a pretty *Fräulein* or *Frau* could earn two fags a night. When a British troopship arrived in the harbour the club would fill up with eager young officers en route for their regiments inland, and they would ask about the going cigarette rate for a *Fräulein*. Cigarettes were the key to the British superiority. A fag was worth four marks, and the average German weekly wage was about thirty marks. The British received 200 duty-free cigarettes a week – fifty of them free – which gave them a bonus of seven times the German wage to spend on girls, Leica cameras or luxuries. Unscrupulous senior officers, including the naval commanding officer in Cuxhaven, could ship cases of cameras and binoculars to Britain at a spectacular profit. The serious racketeers behaved like princes. Once when our motor launch was in Heligoland harbour we were joined by a luxury yacht flying a commodore's flag. We were quickly invited for drinks by Commodore Maund, a big genial man surrounded by floozies, dispensing champagne and canapés, who turned out to be in charge of the NAAFI in Hamburg. He made no pretence of being a serious naval officer: a few months later I noticed in the *Times* that a Commodore Maund had been court-martialled and convicted of racketeering.

The young commanding officer of my motor launch, a year older than myself, spent every night ashore with his 'party', while I often stayed on board, reading novels and Elizabethan plays, and periodically tried to impose some discipline on the unruly crew. But it was a hopeless task. Several seamen got repeatedly and violently drunk on schnapps; the anarchy reached a climax when one of them stole a 3-ton truck, drove it through the dockyard gate and killed a German bystander. He was court-martialled and ended up in Pentonville prison, where I later visited him, wondering guiltily if I could have prevented the disaster.

I was shocked by the glimpses of high-ranking British looters and commanders exploiting their power over powerless Germans, which

11

changed my perception of Englishmen abroad, perhaps unfairly. The British were probably less corrupt and more considerate to their ex-enemies than the French or American occupying forces, and most of the racketeers were not authentic war heroes but reservists who dreaded returning to civilian life and wanted to make a quick fortune first. But I was never again so sure that the British were uniquely fair minded, and less convinced that they were quite different from the Germans, for whom I had some sympathy. I kept remembering the lines from Yeats:

> Those that I fight I do not hate,
> Those that I guard I do not love.[3]

Throughout that eerie winter and spring of 1947 I could make no sense of Anglo-American policy towards Germany: we were still dismantling some factories while rebuilding others, which provided a reminder of German enterprise. A few Volkswagens were already emerging from the wreckage of their big plant in Wolfsburg; British officers and their wives were delighted to buy them very cheaply and to drive them along the empty autobahns, which put British roads to shame. But British car-makers made fun of their comic shape and noisy air-cooled engine in the back, and were confident that they could never compete with traditional British cars.

I was still more baffled by British policy after our motor launch was ordered to sail to Heligoland, three hours from Cuxhaven. The island had opposite associations for the two sides. For the Germans it had been a favourite duty-free resort, reached by pleasure steamers. But the British had always seen it as a 'dagger pointing at the heart of England', and during the war it was a major base for Hitler's U-boats, which made it the target for repeated thousand-bomber raids. The first raid had flattened most of the houses and hotels, and all surviving Heligolanders had been evacuated. But three huge pens for U-boats, cut into the high cliffs, were still intact, and after the war the British government still saw them as a potential base for a future hostile German regime. They determined to finally remove the threat, and in the spring of 1947 a British demolition team arrived to place 7,000 tons of high explosive inside the U-boat pens to prepare for 'Operation Big Bang'. We in the motor launch were told to supervise the operation, ten miles off Heligoland, where a cable ship was conducting two massive explosions. In the second one a spectacular flame lit up the whole island and tiny sparks like fireworks shot up into the sky, followed by a soft thud. The demolition gang were well satisfied with the result – a crater 100 feet wide and 25 feet deep.

The next morning I walked round the deserted island. The U-boat pens had collapsed into a heap of immovable iron and concrete. The two little holiday towns, below and above a tall cliff, had finally been obliterated while the cliff had been reduced to a slope of crumbled rock and the lift connecting them was a tangle of metal. The ground was strewn with masonry, timber, radiators, sewing-machines, lavatory seats. I wandered alone through the rubble for two hours until suddenly I realised I was standing in the ruined kitchen of Heligoland's grandest hotel: I was looking at a blackboard with a handwritten menu above a chef's name and '18.4.45' – the date of the first and heaviest raid on the island. It conjured up a haunting image: of rich German tourists even at the end of the war enjoying a sumptuous meal – until the bombs fell. Now, two years later, the whole town had been destroyed. 'I don't think the island will ever be used again as a pleasure resort,' I wrote that night; 'even if anyone could clear the vast quantity of rubble, they could not put back the cliffs.' We stayed for several days on our motor launch in the harbour, the only human presence among the ghostly ruins, and I began to sense its natural splendour. The guillemots came back to nest in the shattered cliffs and the sea was full of lobsters, with only twenty British sailors to enjoy them. None of us could have imagined that twenty years later Heligoland would be a more popular resort than ever, with all its hotels and restaurants rebuilt, while Hamburg would become more prosperous than any British port.

That demolition in April 1947 was one of the last acts of destruction, for politicians in London and Washington were rapidly reversing their policy towards Germany. Already a year before, Winston Churchill had proclaimed the 'iron curtain' which the communists had drawn across Europe; and in March 1947 President Harry Truman had proclaimed his doctrine which aimed to rebuild the economy of Europe, including Germany – soon followed by the Marshall plan. Industrialists who had been jailed for collaborating with Hitler would soon be released to become the entrepreneurs for the future German miracle. After seeing the devastation of

Hamburg and the demolition of Heligoland, I could only wonder at the suddenness with which our alliances had changed.

> If this was our battle, these were our ends,
> Which were our enemies, which were our friends![4]

Oxford

I was demobilised soon after the destruction of Heligoland, and gratefully exchanged my grand uniform for a demob suit. I had little confidence in my academic abilities but thanks to Westminster I was accepted as an undergraduate at Christ Church, Oxford, which made few academic demands. I was overawed by its beauty and grandeur, all the more after the bleakness of Germany: my rooms looked across to the magnificent college library. But I was unimpressed by the dons, who appeared complacently reactionary, including the historian Hugh Trevor-Roper, the economist Roy Harrod and Lord Cherwell, Churchill's scientific adviser. I read with pleasure how Dr Johnson had shocked the high table two centuries earlier with his toast: 'Here's to the next insurrection in the West Indies.'

Oxford in 1947 was swollen by both pre-war and post-war generations: colonels who had had a good war brushed against teenagers straight from school. It was still gripped by post-war austerity, and the food in college was spartan, with wartime rations only modified by sour Algerian wine, whalemeat and snoek. But the college was already beginning to revert to pre-war class distinctions. The quiet grammar school boys, scientists and swots who put pens in their outside pockets were easily demoralised by loud old Etonians drinking vintage wines and port in the buttery: on summer evenings in the quads they were once again, as Evelyn Waugh described them, 'baying for broken glass' – encouraged by *Brideshead Revisited*, which had been published two years earlier. Was it for this England, I wondered, that the war was won?

The college was full of people who seemed sure of their future careers, round pegs waiting to fit into round holes: for example Sir Edward Boyle, later a government minister, Robert Armstrong, later head of the civil service, and Tony Quinton, later master of Trinity College. The Oxford Union was already resuming its pre-war role as Britain's political nursery, with its customary pomposity. Its office-holders presided over debates in white tie as if they had been born in it; and its successive presidents – Robin Day, Jeremy Thorpe, William Rees-Mogg – competed with old-fashioned rhetoric. Women were then barred from joining the union; hardly anybody had heard of Margaret Roberts, the scientist from Grantham and president of the Oxford University Conservative Association who would become more powerful than all of them. I felt out of place in this assertive world, too insecure to recognise the insecurities of others and tongue-tied with a shyness which sounded like arrogance, and I had moods of depression which isolated me further. I revived my spirits by playing liar dice and darts in pubs with oddball friends, including the enigmatic South African Jim Bailey.

I took a pessimistic view of the world after my German experience, and had few illusions about communists: I bought six copies of George Orwell's *Animal Farm*, which had recently appeared, and sent them to friends, who did not appreciate them. But I was alarmed by the speed with which the West was building up the communist bogey to replace the Nazi enemy. The Scala cinema at Oxford showed a film, four years late, which featured Laurence Olivier as a heroic Soviet engineer visiting Britain in wartime and endearing himself to the British.[5] Now the Russians were already the villains, and Olivier was greeted with catcalls.

I studied English literature, considered a soft option, and imagined my professorial grandfathers and uncles looking down on me with scorn. I was lucky with my tutors and lecturers. I was briefly taught by Professor Tolkien, the Middle English scholar not yet famous as the creator of the hobbits and *The Lord of the Rings*, who gave beery seminars in a pub which opened mid-morning. He assured us that there were excellent linguistic precedents for splitting infinitives and starting sentences with 'and', and gave us his own definition of an intellectual, as 'someone who is never shocked'. Later at Christ Church I was tutored by Jim Stewart, who wrote donnish detective stories as Michael Innes before breakfast. I went to seminars conducted by Lord David Cecil, together with his scholarly protégé John Bayley. I heard Wallace Robson lecture on Pope, Nevill Coghill on Chaucer, Kenneth Clark on Renaissance art, C. S. Lewis on Milton and Plato. It was an extraordinary array of talent, more far-reaching than anyone imagined at the time. Tolkien and Lewis – themselves close friends – both wrote stories which would become perennial best-sellers and Hollywood blockbusters which attracted children all over the world. But I was ashamed how little I really absorbed from it.

I still hoped to be a writer, all the more to express myself among the loud talkers. I wrote some light pieces for Oxford magazines and began a novel about the post-war navy. I wrote an unsuccessful play called *Hoax*, about a charlatan painter who fooled the art world (perhaps it was ahead of its time?), but the play-reading was noisily interrupted by Christ Church hearties in search of booze. I could not depict my characters from life, and I was a writer without much to write about. I kept remembering Roy Campbell's lines about South African novelists:

> They use the snaffle and the curb all right,
> But where's the bloody horse?[6]

The year 1950 was a grim time to enter the job market, and our mood was summed up by the popular song 'Baby, It's Cold Outside'. The Oxford style, disdainful of industry and commerce, was not the best preparation for Britain when the economy was stagnant and the government was retrenching. I was interviewed by corporations including Imperial Tobacco and ICI, my father's firm, but could show no enthusiasm for selling cigarettes or paint. I hankered after a literary life, and thought I could start as a publisher: but publishing was still a 'gentleman's profession' for men with private incomes. I thought I might first become a printer. I was interested in typography: I wrote a pretentious paper on the printing of Shakespeare, and worked briefly at the Curwen Press. Then I took a job at Richard Clay's printing-works in Suffolk, which bored me stiff. I bought a motorbike, which provided an outlet for my aggression and fantasy life, and at weekends I roared through the Suffolk lanes until I reached Walberswick and the sea.

After my time in the navy and at Oxford, I still had no idea where I belonged. I was restless, rebellious, unqualified for any structured career. I did not realise those were in fact ideal qualifications for journalism. But just then I received a telegram from Jim Bailey, and my life was suddenly transformed.

2

Drum

Jim Bailey's telegram, which arrived on Good Friday 1951, read:

ARE YOU IMMEDIATELY AVAILABLE JOB NEW NEGRO
PERIODICAL IN CAPE TOWN FIFTY POUNDS MONTH SAY YES
JIM BAILEY

My father, preoccupied with security, was full of warnings. My mother said: 'You're not taking it seriously?' But there was only one answer: I had to say yes. I sought advice from journalists: I met William Clark of the *Observer*, who urged me to accept: 'If you want to get into Fleet Street,' he told me, 'go as far as possible away from it.' Then Jim mentioned some unspecified problems, but in May he cabled again:

FIX PASSAGE AND COME STRAIGHTWAY BY SEA CABLE IF OKAY
WILL THEN CABLE FARE WRITING JIM.

'It looks as if it will be a tough struggle for some time,' he warned later. 'Your job may be organising distribution, doubling for the editor or selling advertising-space.'

I booked a passage in an aged Edwardian liner, the SS *Llangibby Castle*, which sailed from the Albert Dock, the huge sheet of water in the heart of London's dockland which had always fascinated me, where the great ships and funnels stuck up above the rows of slum houses like images of escape and promise. I embarked with my battered trunk and motorbike and found my tiny cabin in steerage, and then stood on the deck watching the ship leave London behind it, as the sun set over the river. I never forgot that symbolic exit: the liner slowly moved out of the narrow lock which led into the waterway, and steamed at dusk past the landmarks of the still-thriving port: the cranes and warehouses, the tolling buoys and hooting barges, the riverside pubs and the Beckton sewage works, 'the arsehole of London'. We sailed down Gallions Reach, past Creekmouth, Gravesend and Leigh-on-Sea, and my mind was full of Conrad: 'The sea-reach of the Thames stretched before us like the beginning of an interminable waterway.' I was leaving behind all the gloom of post-war London, the austerity and rationing of the failing Labour government, the half-baked celebrations of the Festival of Britain and an unpromising career, to take a risk which, I told my diary, had a one-in-four chance of success.

I was cooped up below decks and snooped enviously into first class, from where a double staircase led down to the imposing dining-room with carved panelling and elaborate meals. But even the tourist class menus seemed luxurious compared to British fare: there were five-course dinners with fancy French dishes and plenty of real eggs. My fellow-passengers were mostly part of a still-confident imperial world. I shared my cabin with a dried-up British colonial officer returning to Northern Rhodesia, where he worked in native education; 'his brains are addled', I reckoned superciliously, 'after years of heat and loneliness.' There were two noisy engine-drivers going out to Southern Rhodesia, encouraged by the Labour government's policy of subsidising settlers; 'they didn't know how to use a knife or fork,' I wrote. There were two young Cambridge graduates going out to hitch-hike to Kenya. 'Could I do any empire-building?' I wondered to my diary. 'Could I lay a single brick?'

But on the slow three-week voyage I was soon caught up in the intense shipboard life, which I already knew from Somerset Maugham short stories, playing deck tennis and quoits, drinking beef tea and guessing the last day's sea miles. As we passed the lighthouses of Ushant and Finisterre into the Bay of Biscay, the land fell out of sight and the life of the liner became more intense: we passed another liner looking like a magical ship of gaiety, with bright lights ablaze in its portholes, and thought: 'Is this how we look to them?' As we sailed southwards towards the tropics, the ship opened up: the rows of folding doors on the top deck were removed to make a sundeck, the swimming-pool was filled and the voyage became like a cruise. Near the equator the relentless sun seemed fixed overhead, casting no shadows and filling me with the aimless lethargy I always dreaded, a forewarning of the African heat to come: the cruder passengers seemed still more boorish. I felt relieved by nightfall, when I saw the stars of the Southern Cross – the constellation I had longed to see – climb further up the sky. I retreated into reading Roy Harrod's life of Keynes and Trevelyan's history of nineteenth-century Britain, but I tried to learn more about Africa. A charming Afrikaner woman with two sweet children tried to teach me her language and explained the logic of the great new policy of apartheid. There were, of course, no blacks on board.

Imperial residues seemed everywhere. We stopped at the Canary Islands and docked at Las Palmas, the faded outpost of the Spanish empire, where hawkers and beggars rushed to the quayside, selling tablecloths, silk shirts and squat bananas. The great fifteenth-century cathedral was crumbling, surrounded by impoverished islanders. We anchored off Ascension Island, the old British telegraph base, and stopped at St Helena, where Napoleon had lived and died; its local inhabitants seemed desperately poor, frantically trying to sell lace handkerchiefs to the passengers, but still fanatically loyal to the British Empire.

At last we reached the bottom of Africa and, after being battered by the Cape rollers, saw the miraculous plateau of Table Mountain and anchored for the night off Cape Town. We celebrated with a sing-song and farewell dance on board ship, and could see the bright lights of the city, the row of liners in the dock and the car headlights lighting up the darkness round the mountain. It looked like a fairyland. What was it going to be like in that remote outpost?

Disembarking at Cape Town I was amazed to find myself in an enchanting fantasy England which did not look like Africa at all. 'It's like travelling 6,000 miles', I wrote home, 'to find oneself back where one started.' And I was equally surprised to find how the English-speaking South Africans took racial segregation for granted. 'The colour bar and apartheid happen without anyone being surprised or shocked,' I wrote. 'That's what one doesn't realise. One must accept that it has been so for a hundred years and can't be changed in a minute – though it may be.' But I quickly realised I would find myself in a contrary world. The magazine, the *African Drum* as it was then called, was only four months old, and in a state of upheaval. Its editor, Bob Crisp, was a popular and genial South African cricketer and war hero who had conceived the magazine as a noble expression of the black soul, filled with folktales, poetry and extracts from Alan Paton's new book, *Cry, the Beloved Country*. White liberals and missionaries admired it, but there was an overwhelming snag: the urban blacks who could afford to buy it were not interested. It was soon obvious why, as Jim Bailey explained to me. They wanted to escape from that idealised rural life, to see themselves as part of the big-city world of showbiz, sport, jazz and American movies.

Jim, who had begun as a minority investor in the little magazine, was determined to intervene to save it. He decided it must move to Johannesburg, where most of the potential black readers lived. After relishing the green paradise of Cape Town I was saddened to leave it. For two days I drove northwards for 1,000 miles with Bob, along the bumpy and desolate sand road, across the Karoo half-desert; on the way I amused myself by imagining the cities and cathedrals we would be passing if this had been the road from London to Rome, but here there were only occasional railway halts with Afrikaner settlements, shacks and filling-stations. At last we saw the tall buildings and factories of the Golden City, but Johannesburg seemed as harsh and inhospitable as the Cape was lush and friendly. I stayed in a bleak and beery hotel in the city centre, with treeless pavements between the concrete canyons, and no river or stream in sight: only patches of brown grass. It still seemed like a mining-camp where men dug gold by day and drank at night to get drunk. It looked like the end of the world.

But the strange challenge of the magazine soon seemed to obliterate the surroundings, and I found myself in a maelstrom of activity. Jim was increasingly at odds with Bob about its future, and after I spent a few weeks as circulation manager, he asked me to my astonishment to become editor. It was ridiculous. I was only twenty-five, with no experience of journalism or Africa. But Jim insisted that ignorance was a positive advantage. 'It seemed better to have for an editor a man who did not know the African world,' he explained later, 'and knew that he did not know it, than to have a white South African, however well intentioned, who was convinced that he knew it and thus could learn nothing.'

Jim and I set out to explore black Johannesburg, to find out what potential readers really wanted. It was an eye-opener for both of us. *Drum* had only one black reporter, Henry Nxumalo, an ebullient sports writer with an infectious laugh and broken teeth who proved the ideal guide into the black world: articulate and gregarious, with a wide circle of friends in the townships. He talked with sharp irony about township life and the absurdities of the colour bar. On the way to Soweto, he pointed out a sign saying 'Natives Cross Here'. Someone had added a word to it, he explained, to say 'Natives Very Cross Here'. He set up meetings in Soweto where black leaders told us what was wrong with *Drum*, with advice which was emphatic and angry. 'It's got the *white hand* on it. It's what white men want Africans to be, not what they are.' 'The boys are screaming for more sport.' '*Drum* must have jazz.' 'We need more babes like that one on the cover.' 'The next magazine must be called "Us".'

There was nothing very original about this formula for selling newspapers. 'Don't be highbrow about using sex, the royal family and babies and animals to pull circulation,' wrote my friend Michael Davie from the *Observer* in London. 'It's the only way.' But in South Africa the idea was revolutionary: it implied that urban Africans were much like city people everywhere. The formula worked, with striking success. The vulgar new *Drum* with its cover girls, crime stories and lonely hearts soon lost us many white friends. 'Anthony, why do you publish such trash?' asked Elena, the resourceful Italian girl who had helped to start it up. But it soon boosted the circulation, which jumped up with each new exposure and crime story.

I was at first ashamed by my own ignorance of journalism. I had never learnt the elementary rules, such as telling the story in the first sentence: 'what, when and how'. When I commissioned the journalist Herbert Kretzmer to write an article, he asked: 'Could I have a by-line?' I had no idea what a by-line was, so I had to say yes. But inexperience had its advantages, as Jim realised. I had no alternative but to let black journalists tell their own stories, which they did with a vigour and freshness which broke all the rules but reflected the true life and spirit of the townships. I wrote only one long piece myself, an exposure of crime in the townships (which was as serious then as it is today); but after that I realised that black writers could describe their own surroundings much more vividly and authentically than I could.

The pictures were more important than the writing for a popular magazine, and we had the luck to find Jürgen Schadeberg, a young and dashing German photographer who had just arrived from the ruins of post-war Berlin. As a restless bachelor, he was fascinated by the black world, particularly the cover girls, and his vivid pictures reflected his own delight. But he also generously trained Africans to follow him, who started a thriving tradition of black photographers in South Africa. The *Drum* pictures, endlessly reproduced over the next fifty years, would provide the chief record of black politics and social life in the 1950s.

I soon found quite unexpected talent was floating into the *Drum* office like flotsam, mainly through Henry. He brought in his nephew Bob Gosani, a lanky and inarticulate schoolboy who was a hopeless journalist but began helping Jürgen in the darkroom and was soon producing superb photographs. Henry also introduced a friend, Todd Matshikiza, an accomplished jazz composer and pianist who turned out to write as well as he played, in a staccato style which we called Matshikese. He conjured up all the vitality and humour of township life, interspersed with glimpses of the humiliations in the white world: when he went to a white music shop to buy Bach's Prelude in C, he was told: 'Bach doesn't play boogie-woogie, you know.' Todd became a close friend: he taught me about African music and Xhosa traditions and we shared recordings of Satchmo. I went to the christening in Soweto of his son John Anthony, as an honorary godfather. I was told about another schoolboy, Arthur Maimane, by the Anglican priest Father Trevor Huddleston; he wanted to be a cub reporter before going to university. He soon proved the most versatile journalist of all, writing sports reports, thrillers or interviews with beauty queens at top speed, and forgot about college.

We launched a short-story competition, which was won by a sardonic tale, 'Mob Passion', which turned out to be written by a schoolteacher, Can Themba. We immediately recruited him and he became an electric presence in the office: a lean bespectacled philosopher, licking his lips as he constructed elaborate theories about women or politics. He was very well read, with a degree from the burgeoning black university of Fort Hare, but he had never found full scope for his talents: 'We were these sensitive might-have-beens who knocked at the door of white civilisation', he wrote later in his poignant essay 'The Bottom of the Bottle', '. . . and had heard a gruff No or a Yes so shaky and insincere that we withdrew our snail horns at once.'

He took refuge in alcohol, which eventually killed him, but in the meantime he cast a spell over young writers, and introduced a group of acolytes including Casey Motsisi, a shy young protégé who soon began his own column with a Damon Runyon humour, which started a new cult.

Ezekiel (Zeke) Mphahlele was an English-teacher with a courteous and sober academic style – his most extreme expression was 'My!' – and an established reputation as a writer; he joined us as literary editor, bringing a new scholarly seriousness to the office. But many contributors just gravitated to *Drum* and stuck around, such as Bloke Modisane, the debonair short-story writer who worked in the left-wing Vanguard bookshop and lived in an immaculate room in a filthy Sophiatown backyard, where he played Mozart and seduced girls.

But Henry Nxumalo was the soul of the magazine. He always had his ear to the ground, with a network of friends along the Reef including musicians, sportsmen and his Soweto neighbour Nelson Mandela. 'It's rather very interesting,' Henry would say at a conference, before he told some extraordinary story of a scandal or atrocity, punctuated with jokes and laughter. Henry had wider horizons than the others: he had served in the war in north Africa and had seen how his life could have been otherwise; he had seen his hopes raised and then dashed, and he covered his bitterness with laughter and brandy. He was erratic and unpredictable, sometimes disappearing for days on end, but his courage and integrity inspired everyone.

It was Henry who undertook our first major exposure when he visited the farming district of Bethal to investigate stories about labourers being imprisoned and flogged, returning with a report which was later confirmed by an official inquiry. For the first time I realised that *Drum* could have a serious influence. Thereafter Henry was always 'Mr Drum' to the readers, always prepared to investigate an outrage. When a black labourer was murdered by his white boss on a farm called Harmonie, Henry volunteered to work on the farm to report what it was like. When we wanted to expose conditions in the notorious Johannesburg jail, 'the Fort', he got himself sent to prison. His terrifying report was backed up by a sensational photograph which Bob Gosani took from the roof of a neighbouring hospital, showing a naked prisoner jumping up in front of a warder to be searched for cannabis.

It was my most thrilling experience in my time as editor to watch that photograph being developed in the darkroom, to provide indisputable evidence of the abuse of prisoners: it would still be reproduced in magazines forty years later, worth more than thousands of words.

The *Drum* writers all told stories with a natural narrative vitality and a mastery of English which they acquired at mission schools, but which had been invigorated by the slang of the townships and the daily dramas of dangerous lives. Compared to the reined-in literary prose of most white South African writers, their language had a freshness which came from their streets and communities, and which made the words spring out of the page. Their stories, together with the jazz, drama and sport that emerged from black Johannesburg in the 1950s – like the culture of Harlem in the 1920s – was the expression of people who were embracing city life as the Afrikaners never did, with a creativity and energy which carried its own political message. As I began to immerse myself in that vibrant society I felt more certain that it did not come from a defeated race: they were bound to win their freedom.

The *Drum* office was in downtown Johannesburg, just next to the *Rand Daily Mail*, but white South Africans – even journalists – saw it as an alien enclave, and few made their way there. White secretaries who had to deliver packages were astonished to see black men using typewriters, discussing books, even using the same tea cups as whites. Sometimes visitors would deliberately linger, to listen with amazement to the flow of repartee from Henry, Can or Todd. For *Drum* was a social centre as much as a magazine: often in the late afternoon the office would suddenly fill up with African visitors who had got wind of a drinking-session, and they would later set off for refreshment at a nearby shebeen. Sitting at my desk amidst this chaos I often felt a cold white fish, quite out of place: 'Is Sampson black?' cabled *Time* magazine when they were preparing an article; I could only hope that my successor would be.

We never needed to search out the news. There were no handouts, press conferences or releases; stories just seemed to come into the office. A gangster needed to tell us how he had been converted. Politicians wanted us to cover the next demonstration. Jazz players hoped for a write-up by Todd. Potential cover girls demanded to be photographed, or waited for dates with

Arthur Maimane or Jürgen Schadeberg. Gang-leaders came to threaten reporters or to offer their memoirs. One day the office boy came up to me with a grin and said: 'Seven witch doctors to see you, sir'. And seven sangomas arrived in full regalia to complain that we had libelled them. It was hard to fit all this activity into only forty-eight pages of *Drum* a month.

It was a long way from white Johannesburg. Prosperous English-speaking South Africans enjoyed a lifestyle which I had only known from Hollywood movies, like scenes from *Gone with the Wind*, living in extravagant mansions with grand staircases, lush gardens and white-gloved black servants. But they still harked back to an imaginary pre-war England. Their suburbs looked like sub-tropical versions of the Home Counties, with names like Bryanston or Hurlingham, streets called Empire Way or Eton Road and country clubs with cricket pitches and bowling-greens. Some families had emigrated from England only recently to escape from post-war Labour austerity, and had quickly been expanded by the sun and luxury to acquire loud hearty voices, blazers and looser limbs. Fired with a pioneering spirit, they became much more socially mobile and enterprising than the English at home; and they embraced every new American import, from Cadillacs and drive-in cinemas to kidney-shaped swimming-pools and private planes.

At first I enjoyed the relaxed and informal style and open life of white Johannesburg. I rode on horseback across the hills outside the city and spent lazy weekends drinking Pimm's round swimming-pools. But I soon felt oppressed by the limitations. Most of the whites showed little introspection or intellectual questioning: there were few introverts and eccentrics of the kind I had enjoyed in Oxford or London. And they nearly all shared the same views about race. As soon as they talked about 'the native' – that significant singular – they were describing the same stereotype. Their casual voices became tenser, as if their confidence and freedom depended on other people's loss of freedom. When I said I worked with black writers on a black magazine they clammed up, or said 'Oh'. An invisible curtain came down.

It was a world which was English, yet not English; and I was disconcerted by this strange mutation, which had transformed people who looked so familiar into a master race. I saw that power could affect people when they dealt with the powerless. As the apartheid government revealed its deeply racist attitudes and policies most English-speakers kept out of politics and busied themselves with money-making. They rarely mixed with the Afrikaners, who dominated the all-white government and parliament, and mocked their crude language and guttural accents. But they voted for the English speaking United Party, which supported each new oppressive law, and they kept their own business offices strictly segregated. Were they really so very different, I began to wonder, from the pre-war businessmen in Germany who had tacitly connived with Hitler at every stage and were happy to be part of the *Herrenvolk*? And would the English in England, faced with this opportunity and predicament, really have behaved more morally and courageously?

I was never sure whether I was ostracised or I ostracised myself; but I felt surges of anger against the white complacency and spent less time in the smart suburbs. I chose to live in unfashionable Yeoville, close to the city, where I could invite black visitors without attracting notice, and where I felt closer to the messy fringe of black Johannesburg. Riding my motorbike, which was always breaking down, identified me as a poor white: one day when it was being repaired I sat on a bus behind two white women and heard one say: 'Of course, if you give the native any machinery, he'll spoil it.' That's me, I thought to myself.

Gradually I was drawn into the township life of the *Drum* writers and readers, where I soon felt more at home than in most white gatherings. It was Can Themba who first lured me into the seductive world of Sophiatown, the multiracial slum where he lived; he called his dingy room 'the House of Truth', where everyone was supposed to be candid with everyone else. And it was Can who introduced me to the shebeens such as Back of the Moon and specially the Thirty-Nine Steps, presided over by the ample Fatsy, where teachers, gangsters, messengers and politicians all gulped down her brandy with growing exuberance: the dialogue became so poetic that I sometimes rushed to the lavatory to jot phrases down before I became too drunk and forgetful. I never felt in danger. Forty years later the writer Don Mattera, who was then a gang-leader in Sophiatown, recalled how he saw this clumsy young white man stumbling up the rickety outside staircase of the Thirty-Nine Steps. He told his gang: 'He must be robbed.' But I never was, and later Can explained that I was known in Sophiatown as 'the Native'. One evening I was drinking in a shebeen with *Drum* colleagues when I heard a sudden cry of 'Police!' and with others I jumped out of the window, to hide among the rubbish until they went away. My black friends saw it as a moment of truth, they told me later, when their white boss shared their indignity and danger. I felt myself increasingly at home in my expeditions to Sophiatown, as I was caught up in strange adventures through a haze of alcohol, never sure where I would fetch up. One morning I was woken up hungover in a narrow bed by a sexy black woman saying: 'Sampson, can you buy me some beers?'

Sophiatown was an impossible place for normal family life, with its people jammed up against each other in hovels, sheds or shacks – even in an old tram. It was a young people's world, where a boy could feel old at ten and be dead by thirty; and Sophiatowners liked to recite the motto 'live fast, die young and leave a beautiful corpse' – from their favourite movie, *Knock on Any Door*. In other countries Sophiatown would have been condemned as a dangerous slum, to be bulldozed in the name of hygiene and safety. But under an apartheid government it acquired a special magic as the urban melting-pot where blacks were mixed up with other races and connected with a wider world, to create a multiracial culture, language and self-expression, reflected in its slang, its jazz or *Drum*. Sophiatown implied that blacks could occupy the cities not just as servants and workers in white homes and factories but as equals in a cosmopolitan world, competing in the boxing-ring or the jazz hall, on the sports fields or the dance floor.

Many white writers, like Alan Paton in *Cry, the Beloved Country*, liked to describe the bewilderment of rural Africans when they first encountered Johannesburg with its bright lights, shiny cars and skyscrapers like boxes piled on top of each other. It was certainly a dramatic transition, from the slow country life of the impoverished reserves to the ruthless fast-moving pace of the mining city. But the newly urbanised blacks were less confused and rootless than whites expected them to be. The huge influx of city dwellers in the 1940s and 1950s included thousands of durable people – such as Nelson Mandela, Oliver Tambo and Walter Sisulu – who retained many of their country roots, which helped them to survive the fierce challenges of urban life. 'The newcomers from the rural areas would find the old residents took them in and they merged very easily,' recalled Zeke Mphahlele, the former country boy. 'You would hardly ever see the difference except in their manner of speech, which was slower and with more metaphor.'[1] The

27

daily battles in the cities – to travel, to survive in the streets, to earn extra money or to outwit white policemen – created a generation of streetwise youths like Dickens's cockneys who had to live on their wits or go under. Their resilience was evident in their language: whether in the slang of the young hoodlums who mixed up Afrikaans, English and tribal expressions, or in the articulate English of the *Drum* writers who echoed Shakespeare or the Bible but borrowed discourse from American movies, jazz songs or the streets or shebeens. Their hazardous lives in the townships brought them into contact with all classes of people: a teacher could find himself pursuing the same girl as a gangster, and the next morning he would be jammed in trains and buses with the riff-raff. They used English with an expressiveness and freshness which the English had lost.

Few respectable whites at that time went to shebeens or Sophiatown; the more time I spent there, the more I felt cut off from the white world. But one of the few intruders was the most surprising Nadine Gordimer, then a young novelist. When I first met her at a white literary party she seemed a world apart: she had just published her first novel, *The Lying Days*, and was writing short stories for the *New Yorker* which subtly described the nuances of white Johannesburg. She was small, elegant and vivacious, like a delicate bird, talking with witty mimicry. I could scarcely believe that she had emerged from a desolate mining-town on the Reef, the daughter of an immigrant Jewish watch-mender from Lithuania. Soon afterwards she married her second husband, Reinhold Cassirer, a businessman and art-collector who had been a refugee from Berlin; at their wedding lunch he raised a glass to me and toasted: 'To the runner-up!' Together they cultivated their own pursuits in their old-fashioned house with Impressionist paintings among the austere furniture and bare floorboards, insulated from the vulgar city; every morning Nadine disconnected her phone and locked herself in her study, dedicated to her writing, and aloof from politics. When I arrived on my motorbike, in my creased and shabby clothes, I felt like a bull in a china shop.

But Nadine was much more adventurous than she looked: she needed bulls in her china shop. I soon introduced her to the *Drum* writers, who showed her a new world. She was fascinated by the vigour and wit of Can, Bloke Modisane or Casey Motsisi, who were far more spontaneous and literate than most white journalists, and she soon spent many evenings with me in the townships. One evening I took her to a print shop owned by my Coloured friend Andy Anderson, a Falstaffian host who in the evening turned his shop into a shebeen, favoured by black politicians including a young Nelson Mandela. Andy welcomed Nadine with open warmth while she was responsive but watchful. Later she wrote a short story called 'Which New Era Would That Be?', which described a white liberal, Jennifer, visiting a black print shop. It ended with Jennifer leaving abruptly and the host kicking over the chair she had sat in. Later I asked Andy, after he had read the story, what had really happened after Nadine left; he answered: 'Tony, I *kissed* the chair.'

Nadine would become my closest friend in white South Africa. We were never lovers but we could open doors for each other. I could lead her into black friendships in a more turbulent city which became increasingly important to her, as reflected in her stories: her novel *A World of Strangers* featured a young Englishman (much gentler than myself) who moved between white and black Johannesburg. But she opened a door for me; with her perceptions about people and her intellectual range she made every occasion more interesting, and she flattered me by taking my writing seriously, as if I were not just a journalist.

One white man was recognised by everyone in Sophiatown: Father Trevor Huddleston, the English monk who presided over the Anglican church and mission and strode through its slum streets with his fine profile and cropped hair, in his black cassock, surrounded by children. His background was patrician: he came from an imperial family and he often dined with the British high commissioner, Sir Evelyn Baring, and the mining tycoon Harry Oppenheimer, who had been to Christ Church. But he was protected from white pressures by his celibate life, and his first loyalty was to his African parishioners. He was the first monk I had met, and at first I felt guilty in his ascetic presence: how could he approve of a sensational magazine? But he admired the courage of the *Drum* writers and sent me promising recruits. I soon found him a sympathetic friend: I could never share his faith, but I was reassured when I visited him in the cloisters of his priory, where he gave me a new view of monkishness. He explained how his three vows – of chastity, poverty and obedience – had given him a new sense of freedom. He had his own human failings: he enjoyed fame, parties and whisky. But he retained his simple dedication to his African parishioners and he was gradually drawn into their political struggle.

As I chugged in and out of Sophiatown on my motorbike it seemed a total contrast to my time at Oxford, where I had learnt plenty about Elizabethan plays but not much about real people. Now this teeming township seemed like a Shakespeare play come to life: sometimes a comedy such as *King Henry IV*, where Falstaff seduces Mistress Quickly in the Eastcheap Tavern; sometimes a tragedy with terror and murder waiting in the wings. Africans too saw the parallel: the young Zulu writer Lewis Nkosi later wrote: 'Ultimately it was the cacophonous, swaggering world of Elizabethan England which gave us the closest parallel to our own mode of existence: the cloak and dagger stories of Shakespeare.' And I soon discovered that my black staff understood *Julius Caesar* much better than I did, despite my degree in English – as a study of revolution. They explained that one scene, which I had thought pointless, really showed each conspirator trying to find out how much the others knew – a familiar precaution for black revolutionaries. But it was not until later that I realised how deeply Shakespeare would influence black politicians.

Drum was probably too obsessed by Sophiatown and by crime. Zeke Mphahlele, the literary editor, later protested in his autobiography about '*Drum*'s arbitrary standard of what the urban African wants to read: sex, crime and love stories; its use of Sophiatown as the yardstick of what the South African non-white should read'. And I soon felt more worried about the hard-drinking lifestyle of *Drum* writers. One evening I had been boozing with Can and Bob Gosani and an intellectual young teacher known as Oubaas, who enjoyed quoting Dante and Milton. After I left them they drove wildly through the townships, where they crashed: Oubaas was killed, Can's face was badly damaged and Bob lost a lung. At Oubaas's funeral, when Huddleston delivered the address by the graveside, I felt overcome with remorse: it was too close to an Elizabethan tragedy. Afterwards in the shebeens Can would recite a typical Sophiatown toast to Oubaas: 'The son of a bitch had no right to lead such a dangerous life.' But the office was never again quite so light hearted.

The apartheid police were steadily closing in on social mixing between whites and blacks, and cracking down more firmly on sex between races, which was forbidden by law. As I spent more time drinking in the townships I lost some of my inhibitions about sex and would find myself relaxed by welcoming black women; but I was haunted by the words of the penalty for being caught: 'six months without the option of a fine'. And there were other dangers of humiliation. One evening in Soweto Todd Matshikiza and his wife Esme gave a dinner party where Esme miraculously produced an English meal of roast beef, Yorkshire pudding and a bottle of sherry from the tiny kitchen. Suddenly six black policemen appeared in the doorway: the sergeant strode up to the table and grabbed the sherry bottle, while the others searched every cupboard for alcohol. We were all marched to the police station, where Todd was fined for possessing liquor, and an Afrikaner detective questioned why I was eating with natives, before he let me go with disgust: 'How can you do it, man, eating with natives? Ag, it makes me sick, man.'

Crossing between black and white Johannesburg, the two separate cities, I was often confused, not surprisingly, about where I really belonged. One evening I would be at a sumptuous barbecue party in a mansion in a northern suburb, making lazy and fatuous conversation round the swimming-pool, served by black servants wearing white gloves and bandoliers. The next night I would be in a box house in Soweto drinking raw brandy by candlelight, listening to far more intelligent and lively talk. When a white woman at a respectable dinner party asked me about my job, my answer caused a deadly silence, as if I had said I was a brothel-keeper.

Jim Bailey, as proprietor of *Drum*, remained caught up in his own contradictions, in his character as well as his predicament. He enjoyed excursions to shebeens and discovering low dives; but he maintained a cool detachment, like Prince Hal in the Eastcheap tavern, egging on Falstaff and his cronies before returning to a life of privilege. He pressed others to play the drinkers' game of Cardinal Puff but stayed sober himself, watching their antics with his loud ambiguous laugh. As a boss he was always stimulating, but unpredictable and erratic: after a few days in Johannesburg he would say casually that the next day he was flying off to the Gold Coast, or to London, or to the farm in the Karoo. He had the imagination of a Northcliffe or a Luce, but lacked the consistent business instinct and found difficulty in finding a manager he could trust. As an old friend from Oxford I could argue and stand up to him, but his black staff were often confused by his alternating camaraderie and detachment. Yet he kept his commitment and vision of a truly African magazine, through all the commercial and political dangers. 'They never had an easy relationship, Jim and those black journos, and they exchanged their fair share of terminal abuse,' wrote John Matshikiza, the son of Todd, after Jim died. 'But they all knew that, somehow or other, they made the damn thing work, like nothing else worked in that accursed space of South Africa.'

All of us saw politics looming larger, and in the townships we could never escape the spreading tentacles of the apartheid monster. Most *Drum* writers were not naturally political: they looked for wider horizons outside the struggle and valued their self-expression. Can, the most brilliant, was also the most sceptical. 'I'm glad not to be mixed up in politics,' he once told me; 'if I was, I'd be one of the most dangerous men in Africa. As it is, it bores me.' In a poignant essay, 'The Bottom of the Bottle', he described how he was canvassed in a shebeen by a huge hoarse-voiced politician: 'The *Ah*frican National Congress is not a political party, it is the organisation of every *Ah*frican.' Can responded by barking 'Afrika!' and hugging his bottle, while the Congress man said: 'He's drunk, that's all.' But Can realised, as he put it, that 'the machine that was ploughing up the country could not leave one square inch undisrupted'. And politics was even penetrating Fatsy's shebeen.

For myself, South Africa provided a crash course in political theory which I had never learnt in England. At Oxford I had been a political innocent, vaguely High Tory, and sceptical about socialism. Power and wealth in Britain seemed diffused and divided, rooted in ancient institutions and foundations; but in South Africa they were recent and raw, and among the *Drum* writers I saw the receiving end of brute power, witnessing oppression at first hand. Johannesburg was almost a caricature of Marxist theory, with the capitalists all white, and the workers black. The Afrikaner government controlled the machinery of the state through the army and the police, while the great mining-companies controlled the finance. On the white side, the whole city looked like a masterwork of capitalism, building extravagant mansions and tree-lined suburbs with the money from foreign investors exploiting the goldfields, transforming the bare veld into an oasis of luxury. But the black side looked like a proletarian nightmare, with its straight rows of tiny houses and shacks spreading between the mine dumps.

I never became a Marxist, but I soon moved leftwards: I immersed myself in black South African history and I took a new interest in the history of the British working class. I could understand why Lenin saw South Africa as the extreme case of capitalism. It was easy to answer his questions about power: 'Who? Whom?' The whites had the power, and the blacks were without it. I had to keep asking myself: when and how would power ever change hands?

And as I came to know black politicians, I found them more interesting than any white politicians in South Africa, or in Britain. For their lack of power and privilege put a premium on more fundamental qualities of courage and identification with their people. Without money, there was little scope for corruption or even patronage. They had to remain close to their roots to survive, to develop political antennae without help from opinion polls or party agents; and like any subject people they had to watch their white masters like hawks.

As the apartheid government tightened the screws black politicians were becoming more militant, but the white newspapers did not take them seriously – which gave *Drum* a special opportunity. Soon after becoming editor, in December 1951 I drove down with Henry Nxumalo and Jürgen Schadeberg to the annual meeting of the African National Congress, in a sweltering tin-roofed hall in the Bloemfontein township. The delegates were not very welcoming, and many resisted Jürgen taking their mugshots: I could spot only four other whites in the audience. I was exasperated by the delays, the incompetence, the slow speeches in three languages which seemed to lead nowhere. I could hardly imagine this slow-moving organisation ever coming to power. But Henry was more impressed, and I was surprised by the intelligence and commitment of the younger leaders – most of all by quiet, bespectacled Walter Sisulu, the newly elected secretary of the ANC, who was friendlier than most. And by the end of three days I was astonished to find that Congress had somehow committed itself to a historic decision: the ANC would launch a passive resistance campaign in protest against the new apartheid laws, which put it on the road to outright confrontation with the government.

Over the first months of 1952 I watched the black leaders gradually shifting from passivity to militancy, as they mobilised volunteers to launch the Defiance Campaign, which *Drum* covered at length. The provocative campaign provided a test for the attitudes of liberal whites. The apartheid regime was beginning to look like a menacing replay of the Nazi regime in Germany, which had collapsed in ignominy a decade earlier; but most liberal whites could not manage to ally themselves with black politicians who threatened to undermine their comfortable security by asserting their power. Most of them saw themselves as leading the blacks, rather than joining their cause: even Helen Suzman, the courageous and feisty MP whom I much admired, or Ellen Helman, the dedicated chairman of the Institute of Race Relations. Harry Oppenheimer, who controlled Anglo American, the biggest gold combine, was much praised as a liberal patron, but he was very hostile to the ANC, which he saw as dangerously revolutionary.

I came closer to the few liberal whites who identified themselves with the ANC cause. One of them was Patrick Duncan, who had an impeccable background: educated at Winchester and Oxford, son of a former governor-general of South Africa, and former private secretary of the high commissioner Sir Evelyn Baring. But he had developed a deep sympathy for blacks ever since he had made friends with black servants at Government House, and he became a close friend to Jim Bailey and me, while his sister Deborah worked for a time on *Drum*. Pat was a charming and inspiring companion, an idealist who talked with the boyish enthusiasm of a John Buchan hero, and he was soon moving closer towards black politicians. I helped to persuade him to join the Defiance Campaign, and he illegally entered a township on crutches, alongside Manilal Gandhi, the son of the Mahatma, to be sent to prison. But he was soon worried by the communist influence within the ANC and instead he quixotically joined the more extreme but anti-communist Pan Africanist Congress.

Trevor Huddleston had followed a very different route to commitment. When he first came to South Africa in 1943 he had been politically naïve and cautious, disapproving of militant clerics such as Michael Scott; but as he became more identified with his black parishioners he was provoked to 'holy anger' against apartheid and its appeasers. He became more outspoken until by 1953 he finally committed himself to support the ANC. I listened to him in the Trades Hall in Johannesburg making his bravest speech, saying that 'when government degenerates into tyranny . . . laws cease to be binding on its subjects'. His black audience were amazed that a white clergyman should ally himself with their cause.

I was moved to see Huddleston, Duncan and other courageous white liberals stand up to be counted: many ordinary people, who would normally have led safe commonplace lives, suddenly rose to the challenge and seemed larger than life, throwing long shadows on this African stage; and they played an important historical role in persuading black leaders – including Nelson Mandela – that they had serious friends among whites. But most white liberals were too preoccupied with their own rivalries and policies, arguing endlessly about limited franchises and voting rights, to have much time to listen to the black leaders themselves. As I spent more time in the townships, I was more convinced than ever that the future of the country lay with the black leadership and the decisions within the ANC. Surprisingly little was known or written about it, but *Drum* provided a wonderful listening-post. I was still unversed in political history, but I had a good view from the ground. My main insights came from the shebeens, through a haze of liquor and laughter, but they had their advantages.

It was at Andy Anderson's print shop that I first encountered the young lawyer-revolutionary Nelson Mandela. He was not a frequent shebeener or drinker, but forty years later, when he was president and I was his biographer, he would often introduce me to others – including Prince Charles – by saying: 'I first met Tony in a shebeen.' The encounter should have been imprinted on my mind; but my memory was shaky, I was probably quite drunk, and he recalled it better than I.

Soon afterwards I saw Mandela on a much more memorable occasion when I watched him launch the Defiance Campaign, of which he was chief volunteer. On 26 June 1952 I drove out to Boksburg, a grim mining town outside Johannesburg, to watch him assembling the first batch of fifty-two 'defiers', including Indians as well as Africans, who gathered outside the township and then walked through the gates with quiet dignity, to be arrested by the police for illegally entering – while Mandela stood by calmly. It was the beginning of the open resistance to apartheid which would culminate in Mandela's imprisonment ten years later, but it was a low-key event, designed to offer no provocation, and few people recognised its significance. Two months later I commissioned Mandela to write a short article in *Drum* called 'We defy' – his first major contribution – which spelt out his commitment: 'Though it takes us years,' he wrote, 'we are prepared to continue the campaign until the six unjust laws we have chosen for the present phase are done away with.' After some copies had been printed we had to scrap the article because it became illegal after Mandela and others had been arrested.[2]

I would love to recollect that I recognised Mandela from the start as a true leader of his people, destined to change the course of history. But in truth at that time I sadly underestimated him: he seemed to me too flashy and vain, with his immaculate suits and his wide smile, and he kept aloof from most white observers; I found his rhetoric too formal and stilted, full of anti-colonialist clichés. I was much more impressed by his mentor, Walter Sisulu, and by his legal partner, the intellectual Oliver Tambo. It was not until 1962, when he made his first great speech in court before going to jail, that I realised his true courage and total commitment.

*

There were many extraordinary expatriates working in South Africa. One Christmas I drove down on my motorbike to stay with one of the most remarkable of them, Dr Anthony Barker, a well-qualified British surgeon who ran the famous Charles Johnson Memorial Hospital in Nqutu, a remote settlement in one of the poorest parts of Zululand, then a 'native reserve' adjoining Natal. Zululand possessed a beautiful landscape which conveyed all the splendour of Africa untouched by urban influences, but it was desperately poor, with only a thin layer of soil above the rock and ravines formed by soil erosion. The patients, from a population of 40,000, arrived either by foot or by an infrequent rackety bus, known (so Anthony told me) as 'the Lady of Easy Virtue' because it picked up so many men on the way.

Anthony was a charismatic leader, a stocky, bearded man, still with a rich Birmingham brogue; he had come out from England to work at the hospital and had fallen in love with a beautiful young missionary doctor, Maggie, who had contracted to work there in return for her medical education, paid for by the Christian Medical Society. He was determined to stay with her, so he took over her contract and remained in Zululand. He became a dedicated missionary with a confident paternalism and a pioneering enterprise, and as a hobby he made his own beautiful furniture; but he retained a wide interest in the world, and a robust humour and enjoyment of life: when he drank whisky in the evenings he would give a toast 'to the Reverend Doctor Alcohol!' He spoke fluent Zulu, with all its clicks, and was well versed in Zulu culture and traditions: he often talked impatiently of the frustrations of trying to convince his patients about the benefits of scientific medicine, and their ingratitude for their cures, which they regarded as acts of fate, rather than the results of rational treatment; but he had long ago come to respect the local witch doctors, who could often cure hysterical patients, by throwing bones and muttering chants, much better than he.

Anthony immediately involved me in hospital life, enlisting me as an orderly to help with his operations in the makeshift theatre, and I followed him on his rounds with his black bag through his patients' tiny thatched huts: he helped a Zulu woman in labour, lying on her straw mat on the ground, with no furniture or decoration except the jawbone of an ass hanging over the entrance to keep the evil spirits away. On Christmas day there were celebrations, half Christian, half pagan, in which Zulu women sang with their high-pitched ululations.

Anthony disapproved sternly of *Drum*'s depiction of that undisciplined world, and of the communist revolutionaries of the ANC who were threatening to disrupt the missionaries' dedication. 'You and Jim are like people at a boys' club determined to show that you can be one of the boys.' Watching the tangible achievements of doctors and nurses at that hospital – the lives saved, the miseries averted – I could not but feel the uselessness and irresponsibility of my own dubious profession as a journalist. Yet I still felt, as I argued with Anthony, that I had found my way into a world that was more relevant to the future of Africa.

As I sat in the *Drum* office listening to the excited stories of black resistance I was still astonished by the lack of interest of white South Africans in the leaders who were beginning to show their strength. Most whites, encouraged by the government's propaganda, were convinced that the ANC was merely a tool of Moscow. And the British government largely followed the Pretoria line. British diplomats and foreign correspondents rarely made contact with the ANC leaders, or even with the *Drum* reporters. When I occasionally encountered British diplomats they were preoccupied with getting closer to Afrikaner ministers, or with all-white social functions, and they asked me no questions about the black world: the annual Queen's Birthday Party admitted no black guests. When forty years later I read through the confidential British despatches, I noticed that the high commission took its view of black politics entirely from the South African police, who were convinced that the ANC was run from the Kremlin. The prime minister, Winston Churchill, commented on a report on the Defiance Campaign in 1952: 'What the communists and Indian intriguers are doing is really to help Malan,' who was the staunchly pro-apartheid politician who rallied support by his anti-communist stance. Churchill continued: 'They must be very stupid not to see this.'[3] But the British diplomats had no personal contacts with black politicians: when a few years later the high commission was asked by London for more information about Congress, all they could do was to send them two paragraphs of a book I had written, *The Treason Cage*. It confirmed my suspicions about the limitations of British diplomats.

I had my own mixed feelings about the white communists who worked closely with the ANC. At every Congress gathering I encountered the same comrades, such as Joe Slovo or his journalist wife Ruth First, whom I came to know well. I enjoyed the Slovos' parties, in their modern house in a Johannesburg suburb, where white and black communists drank and flirted together, with all the camaraderie of shared commitment and danger. I had to admire the courage of the white comrades whose party had been the only multiracial force before it was banned in 1950: they still kept together, sharing the danger and persecution of their black colleagues. Many of them were successful professional people who had sacrificed promising careers to join the struggle. But they had such a different outlook from mine: mostly from Jewish families who had been refugees from Lithuania and elsewhere in eastern Europe, they were convinced by the Marxist dogma to build a new Utopia in South Africa, which I could not believe in. To most white liberals, as well as the government, they seemed to threaten the whole fabric of capitalist society.

Yet from my *Drum* experience I could not believe that black South Africans, with all their individuality and pride, would in the end be attracted to the communist system. The ANC itself had much deeper roots in Christianity than in communism and the new president of Congress, Albert Luthuli, a former tribal chief, was a devout Christian. Mandela was close to the communists, but his law partner Oliver Tambo, who would himself later become president of Congress, was another convinced Christian, nearly becoming a priest. It is true that the Christian churches in the early 1950s were cautious and compromised by their segregated congregations and clergy, but a few priests such as Trevor Huddleston were already becoming more militant; and later church leaders such as Archbishop Desmond Tutu could depict Christ as a revolutionary with a more powerful message than Marx. But ultimately it was nationalism which was the driving-force of African politics, and the humiliations and provocations of apartheid were making blacks all the more determined that they must rule themselves.

In South Africa it was Sophiatown that first felt the ruthless physical impact of the theory of apartheid, when the government decided to knock down the 'black spot' and to forcibly remove its African inhabitants to Meadowlands, on the edge of the sprawling mass of Soweto. The *Drum* writers who lived in Sophiatown saw its removal as a personal outrage, but to the ANC it was a major political challenge. The walls were scrawled with 'We Won't Move', young gangsters were converted into agitators, crowds listened to protest meetings until they were banned. Mandela made an explosive speech, telling the crowd to prepare for violence. The tension mounted as removal day approached in February 1955. Foreign correspondents flew in, the police issued warnings, the tsotsis or gangsters chanted down the streets. Even Can Themba at the House of Truth was infected with the revolutionary spirit, reciting Dickens: 'It was the best of times, it was the worst of times.' Many Sophiatowners still believed that their spirit could prevail against force; but they were quite unrealistic. I arrived there at dawn on 9 February to find 2,000 police; at 6 a.m. lorries and motorbikes roared into the township, carrying people who began taking furniture out of the first houses scheduled for demolition, while the occupants offered no resistance. Four days later the tsotsis tried to organise a strike; the whole township shrieked as they hit the metal telephone poles – the signal for revolt. But the streets quickly filled up with police cars, which chased them down the alleys, while the workers meekly queued up to take buses to work.

It was my first grim view of how ruthless power looked from the receiving end: how a crazy ideology could uproot a community and ruin people's lives. 'Sophiatown was preparing the people for a new frontier,' wrote the ex-gangster Don Mattera, 'and then it was just wiped out.' For Mandela it was a turning-point: 'Sophiatown died not to the sound of gunfire but to the sound of rumbling trucks and sledgehammers,' he wrote later; and it was then that he first recognised that 'we had no alternative to armed and violent resistance'.

On the day of the abortive strike I experienced my own moment of truth. I was watching the police cars charging towards the protesting tsotsis with apprehension, when I noticed that the tsotsis were dancing and dodging between the cars, laughing as if they were playing a game rather than confronting an enemy. I felt suddenly very English, as if I were blundering into a strange sport between black Africans and Afrikaners whose violent rules I would never understand. And just then, a police car pulled up and I recognised the pug-face of Major Spengler, the head of the Special Branch, whom I had often observed at ANC meetings. There would be no trouble, he assured me, and then added, with a smile: 'I hear you're going back to England very soon?'

He was right. After four years in South Africa I felt I had achieved what I could; I was not prepared to go to jail for the cause, and at twenty-eight I wanted to try my luck as a journalist in London. It was a painful decision and separation, and my farewell party at the House of Saints in Sophiatown, which was already being demolished, reminded me of the splendours I was leaving. The small dingy room filled up with the *Drum* staff, a few white friends including Nadine Gordimer and Reinhold Cassirer, and local black stars, including the famous singers Dolly Rathebe and Thandi Klaasen, the guitarist Alpheus Nkosi and the saxophonist Ben Gwigwi. The music started and everyone sprang into jive; the room was full of writhing bodies like a snakepit. Dolly sang 'Stardust', like a black Marlene Dietrich, then jived with the amazed Scots advertising manager. Ben played his own jazz composition and imitated Caruso. Alpheus sang a Zulu song. The floorboards shook and the lights swayed. Can jived by the doorway alone, his frail body curled forward, one arm curved behind him like a spring, vibrating and tense with energy. The band worked themselves up into a frenzy and strode round the room pointing their instruments in the air and playing to each guest in turn. The walls seemed to disappear altogether, spirited away by the music, as the room was filled with fast-moving shapes – bodies, legs, trombone tubes flashing in the light. 'I suppose you find this very savage,' said my neighbour; 'how would *you* describe it?' I referred him to Nadine, who expressed her delight. 'You're lucky,' a rueful bespectacled girl said to her. 'You can enjoy yourselves. My husband won't let me'. Someone said: 'And you whites are getting rid of Sophiatown!' At the end Todd Matshikiza presented me with a briefcase and two beer mugs inscribed with *Drum*. Can made a fulsome speech of praise, and I replied: 'I didn't make *Drum, Drum* made me.'

I returned to London in March 1955 as I had arrived, by sea: I gave a little party on the SS *Rhodesia Castle* in Durban Dock, seen off by old *Drum* friends, thinking I would never see South Africa again. I was very conscious that *Drum* had made me into someone more confident and experienced, more understanding of the effects of politics and power. But I saw it as an adventurous prelude, before I started a more serious career, a sowing of wild oats: yet another story of a young white man's self-discovery by losing himself in Africa. It took me some time to realise that my view of the world – and of Britain – had been turned upside down by my Johannesburg experience and would never revert; and I never imagined that South Africa would remain a consuming interest for the rest of my life.

The *Rhodesia Castle* was a cargo liner which took six weeks to reach England, stopping a few days in each port up the east coast. Lingering in Lourenço Marques (now Maputo), Beira, Zanzibar, Dar es Salaam or Port Sudan, I had time to glimpse the splendours of colonial Africa, with its imperial palaces, gymkhana clubs and military police, which were already feeling less secure. From Mombasa I took the romantic night train to Nairobi, which had been militarised by the Mau Mau rebellion. The white settlers, wearing revolvers, were swaggering at the bar of the New Stanley Hotel, while the Kikuyu boys were less obedient and the black politicians were conspiring for power. But I found them much less articulate and interesting than the blacks in Sophiatown.

The liner was full of white settlers and colonial officers who were liberated and stimulated by shipboard life as if playing out a Somerset Maugham short story, with wild drinking, wife-swapping and passionate affairs. I breakfasted every day at the table of the first officer, who fed me with sea stories every morning: how he had seduced a settler's wife the night before; how he extracted commissions from the trinket-sellers who came on board; how the bluff colonel at the captain's table was really a homosexual who picked up sailors in Dar es Salaam; how on the previous voyage a settler was so drunk that he dived into the swimming-pool without noticing it was empty, and killed himself. I shared a small cabin with three Afrikaner youths who complained that they might be made to sit next to kaffirs in London: 'If we do, there'll be war.' I retreated into daily games of chess with an Irish lawyer and began to write a book about *Drum*.

After steaming through the Suez Canal and Port Said the ship stopped at Genoa, Marseilles and Gibraltar, and became part of Europe. When it docked in Genoa alongside the Renaissance city I suddenly realised how much I had been missing Europe through my four years of bleak Johannesburg. Taking the bus to Rapallo, winding through the enchanting hillsides of vineyards and olive groves in spring, my American fellow-passenger said: 'You can keep the whole of Africa; I'll just take this.' I half agreed; but I also knew that I had learnt more about the mainsprings of history and power in Johannesburg than I would ever understand from looking back on the past glories of Italy.

3

Observer

As we steamed towards England, I felt increasingly anxious about my lack of qualifications for any serious career in journalism, after my amateur adventures. I contracted toothache and, after having a tooth painfully extracted in Aden without any relief, I realised it was psychosomatic. But once back in London I was astonished to find that I was marketable. My friend William Clark's advice had been precisely right: 'If you want to get into Fleet Street go as far away from it as possible.' I realised that, having been away from England, I saw it more clearly; and by huge luck South Africa was now a fashionable subject, on both the left and the right. To my surprise I was summoned by Stuart Maclean, a nephew of Lord Northcliffe who was managing the *Daily Mail*, who immediately offered me a highly paid job. But just before I said yes, I went to see David Astor at the *Observer*.

I had first known about David through *Drum*, which had attracted his interest as a champion of African rights. He had cabled Jim Bailey in Johannesburg to tell him more, and I hastily wrote some notes – which I was soon startled to find printed verbatim on the next leader page of the *Observer*. (It was a useful lesson, that journalists often write best when they don't expect to be in print.) When I came back to London David asked me to lunch at his house, which overlooked Lord's cricket ground and had a Henry Moore in the garden. At forty-three he still looked boyish, with his questioning eyes, a thatch of hair and diffident mumbles. I was a gauche 29-year-old, but he was immediately disarming: he questioned me about *Drum* as if the popular magazine was as important as his newspaper, and asked me how to improve the *Observer*. Half-way through lunch he murmured that he needed some kind of organiser, and perhaps I could join the paper as an 'assistant to the editor'. I said yes before he could find out how little I really knew. When I told Maclean about my decision he was baffled: 'I can't see the connection between *Drum* and the *Observer*.' Nor at that moment could I.

The *Observer* was then at the peak of its influence as a highbrow political and cultural organ, respected almost equally on the right and the left. Its sixteen pages every Sunday seemed to be at the centre of all serious debates, discussed at dinner parties and setting agendas for politicians. It was original and unpredictable, linked to neither major political party, and defying conventional wisdom. Coming from South Africa I felt I had joined a topsy-turvy world where black was white and left was right.

How did the *Observer* command such authority and influence? Arriving at its quaint building off Fleet Street, tucked behind the *Daily Mail*, I was amazed by its apparent casualness: it seemed more like a family charity or an eccentric college than a commercial newspaper. The manager, Tristan Jones, was an ex-communist and David's childhood friend, whose real interest was collecting antiques: he projected a deep negativity behind a big deadpan moustache. The front office was run by a jovial cockney, Charles Vidler; he had been the butler at Cliveden, the Astors' great country house, but had been fired for being found asleep in Lord Astor's bed. The manager of both circulation and advertising, Norman Berridge, a nervous man whose father had been general manager, felt harassed by advertisers clamouring for space – because newsprint was strictly rationed. David, as he himself explained, preferred not to know about circulation figures yet they went up and up without apparent effort.

I had a ringside view of the strange workings of the paper. I was put in an office just opposite David's open door, watching visitors coming and going like a concierge. I saw David almost every day over two years, and often in the evenings or at lunch. I was fascinated by my improbable boss, who came from such a different background, and would always be surprised and amazed to enjoy his friendship over the next forty-five years. The Astors at that time were regarded almost like royalty. David's father, Waldorf, the second Viscount Astor, had been one of the richest men in the world, inheriting a fortune made in fur-trading and multiplied by investments in Manhattan real estate. His mother, Nancy, the first woman MP to take her seat in the Commons, was the dominating hostess of Cliveden. And David was part of an extended cousinhood which moved in the heart of the transatlantic power world. David was much influenced by his father, whose photograph sat on his desk, and often talked about him (he favoured the Waldorf Hotel for office lunches, he explained, because it reminded him of his father and the Astor home village in Baden-Württemberg). But he had rebelled against his formidable mother while he was at Eton; he had a breakdown while at Oxford and never took a degree (though he later showed every sign of an alpha mind). He was psychoanalysed by Anna Freud, with unusual success – though he sometimes went to sleep, he told me, during sessions. He discovered himself through artists, intellectuals and Labour politicians, not through Tories or aristocrats. At grand social occasions he was visibly shy: 'David doesn't even know how to get out of a room,' complained one of his Tory cousins. But on his home ground he was relaxed and completely unstuffy, using schoolboy phrases like 'hols', 'chums' or 'okey-dokey'. His perfect manners were based not on etiquette but on sensitivity to others. Once when I asked for a beer at his house he disappeared for an age before returning with a pint glass: I was convinced that he had gone round to a pub rather than say he had none.

He had taken over the *Observer* when he was just twenty-nine, after only a year's training on the *Yorkshire Post*. But he had been brought up in Cliveden and London against a background of Cabinet ministers, diplomats and intellectuals constantly arguing and explaining events: as other children played nursery games, he overheard statesmen and politicians playing the world's game of high diplomacy. He remained surrounded by talkers and fascinated by ideas, all the more because he had failed at Oxford: he saw his *Observer*, he explained later, as 'the Balliol I never had'. As I had also wasted my Oxford years, the paper also gave me a second chance, providing the intellectual stimulus and camaraderie that I had never felt at Christ Church, and much more fun. Was I being paid, for *this*?

David had personally picked most of the *Observer* journalists, who seemed to reflect each stage of his development: 'We are all part of the litter of his past,' said Patrick O'Donovan. He was an ex-Guards officer whom David had recruited at the end of the war. Nigel Gosling, the features editor, had been his friend at Eton. Philip Toynbee, the chief reviewer, was the son of his father's friend Arnold Toynbee. Terence Kilmartin, the literary editor, had helped to rescue him in France during the war. Sebastian Haffner and

Richard Lowenthal, the international pundits, had been recruited by David to join his wartime brains trust. Colin Legum, the Africa correspondent, had been picked when David became passionately concerned with South Africa.

I was very conscious that I owed my job to David's passionate interest in South Africa. He was always repelled by racism, certainly partly in reaction against his mother – though he would deny that. When the apartheid government came to power in Pretoria in 1948 he was appalled at the promotion of a racial doctrine so soon after the death of Hitler and wrote an eloquent leader in the *Observer*. He followed South Africa closely and his knowledge was all the more remarkable since he had never been there. I often felt that he understood it better than I did. David was concerned that British anti-apartheid campaigners like Trevor Huddleston and Canon John Collins were being duped by communists, and he gave some support to anti-communist black rebels against the ANC. But his main concern was coming to terms with African nationalism and avoiding the mistakes the British had made in India, which George Orwell had warned him about after the war; in this he was far ahead of governments, whether Conservative or Labour.

From my strategic desk I watched the week slowly maturing. David would start work on Tuesday morning, but many journalists did not turn up until Wednesday and the paper only began to take shape on Thursday. On Friday contributors would arrive, bringing their handwritten copy and staying for drinks at 'Auntie's', the *Observer* pub. Then the managing editor, Kenneth Obank, a masterly and long-suffering professional from Yorkshire, began to transform the messy paragraphs and wild ideas into a proper newspaper, which a team of sub-editors from other papers finally knocked into shape on Saturday. It was a weekly miracle to watch the hot air distilled into cold print.

For David edited the paper through talk which was transmuted into journalism. He held interminable conferences, about editorials, features and special projects, nearly all of which I attended as his assistant. 'Mao invented the permanent revolution,' complained John Pringle, later the deputy editor, 'but David invented the permanent conference.' I listened bewildered by the passions and range of debates ranging across the whole world. Rix Lowenthal, with one eye rotating round the room, worried about outposts like Quemoy or Yemen as if they were his own big toe. William Clark, the diplomatic correspondent, brought titbits from embassy dinners, high tables or episcopal gatherings. Nora Beloff argued with Bob Stephens about Israelis and Arabs across the table as if it were the river Jordan itself, while David – who had both Jewish and Arab friends – wrestled with an editorial which could be fair to both sides.

General elections generated still more conferences. David was determined to maintain the paper's independence from either party: he published views from all sides, and wrote contorted editorials which sat precariously on the fence. He was pro-Labour over issues which concerned him most passionately, including Africa, hanging, censorship and human rights, and he was a friend of Hugh Gaitskell, the Labour leader. But he was closer to the Conservatives on taxation, trade unions or nationalisation. To many people David appeared as a socialist millionaire, a contradiction in terms: why should an Astor want to get rid of his fortune? But he was never a socialist, and his combination of views was more in keeping with American Democrats.

David's range of interests seemed limitless; but his eyes glazed over at the mention of economics and industry, which he delegated to successive economics editors – Susan Strange, Andrew Shonfield and later Sam Brittan. Most of the other pundits, I noticed, hardly seemed worried by Britain's industrial decline: they seemed too preoccupied with Britain's responsibilities in the world to notice that she could not afford much of a role. I kept sending David memos about covering business more seriously, and later started my own column called Mammon; but I felt David's heart was not in it. It was the discussions about traffic, I noticed, which revealed the paper's real lack of understanding of industry. Why didn't they ban lorries from the new motorways, asked Philip Toynbee.

The stately masthead of the paper, with its royal crest, and the dignified by-lines concealed some very undignified goings-on which might have come from Evelyn Waugh. Admiring readers would turn up at the office expecting to meet a solemn pundit, to find a dishevelled shape slumped in a pub. Many famous contributors were heavy drinkers who were escaping from themselves or dominating fathers, while still taking themselves very seriously. Philip shambled in wearing his old duffel-coat, and told comic stories against himself, giggling like a soda siphon, until he collapsed in a deep chair for the afternoon. He relished his own fiascos: after the Hungarian uprising of 1956 he recruited a band of young idealists to follow him in a protest march across

Europe; but he got no further than a West End pub. One drunken night he returned to the *Observer* offices to sleep: the caretaker complained and next morning Tristan Jones reprimanded him. Philip was furious and went on to David's office to complain, but David just said sadly: 'Philip, you peed in the lift.' Behind all his clowning Philip still saw himself as a moral prophet, like his father Arnold and his daughter Polly, from an intellectual aristocracy – as emerged in his verse memoir *Pantaloon*.

Patrick O'Donovan, the son of an eminent surgeon, was likewise divided: with his ruddy Irish face and strong physique he was a legendary war correspondent, writing vivid reports in sharp staccato sentences. But he was a formidable drinker and later he went on more destructive binges – 'occasional touches of Gaelic abandon', David called them in his obituary – and was confined to quiet reporting of country life or ceremonials. He was frequently hospitalised: 'I have just come out of hospital again,' he wrote to me in 1974. 'I don't think I shall ever be able to respect anyone of any position again. I know the ritual humiliations they all go through at one time or another in their lives.' But he was kept going by his wife Hermione and their faith and loyalty to the Catholic Church; and his funeral was a major Catholic event.

Alistair Buchan, the diplomatic correspondent, was still more surprising. He was the son of Lord Tweedsmuir, a former governor-general of Canada, better known as the author John Buchan. Alistair had a military moustache and voice; but he went on violent drunken escapades: one night the *Observer* had a call from the local police asking them to collect him from the station, where four officers were needed to hold him down. He seemed bent on self-destruction before he gave up drink and went on to found the Institute of Strategic Studies, later becoming a professor at Oxford.

Few of the *Observer*'s writers seemed altogether stable, behind their confident pronouncements. I joined the paper expecting to be one of its most neurotic employees, but soon found myself outbid. John Gale, the reporter I most admired, projected a boyish enthusiasm and openness, conveyed in his autobiography *A Clean Young Englishman*. He delighted in recording the talk of ordinary people, questioning them with wide eyes and scribbling on a big clipboard. But he was increasingly manic-depressive, and after he was sent to report the horrific Algerian War he never fully recovered. David protected him from future ordeals, but he kept sinking back into depression and eventually committed suicide on Hampstead Heath.

Among such wobbly talents David appeared more like a Renaissance patron than an editor: 'we are all Astoroids', said John Silverlight, a colleague on the paper. Many of us doubted who else would employ us, and for myself I could never work out what he saw in me. We were always talking and speculating about David, his latest craze, theory or guru. He had a touch of the impresario: the last great actor-manager, we called him. 'Showbiz made him who he is,' said the theatre critic John Heilpern. He had always loved the theatre: he had briefly run a troupe of performers touring seaside resorts in Yorkshire, and he brought his own kind of showmanship to Fleet Street; he seemed to regard his journalists as temperamental actors, to be humoured, reassured and given their cues, sometimes their lines. He was a constant father figure, always prepared to discuss emotional problems or to intervene in a crisis.

The *Observer* was sometimes known as 'Dr Astor's Clinic' or 'that hospital for lame ducks'. David seemed to welcome the challenge of impossible people: for example Brendan Behan, the alcoholic playwright whom he tried unsuccessfully to stop drinking himself to death. He appeared to understand his staff better than they understood themselves, as Michael Davie complained. He regarded much illness as psychosomatic and explained most difficult behaviour in psychological terms: Kenneth Harris blustered because he was insecure, Katharine Whitehorn suffered from penis envy, Lord Hailsham was 'running away from love'. He remained a convinced Freudian after his own analysis: 'I don't believe in God,' he told Susan Strange, 'but I do believe in Freud.' It was wiser not to mention heretics like Jung, or to criticise Dr Benjamin Spock, whose book *Baby and Child Care* was serialised in the *Observer*.

David depicted aggression – whether by people or nations – in nursery terms, and he was always telling people to be 'adult'. He himself was always adult in arguing with his colleagues, disarming them with quiet reasoning and a diffident style, but he was, as the philosopher Sir Anthony Kenny observed, 'most dangerous when most diffident'. Sometimes he tried to use me as a troubleshooter to sort out office problems and he would give me advice about handling awkward members of the staff. He hoped I could persuade Mechthild Nawiasky, the fiery picture editor who had once been a lion-tamer, to use news photographs as well as the moody, soft-focus pictures she favoured on the front page. 'Handle Mechthild carefully and straight-forwardly,' he advised in a note, 'and I think you'll find she will try to co-operate. (None of us is responsible for our temperaments – only for our efforts to master them.)' But he could resort to psychological tricks when other means failed, and attack motivation instead of arguments. He was once in a difficult fix, he told me, when the veteran film critic Caroline Lejeune was spotted walking out of a movie by the director Roy Boulting, and then rubbished it in print. When Boulting called to complain David had no real defence, so he replied: 'You're enjoying this too much.'

With all his tolerance, David was stubborn about pursuing policies he really believed in, and defied anyone who crossed him on questions like nuclear disarmament, African independence or Freudian interpretations. Terry Kilmartin, who had known him in the war, would warn: 'David's as tough as old boots.' Behind all its variety the paper always reflected David's own personality and interests: it was as loveable or hateable as a single human being. David resisted market research to find out what readers really wanted: when a survey *was* conducted it depressingly recorded how readers lost interest in editorials or book reviews with each new paragraph, but he refused to show it to the journalists. When he complained to Cecil King, the chairman of the *Daily Mirror* about how the *Mirror* distorted the news, King said that he had to keep worrying about the sales. David had replied: 'I edit the *Observer* for myself and my friends.' He was always prepared to take risks with his readers. When Nikita Khrushchev made his speech denouncing Stalin, David was persuaded by Ken Obank, the managing editor, to devote most of the newspaper to printing the whole 26,000 words, leaving out advertisements and much topical news. But the readers agreed: the whole issue sold out and had to be reprinted.

'It's a great life if you don't weaken,' David liked to say, and I could not see him weaken. Despite his unhappy adolescence, he never seemed insecure or un-adult. One day when he was irritable, he explained that he had been arguing with his first wife; but his home life with his second wife, Bridget, seemed entirely tranquil. Yet he was never sure about how much he had achieved independently of his rich inheritance: when much later he tried to write his autobiography he gave up because he could not face the word 'I'.

It was an awesome inheritance. Every summer the *Observer* staff had its annual outing at Cliveden, the great country house on the Thames over which his parents had presided, where his brother Bill, the third Viscount Astor, uneasily welcomed the odd mixture of printers, secretaries and journalists. Wives, husbands and children wandered along the lawns, listened to the band of the Grenadier Guards and swam in the pool which was soon to become notorious. It was at Cliveden that I first met David's mother, Nancy, who had dominated the house in the 1930s, and who was still intimidating in her seventies. 'So you work for my son David,' she said, 'with all those niggers and communists?' Her influence was still felt: the *Observer* refused to accept alcohol advertisements because she was a Christian Scientist.

But David had long ago rejected most of his mother's fierce beliefs, beginning with Christian Science. One evening at dinner I heard him mocking its founder, Mary Baker Eddy, with Patrick Duncan and Mary Benson, a South African writer and activist who also had Christian Science parents, and speculating how such a dotty religion had produced the *Christian Science Monitor*: 'How amazing that a crazy woman should help to found one of the world's great newspapers,' he said. 'It's hard enough to do when you're sane.' He had reacted strongly against Nancy's racial attitudes, but he always defended his mother. He rejected the view of southerners in the United States as racists: his aunt Nancy Lancaster had explained that the style and dress sense of the Virginians was really derived from the black servants who had brought them up. Above all, David was infuriated by left-wing attacks on his mother as a pro-Nazi anti-Semite; she was after all often fiercely critical of the Nazis, and her husband protested to Hitler about his treatment of the Jews. David would never forgive Claud Cockburn and his news sheet the *Week* for spreading lies about the 'Cliveden set'. His own record as a critic of Hitler was clear: 'The only member of the Cliveden set whose opinion was never sought,' wrote his brother Michael, 'who was right about Germany as well as Russia, was . . . David.'[1] David was deeply hurt by the recurring stories about the Astors encouraging appeasement, and then by the scandal surrounding John Profumo, the Tory minister who had an affair with Christine Keeler (whom I was to meet later), which began at the Cliveden swimming-pool. 'All that people remember today of the Astors is the "Cliveden set" and the

"Profumo set",,' he wrote later. 'Both stories were inventions, but it appears that they'll be with us for ever.'

The Astors were less prominent in the post-war years, but they remained very rich. They still inhabited a separate Astorland, in stately homes with butlers and chefs, apparently invulnerable to high taxation and death duties: even distant relatives, ex-wives or in-laws, seemed still irrigated by underground streams of money. David himself was discreet about his wealth, and lived more modestly than his three brothers, who all had big country mansions: his London houses got smaller as he got older, and he ended up in a quite ordinary narrow terraced house in St John's Wood. But he often seemed to forget that journalists had a different standard of living: one evening he suggested taking me to dinner at 'a little place I know' which turned out to be the Connaught, then the only really grand restaurant in London; he handed me the extravagant wine menu and asked: 'Do you play the grape game?' The *Observer* journalists, who were not overpaid, were puzzled by David's attitudes to money: we envied his security and opportunities, but he seemed to envy middle-class intellectuals and never quite understood the problems of ordinary life outside his gilded cage. He was fascinated to hear from his chauffeur about mortgages, of which he then became a keen advocate and he complained that we did not realise how bored most rich people were: 'They've got nothing to do but change their houses.'

Outsiders saw all the Astors as part of a close network, but David was never close to his uncle John, Lord Astor of Hever, who then owned the *Times*, or to the Hever cousins, who were stuffier than David's side of the family and more linked with the conventional rich world. Once, when the *Observer* was sharing a building with the *Times*, David invited me to join him at lunch with his cousin Gavin, who had become the chairman of the *Times*; I was surprised to find they hardly knew each other.

Through David's younger brother Michael I came to understand more about both the splendours and the miseries of Astorland. Michael had never really found a proper career: after a stint as a Tory MP, in the family tradition, he wanted to become a journalist, and asked me to help him. After a few breakfasts and lunches he invited me for the weekend at Bruern Abbey, his Cotswold pile. It was my first glimpse of a country-house lifestyle which I had only known about through P. G. Wodehouse. I arrived in a rainstorm in my battered Ford, which got stuck in a ditch. I reached the front door bedraggled, carrying my old suitcase, to be greeted by the butler, who calmly took my car keys and showed me into the great hall full of Impressionist paintings and Tory grandees in dinner jackets. I felt totally out of place in my creased Marks & Sparks suit; but Michael, like David, could put anyone at his ease, and he turned out to be more interested in writers than in politicians: he had installed Stephen Spender in the dower house and liked to invite Oxford dons and artists to dinner. I was soon spending frequent weekends with Michael and noticed in the midst of all the entertainment that he was often subject to fits of desperate boredom. Sometimes he would simply disappear in the middle of a house party to play golf; and when I stayed over until Monday morning the façade of fun seemed to collapse into ennui. I would feel guilty, after enjoying all Michael's hospitality and friendship, that I could not reciprocate by rescuing him from his isolation, particularly in his lonely interval between wives: it was only with his third wife, Judy Innes, that he seemed to find peace. Michael would often ask me about life on the *Observer* and I realised that he envied David for having a real job. I recalled Dr Johnson: 'Money cannot buy occupation.'

Stephen Spender was succeeded in the dower house by Roy Jenkins, who spent many weekends there. He and his wife Jennifer often came over to dinner at the big house, where the parties typically included Tory MPs, Oxford dons and writers or artists from London. Roy seemed in his element, always smooth, well informed, at ease with almost everyone. He was very friendly to me as a gauche young journalist, but I was rather in awe of him. I preferred talking to Jennifer, who was more detached from the scene, and she quietly made it clear that she had a strong mind of her own. I found Roy's views liberal, not radical. I remember once trying to interest him in a proposal for a boycott of oil to South Africa which I had published in the *Observer*; he read it carefully, but without response. (But he had no reason to be especially interested in South Africa.)

David had escaped on a silken ladder from this world of bored luxury. He had found an absorbing occupation, engrossed in ideas and causes, peopled by intellectuals and writers from other backgrounds. He used his money in much more interesting and creative ways than most rich men: not just through the *Observer* but also through a network of benefactions and charities which I only discovered later. He became expert in setting up small committees and lobbies – in a few of which I became involved – to discreetly press for reforms and create new institutions. He had developed the art of lobbying he had learnt from his father – to subtly transform ideas into execution. He would put together a small group under a convincing chairman; then he would prompt letters to ministers or the *Times*, arrange meetings at Chatham House (which his father had helped to found), or set up lunches or dinners at one of his five clubs. Then he would retreat into the background, leaving the chairman to take over. Many new institutions which appeared to have emerged autonomously, such as Index on Censorship, the Butler Trust for prison warders or the Minority Rights Group, were the fruits of David's seed.

*

David Astor's privileged background put a special premium on political courage. He needed to prove himself; and the real test of both his editorship and his fortitude was the Suez crisis of 1956 – his 'Agincourt', as he called it. When President Nasser nationalised the Suez Canal the *Observer* was immediately in the eye of a political storm, for the crisis brought to a head the issues David felt strongest about: Africa, nationalism, anti-colonialism and the American alliance. He had some friends in the Tory government of Sir Anthony Eden, and Eden's press secretary, William Clark, had recently left the *Observer* for that position. William gave some warnings that Eden was becoming overexcited, while Rab Butler, then Lord Privy Seal in the Cabinet, told the political correspondent Hugh Massingham that he sometimes felt 'surrounded by madmen'. But David, like the other journalists, never thought that Eden would go to war. He was appalled when British troops invaded the Suez Canal, on the pretext of peace-making between Israel and Egypt, and rightly guessed that Eden had secretly colluded with Israel. He thought that the war would set back all the peaceful decolonising of Africa and cause a rift with Washington. His friend Dingle Foot drafted an editorial which David then sharpened up, inserting phrases which summed up his outlook: 'We had not realised that our government was capable of such folly and crookedness . . . It is no longer possible to bomb countries because you fear that your trading interests will be harmed . . . this new feeling for the sanctity of human life is the best element in the modern world.'

From my office facing his I watched David taking the strain. The *Observer*'s leader appeared just when British troops were landing in Suez, and aroused furious accusations of treachery from conservative readers. Three of the seven trustees resigned in protest: if another had gone, David told me, he would have had to resign, and he always felt grateful to the smooth chairman of the trustees, Sir Ifor Evans, for standing firm. David remained undeterred: when he wrote an unrepentant second leader he headed it 'The government's war' and explained with relish: 'That's a mutinous headline.' Many advertisers were upset: J. Walter Thompson, which handled the *Observer*'s own advertising, gave warnings which I passed on to David but he was unimpressed. Some advertisers withdrew, including Jewish tycoons who resented the criticism of Israel – which saddened David, who had always supported the Zionists. But David's brothers, influenced by their American connections, remained supportive. John Jacob Astor made a speech in Parliament which made him so nervous that he first went to the lavatory to be sick. The historian Hugh Trevor-Roper (later Lord Dacre) was staying with Michael Astor at Bruern and referred to the *Observer* as 'the traitor's paper'; Michael (he told me) told the butler to pack Trevor-Roper's bags.

For weeks the Suez Canal seemed to overflow through the *Observer*'s offices, as it flowed through Eden's drawing-room. Only two of the staff supported the government's policy: the veteran Asian expert O. M. Green and the cartoonist Haro Hodson. I felt myself for the first time watching history with a ringside seat. I heard Eden defending his invasion in Parliament, and I joined the crowds of protesters in Trafalgar Square, who hailed anyone from the *Observer* as a hero. David sent me out to report on the scene in Port Said. I had last seen it as a thriving entrepôt two years earlier on the way back from Africa; now the canal was blocked with sunken ships, the emporia were deserted and the streets were patrolled by nervous British conscripts who sounded confused about their mission. Soon afterwards the British government was compelled to withdraw by American pressure, and faced huge economic losses, while before long all David's suspicions about collusion with Israel were vindicated.

The *Observer* achieved notoriety and attracted many young readers, many of whom were first politicised by the Suez war. At the beginning of the crisis, it had just overtaken the *Sunday Times* in circulation, to the dismay of that paper's owner, Viscount Kemsley, many of whose journalists felt deeply envious of their rival's courage. But the *Observer* also lost many conservative readers and advertisers, and ended up with more impecunious readers who were less attractive to advertisers. Tristan Jones was gloomy, but David was undeterred. He wrote to me:

> Don't let Tristan get you scared. The one way to get into real trouble is if we lose our self-confidence. After all, we've been right over this crisis and will be proved so. We only need not to get alarmed, and should of course avoid saying 'I told you so'. All will be well if we keep our heads.

David reckoned later that his attacks had been too emotive, going beyond reasonable argument, though he was unrepentant. 'I think I would do it again,' he said thirty years later. 'You couldn't keep quiet.'

It was not primarily Suez which damaged the *Observer* in the coming newspaper war, it seemed to me, so much as the lack of commercial drive. David was mainly interested in political influence and despised the commercialism of Kemsley, whose *Sunday Times* was conventionally conservative and printed reverential editorials about the royal family in italics. 'Kemsley orders his politics from Central Office as if it were a commodity like newsprint,' he said; and when he showed me a stuffy letter from Kemsley he commented: 'There are generations of capitalism behind that style.' (There were generations behind David's own style, with a different outcome.) But just after Suez, the *Observer* faced much fiercer commercial competition when newsprint rationing was lifted, allowing newspapers to carry as much advertising as they could get. The *Observer* was caught napping while the *Sunday Times* rapidly increased both advertising and circulation, which they boosted with extracts from war memoirs which captured the mood of military nostalgia. The competition was soon intensified when the *Daily Telegraph* launched its own Sunday paper. The battle for advertising changed the whole character of newspapers, demanding features about consumers, lifestyles and fashion to encourage spending.

David remained aloof from commercial pressures. He talked about businessmen rather as racehorse-owners discussed bookies: 'lovely people' but always watching the odds. When we were given a lavish lunch by J. Walter Thompson, one executive gave a long account of the economic situation, and David whispered to me: 'What should I say: yes or no?' He had always distrusted advertising: when in 1953 the Tory government planned to establish commercial TV to break the BBC's monopoly, David strongly supported the lobby to protect it, led by his friend Lady Violet Bonham Carter. When several of the first commercial TV syndicates invited the *Observer* to join their consortia to give them respectability David turned them down – thus missing a potential windfall which could have transformed the paper's financial fortunes. But he enjoyed the first commercial programmes and quickly admitted his mistake. 'That's one more case where the *Observer* has been totally wrong,' he said to me. 'Not only has commercial TV been a success, but the commercials are the best part.'

He remained relaxed and lofty towards newspaper competition even after Roy Thomson, the ebullient Canadian newspaper tycoon, bought the *Sunday Times*. Thomson swiftly raised the stakes with more investment and commercial drive, but David welcomed the arrival of this genial newcomer with pebble glasses who was prepared to give his editors independence; he was furious when the *Observer* published a critical profile of Thomson while he was on holiday. David gave a grand dinner for Thomson at the Savoy to meet some of his journalists: he helped to persuade him of the need for 'salaried eccentrics', as Thomson called his cultural columnists, and Thomson picked up some ideas from us. He was particularly interested, he explained, in the Mammon business column. But within a few months the *Observer* was feeling the full force of North American competition when Thomson started up the *Sunday Times* magazine, which challenged even the Astors.

The two newspaper-owners represented opposite views of the power of the press. David Astor saw his paper primarily as the means to disseminate his own ideas and policies; Thomson was uninterested in politics and saw his papers as money-makers – which would become part of an empire including television, holiday tours and Yellow Pages. In commercial terms Thomson won decisively, while Astor's *Observer* looked more like the end of the line of old 'journals of influence', financed by rich families to pursue political goals. But money power was more ephemeral than political influence. Thomson left little behind him after he died: his empire disintegrated, while his newspapers were later sold to Rupert Murdoch and became part of a much more ruthless contest between global media empires. Astor's ideas had helped to shape the character of Britain in the late twentieth century in both politics and culture.

*

David Astor extended his paper's influence through good writing, and the *Observer* was above all a school for writers. He had seen how intellectuals like George Orwell and Arthur Koestler could project their ideas, and he maintained his respect for creative people with all their egotism and neuroses. He saw talent-spotting as his metier. 'Writing talent will always be as rare as gold', he wrote when he retired, 'and will always turn up in unlikely places. Finding it – and being allowed to employ it – doesn't become easier. It's to me the most thrilling part of the job.' He depicted himself as a head chef who knew how to find and mix ingredients, provide sauces and devise tasty menus. He often discussed how to devise a new 'throne' for an ambitious journalist, giving him a high-sounding title like 'home affairs editor'; or how to play 'musical chairs' while leaving no-one without a seat.

He was always looking for original thinkers who cut across conventional ideas. His friend John Strachey, the Labour politician who became war minister, had told him how his civil servants were always describing the people he disagreed with as 'sound', so he began to look for people who were *unsound*; and David followed the same principle. When a friend of mine applied for a job, but received an unpromising reference from his Eton housemaster, David was all the more determined to hire him.

David's respect for good writing infected the whole paper: he never really distinguished between writers and journalists; he liked to turn novelists, poets or academics into reporters or columnists. The weekly deadlines gave plenty of time to experiment: we could spend a whole afternoon discussing a metaphor or turn of phrase, or the merits of commas or colons, and we all watched each other's tricks of style. The anonymous profiles, which would often pass through several hands, were a special challenge to meet David's standards of critical candour: he would often insist: 'What's wrong with this guy?' And David was assiduous in sending congratulatory cables to exceptional reporters, particularly to isolated foreign correspondents.

Good writing was much encouraged by Michael Davie, whom David had recruited while still an Oxford undergraduate, who became my own mentor.

As sports editor Michael recruited an unlikely team of football and cricket reporters including the philosopher A. J. Ayer, John Jones, later professor of poetry, the art critic David Sylvester, John Sparrow, later warden of All Souls, and Norris McWhirter, who went on to co-invent the *Guinness Book of Records*. Later as news editor Michael became the champion of many other writers, including John Gale, Gavin Young and Colin Smith.

Michael could transform dull copy with some vivid phrases: when he edited a short agency report about Arthur Miller arriving in London with his new bride Marilyn Monroe he added: 'Few intellectuals in history could have been as widely envied as Miller.' The piece was noticed by Lord Beaverbrook – another sharp talent-spotter – who invited Michael to the south of France to try to lure him over to the *Daily Express*.

As a reporter himself Michael developed his own light-hearted style, influenced by the *New Yorker* and his friend Joe Liebling, who had warned him: 'Never forget to be funny.' Like Liebling he liked to relate everything to sport: when he noticed that Groucho Marx was in London he invited him to visit Lord's and introduced him to the secretary of the MCC, who asked: 'Are you on holiday, Mr Marx?' Groucho took out his cigar: 'I was until I saw this game.'

The most controversial of David's recruits was the *enfant terrible* of theatre criticism, Kenneth Tynan, who was employed by the tabloid *Daily Sketch*: Tynan saw the promotion as 'not unlike moving from a brewery to a vineyard'. David reckoned Tynan's appointment as 'the bravest thing I did', and his flamboyant arrival brought a new sense of drama both to the theatre reviews and to the other journalists. He made everyone feel larger than life, arriving at the Feathers on Saturdays with a new batch of jokes and Hollywood gossip about Orson, Larry or Tennessee. David enjoyed his theatricality and intellectual fireworks, though he was more doubtful about Tynan's concept of sexual liberation in his production *Oh! Calcutta!*.

A few of the *Observer*'s writers found themselves at loggerheads with David. Hugh Massingham, the political correspondent in the 1950s, had acquired valuable sources and a subtle Swiftian style (later developed by Alan Watkins) which disguised scoops as humorous fiction; but David disagreed with some of his views and carefully edited his unsigned column. I would watch Hugh emerging tensely furious from David's office on his way to

Auntie's, where his friends would warn: 'The stiletto's out.' He became so bitter against David that he called his dog Astor so that he could shout insults at it. He was always threatening to resign, but never did. Years later Anthony Howard was also at odds as political columnist: when he moved on to become editor of the *New Statesman* he wrote a critical profile of David called 'The Silver Spoon', which accused him of having 'shown unmistakeable signs of going over to the enemy'. 'It's strange to think we ever employed Tony H.,' David wrote to me afterwards. 'But my motive was always commercial – I thought he was light and would help sales.'

It was one of my jobs to sift through job applications, while at parties I would often be accosted by would-be recruits. Most talented young writers seemed determined to join the paper. '*Granta* now thinks that I am the only good writer in Cambridge,' wrote the undergraduate Michael Frayn (who joined the paper much later). 'This letter is outrageously conceited and self-important, but I suppose letters for jobs have to be.' 'I owned and edited *Cherwell* while still at Oxford,' wrote Michael Sissons, who later became London's master literary agent. 'Grey Gowrie wants to make a career in this trade and would like to work for your column,' David told me. There were never enough vacancies, but I did help to introduce Neal Ascherson, Godfrey Hodgson, John Thompson, Richard Hall, Thomas Pakenham, Virginia Makins (who was later to work with me on *Anatomy*) and John Heilpern. When I brought Kathleen Halton onto the paper I introduced her to Ken Tynan and they were later married.

I soon had my own chance to turn to writing. After two years David had clearly realised that I was not organising things as he had hoped. It was probably an impossible assignment anyway: I remembered how James Thurber had described Harold Ross, the founding editor of the *New Yorker*, welcoming each new recruit as a master-manager who would bring order to the editorial chaos; and I was no great organiser. But David, like a hopeful father, believed that everyone must be good at *something*; and he began tactfully suggesting other jobs: sending me abroad as a roving foreign correspondent, or asking me to write profiles. I soon realised David's skills as a hands-on editor. He had an instinctive sense of communicating with readers, and he knew how readers could suddenly be persuaded to read about a subject which they had thought boring: 'a peg', he explained to me, 'is just a curiosity in the mind of the reader'. He knew how to get the reader's attention, to avoid clichés, to cut out verbiage. When I wrote my first profile, of the mission doctor Albert Schweitzer, I laboured for hours on the perfect opening. David congratulated me on the piece but said: 'Just leave out the first paragraph. It's like a cough at the beginning of a speech. You just have to get it over with.'

Then he asked me, prompted by Michael Davie, to take over the gossip column, called Pendennis. He sounded apologetic about this sideshow, while explaining that it was the most popular part of the paper. But I seized the chance to meet and interview anyone I wanted to, and sum them up in 200 words. The pseudonym allowed me to pick everyone's brains, and build up a fantasy personality: a worldly know-all who picked up juicy titbits from London drawing-rooms. The anonymity also gave David the right to interfere, but I never resented that: the worst thing an editor can do to a journalist's copy, I realised, is to ignore it. David read Pendennis carefully every week, his fountain pen poised over the high desk, sometimes grunting, laughing or suggesting another phrase – Roy Jenkins's 'clever grin' or the Labour-turned-Tory MP Aidan Crawley's 'comic chin' – or protesting: 'A bit too cruel?' He enjoyed the irreverence and only occasionally complained if I mocked a friend, as when I mentioned French jokes about the first name of Sir Con O'Neill, the diplomat who was negotiating in Paris, or criticised Anthony Armstrong-Jones, who had become engaged to Princess Margaret.

As the column prospered I was allowed to take it abroad, and wrote about Harold Macmillan's visit to Moscow and his tour of Asia and Australia, which gave me new insights into the prime minister's job.

I spent four happy years writing in my disguise as Pendennis. It gave me a precious education as a journalist: it taught me how to describe people and places succinctly, to make facts readable and difficult subjects comprehensible: to become what David grandly called an '*haut vulgarisateur*'. Stimulated by the adrenalin of deadlines, I came up with words and phrases I didn't think I knew, and found a talent which was limited but marketable. The column was only a side dish in the paper, a salad in the editor's cuisine, dressed with oil and vinegar: the real *plats du jour* were the arguments about high diplomacy or human rights. But David provided both the kitchen and the table for aspiring writers – the context in which they could develop their skills. And like many other journalists I doubt whether I would ever have found my talent without him.

I was very conscious of the many alphas of the *Observer*, but I realised it was often easier for a less rarefied mind to explain ideas to ordinary readers and to pick others' brains. 'Educating yourself in public' was the most natural way of educating readers too. I was still a poor talker, but good talkers were often poor writers, because they did not understand the difference: and I remembered Garrick's epitaph for Oliver Goldsmith, 'who wrote like an angel but talked like Poor Poll'. I loved the easy access which the paper gave me to all kinds of worlds.

I felt fulfilled but bewildered by my role as a social spy, intruding on such a contrasted world, like a theatregoer who could wander onto the stage. I was never sure on which side of the proscenium I stood, but it was exciting to be slipping in and out among the different props and scenery which suddenly changed as if on a turntable: one day there were diplomats in ballrooms under chandeliers, the next there were noisy trade unionists in seaside conference halls. I loved the variety of their rituals and styles, each coming from a different strand of British social history, and tried to convey in print how they looked and talked and interacted. They nearly all seemed glad to talk to a journalist who listened, and I was bemused by the interaction between the observer and the observed. 'The gentleman from the press' was always an ambiguous guest, traditionally below the salt. But they nearly all craved publicity and a mirror to remind them of their own identities, and they hovered round journalists like moths round a candle. A gossip columnist was especially infra dig. 'I thought you wrote best when you were Pendennis,' a senior politician told me years later, adding, 'if you don't mind my saying so.' On the contrary I was flattered: I saw gossip as the origin of lively journalism, going back to John Aubrey or Samuel Pepys, who did more than any formal historians to bring characters to life, recognising that history was made by the oddities and foibles of human beings. I was not surprised that some of the most successful editors first found their feet writing gossip columns or 'diaries', as they are more politely called; and I would always look back at those years with gratitude and nostalgia.

The launch of the *Sunday Times* magazine, to attract more advertising, had abruptly raised the financial stakes, and David felt impelled to follow with the *Observer* magazine. After its first year I took over editing it, and enjoyed the challenge to popularise and push up circulation – which at one point topped a million – but I felt frustrated by the lack of entrepreneurial drive from Tristan Jones, and after a year I went back to a more rewarding career as an author.

David was soon beset with problems on all sides, as the competition intensified while the economic background worsened. The paper was losing serious money, and the unions were still more obstructive: printers were constantly demanding more jobs and more pay, suppressing any public criticism by threatening to sabotage the print run; while the journalists' union was imposing its own closed shop, which prevented the editor from hiring the talented amateurs he favoured. David had brought in Lord Goodman as chairman of the paper's trust, who battled with the unions, but for the first time he was showing the strain: when Michael Davie and I proposed some new editorial ideas he only responded: 'Thank you for trying to save us.' The Labour Party, now lurching to the left, saw the *Observer* as betraying it. By 1975 the crisis was being publicised on television and in other papers; the *Times* prepared an obituary. The paper was known to be up for sale and many possible buyers were approached, from the *Age* in Melbourne to the *Washington Post*, but none could face the heavy losses.

Then in September 1975 David announced his impending resignation as editor. I found myself suddenly a contender when some *Observer* writers whom I most admired, led by Michael, asked me to stand for the editorship. I had a casual breakfast interview with Goodman in his flat; wearing a flamboyant red dressing-gown, he was flanked by another trustee, the Countess of Albemarle, and interrupted by long phone calls. Goodman stressed the grave financial crisis: did I realise what a gamble it was? I insisted I could turn it round, provided the management was completely reorganised. But the decision, it turned out, had already been made; David explained later that in other circumstances he would have favoured me as a 'writing editor', but the commercial crisis now required an 'organising editor': that is, his deputy, Donald Trelford.[2] I could not seriously regret the setback, and the *Observer* would become much more circumscribed by commercial pressures.

At the end of the year a small group of old friends, inspired by Terry

Kilmartin, gave David a farewell dinner at the Gay Hussar. He was less regretful than we had expected, and very aware that his own ideas of a newspaper clashed with the commercial imperatives. Afterwards he wrote a thank-you letter to Kilmartin which provided a kind of epitaph for the old *Observer*. David explained how his real interests — such as the ecology crisis, war prevention, the limitations of the European Community and the misdeeds of India or Indonesia – were not popular with most readers:

> If I were to have gone on editing the paper, giving full rein to whatever were my strongest feelings, as I tended to do in our early days, and if the paper had consequently appealed to fewer and fewer readers, and had by now died, you would have given me no dinner.[3]

David was still a trustee and major shareholder of the paper, which was making yet heavier losses. Goodman was again talking to potential buyers, including Sir James Goldsmith and Robert Maxwell; and the trustees were pressing to sell it to Rupert Murdoch, the 'efficient Visigoth' as David called him. Then suddenly an apparent white knight arrived from California, in the unlikely guise of Robert O. Anderson, the chairman of the upstart oil company Atlantic Richfield, who quickly agreed to buy it. I was sceptical about Anderson's motives, having written a book about oilmen (see Chapter 10): he had a major interest in North Sea oil, and I suspected that the *Observer* would become a pawn in global oil plays. But Anderson appeared as a Pickwickian benefactor, beaming under his side whiskers and a wide Texan hat, apparently undeterred by the mounting losses; and David saw him as a saviour.

The *Observer* remained a kept newspaper with continuing losses, like a kept woman at the mercy of a rich man's whims; and it was soon caught up in intrigues like a medieval court. The court favourite was Kenneth Harris, a former *Observer* journalist, who had first introduced Anderson to the paper and was known as a master-flatterer. He now dedicated himself to massaging Anderson's ego: he arranged grand occasions, seminars and clubland invitations to establish Anderson's prestige, culminating in an annual 'Astor–Goodman' dinner where top people gathered to pay tribute to his words of wisdom.

Anderson soon wanted to toughen up the *Observer*'s editorial line, and imposed an 'editor-in-chief' above Trelford. He had chosen at David's suggestion Conor Cruise O'Brien, the brilliant but erratic Irish politician who combined genial beer-drinking with a sharp intellectual mind, and was suitably anti-communist, anti-terrorist and pro-Israeli; but O'Brien was in no mood to edit the newspaper seriously and confined himself to writing brilliant fortnightly columns, alternating with milder columns by myself. And he was soon at loggerheads with Harris, who had wanted himself to be editor-in-chief and kept trying to pressurise O'Brien, who laughed in his face. O'Brien saw himself in a deadly duel with Harris, like Sherlock Holmes wrestling with Dr Moriarty before they fell down together over the cliff into the Reichenbach Falls.

Anderson became more impatient with the *Observer*'s leftish tendencies, particularly after it endorsed James Callaghan's Labour Party before the 1979 elections, and he was beginning to lose interest. To supervise the paper he used his chief executive, Thornton Bradshaw, who invited me to lunch and to my amazement proposed that I replace O'Brien as editor-in-chief. I stalled, and soon afterwards Bradshaw resigned to take over the American giant RCA, after which I heard no more. But behind the scenes, Anderson was pursuing his own agenda: he now wanted Harris to become vice-chairman and effective boss; but Goodman and the other directors refused. Anderson was furious and decided to sell the paper, settling on a buyer, with Harris's help, who stood for almost everything the *Observer* was against. When Goodman heard the news he was for once speechless, realising he had been outployed by Harris: 'We thought he was Malvolio', he said afterwards, 'but he turned out to be Iago.' For David it was a betrayal of much of his life's work. That evening we met at a BBC studio, where we both denounced the new owner on television, and David seemed close to despair. He appealed to the Monopolies and Mergers Commission, but in 1981 the sale went ahead.

'Tiny' Rowland was a tall, domineering ex-German entrepreneur who had amassed his fortune largely in Africa, where he had built up a network of companies with the help of large bribes to black politicians; and he needed the *Observer*'s reputation in Africa to give him credibility and leverage. For a crusading journalist he appeared the ultimate nightmare. I was reminded of the scene in John Buchan's *The Thirty-Nine Steps* when the hero Richard Hannay takes refuge with a genial host to whom he confides that he is being

pursued by a villain with a missing little finger, at which his host holds up his
hand – missing its little finger.

Rowland did not immediately undermine the *Observer*'s character and
policies, as many had dreaded he would. As editor he kept Trelford, who
retained many fine journalists and even defied Rowland by publishing an
exposure of the brutal methods of his friend Robert Mugabe in Zimbabwe.
But Rowland could still use the paper as a weapon to support his devious
world operations, whether to boost his other allies in Africa, to discredit his
arch-enemy Mohamed al-Fayed at Harrods, or to expose rival arms dealers
in Saudi Arabia. And Rowland was more interested in suppressing news
than publishing it. 'The power of the press is very great,' Lord Northcliffe
once said, 'but not so great as the power of suppress.'[4] He had no love for
investigatory reporters: I had already crossed swords with him over Africa,
and when I was reintroduced to him – at an *Observer* gala at Covent Garden
to celebrate its 200th anniversary – he glared at me and said: 'You're against
everything. Have you ever done anything positive?'

I could only reply: 'I've backed Mandela ever since he went to jail.'

'Anyone could do that,' he snorted.

Could no newspapers escape the influence of big money and proprietors
with their own agenda? I felt alienated from Rowland's *Observer* and soon
gave up writing for it. I felt lucky to have an alternative income; but as a
journalist without a journal, I was worried by the growing vulnerability of all
newspapers to crude commercial pressures.

I learnt some more lessons about owners and editors when I spent three
years as a director of the *New Statesman* from 1980, under the chairmanship
of Graham C. Greene. The title still commanded loyalty and respect from
ageing readers, but its circulation was falling below the point of profitability:
it had an elaborate constitution devised by John Maynard Keynes, a
previous chairman of the board, to protect it from predators, but no
safeguards could protect it from bankruptcy. When I joined the board it had
just appointed a new editor, 'Colonel' Bruce Page, a dynamic Australian
investigator from the *Sunday Times* who was determined to popularise the *New
Statesman* with exposés; but the resources were slender and the sales fell faster.
With much anguish the board decided to change the editor, but it was a
difficult process: the journalists commanded three out of the seven votes on

the selection committee, and the outside directors could not accept a purely internal choice. When we eventually achieved a majority in favour of Hugh Stephenson, a more business-like editor who had plans to stem the paper's losses, the journalists went briefly on the rampage. It was painful to be confronting talented and dedicated young writers including Francis Wheen and Duncan Campbell; but I learnt a lot about the harsh realities of newspaper ownership.

I looked with some envy at the one paper which could combine fearless independence with commercial success: the fortnightly *Private Eye*, founded in 1961. I could claim to be a godfather since I was one of the first to publicise it, in the *Observer*; and over the years I would often slink into the Coach and Horses in Soho for the *Eye*'s fortnightly lunches, where the editor, Richard Ingrams, presided, with his craggy face and deadpan expression occasionally breaking into a grin, as he pressed guests into indiscretions. I was often exasperated by the *Eye*'s irresponsibility, its vendettas against gays and innocent victims, but I had to admire its courage and investigations into scandals which no-one else dared touch; and it showed up all the limitations of other papers, constrained by proprietors and libel lawyers. It harked back to the first disreputable but brave scandal sheets, as a whistle-blower warning about corruptions which had been suppressed. The *Eye* sometimes came close to financial ruin from exorbitant libel costs, but it attracted unique loyalty from its readers, who often bailed it out, and its circulation shot far ahead of that of the *New Statesman* or the *Spectator*.

I made my own small bid for independent journalism in 1984 when I started my own fortnightly 'Sampson Letter', analysing world affairs. I wanted to show how closely world politics was interlocked with multi-national companies and banks and I was always attracted to the newsletter formula as the most natural form of communication, without the artificial rules of newspapers; I was making enough money from books to take a risk, and I was backed by enterprising friends including Robert Loder, Ronald Dworkin and the Arab banker Abdlatif al-Hamad. But there was a catch which I did not fully foresee: a small circulation dictated a high price, too high for most individual subscribers, while the companies that could most afford it and benefit from it were the most averse to criticism. We could not sell enough copies to break even, and after two years I abandoned it and returned to book-writing. I still believe that newsletters are the best way of intelligently covering world affairs; today the internet provides a much greater opportunity for the formula.

Ten years later I received a more serious education in big-time newspaper ownership, back with the paper where I had begun my journalist's career. In 1993 Tiny Rowland's board finally tired of losing money with the *Observer* and sold it to the owners of the *Guardian*. It seemed a marriage made in heaven: the *Guardian* shared many of the liberal principles of David Astor's original *Observer* and it was owned by the Scott Trust, which guaranteed its editor's independence and now had ample resources thanks largely to a far-sighted investment in a secondhand car magazine, *Auto Trader*. Soon after the marriage Hugo Young, the chairman of the Scott Trust, asked me to join to represent the *Observer*'s interests. I felt privileged and awed but the problems were harder than I had expected. The *Guardian* management had been too optimistic about turning round the *Observer*'s losses, which continued to grow, and the trust was required to keep its hands off editors, who were regarded as sovereign. The founder of the trust, C. P. Scott, whose benign ghost still hovered over the *Guardian*,[5] had told it very simply how to pick editors: 'Take time to find your man and then give him his head.' The process had worked very well for the *Guardian*, which had maintained a confident character and was required by the trust deed to continue 'upon the same principles as they have heretofore been conducted', but the *Observer*'s character and principles were now less certain, and the trustees were too hasty in choosing editors:[6] they had painfully to fire three within as many years, before finding the right one. I felt myself an uneasy relic of the old Astor paper with its dedication to foreign news and intellectual argument, facing the new journalism of celebs, confessions and egos; I was doubtful about my usefulness and withdrew from the trust. But I retained a great respect for the *Guardian*'s system of ownership without proprietorial power.

4

Anatomy

On my thirty-third birthday I was still a bachelor journalist restlessly pursuing both news and women. I went to El Vino's in Fleet Street, the old-fashioned bar which had undone so many journalists' and barristers' careers, ordered a hock-and-seltzer, and looked round at the vista of drinkers. I had a sudden moment of truth: most of the journalists in their mid-life were already in decline as they lost their first curiosity and enthusiasm and were challenged by younger rivals. I made a vow on the spot: by the time I was thirty-five I must have an alternative livelihood. I must try to write a bestselling book.

Ever since I had returned from South Africa I had been puzzled by the question of who really held the power in Britain. In Johannesburg I had seen power being exercised nakedly and visibly: whites dominated blacks; mining magnates dominated workers; people with guns shot people without them. A few individuals could affect the course of history, while the future looked wide open: it could go in any direction, whether to dictatorship or to revolution. But back in London I found the workings of power as foggy as the weather, full of blurred shapes and groupings; while the established hierarchies and class divisions seemed to get in the way of all change. And after six years of Labour government, the old ruling class was reasserting itself under Conservative governments led by old Etonians and aristocrats who seemed to defy all the post-war expectations of social reforms which I had shared at Oxford. After my African interim, Britain looked much odder, but also clearer, viewed from outside. I looked back on my own privileged education as if it belonged to someone else. I felt like a colonial anthropologist studying the white tribes of Britain.

I had learnt more about Britain's rulers on the *Observer*, and I had begun writing columns about clusters of top people – bankers, governors, bishops or headmasters – trying to describe their characters and backgrounds. Could I take it further, and write a book which tried to answer the question: Who runs Britain? I went to see my school friend Robin Denniston, who was now a senior editor at Hodder and Stoughton, and over dinner we jotted down thirty-nine chapter headings for *Anatomy of Britain*, which would explain British institutions and their leaders, all the way from the palace to the shop floor. Robin was enthusiastic; my agent, Michael Sissons at A. D. Peters, extracted a sufficient advance; and David Astor agreed to grant me a year's leave. I launched myself on the absurdly ambitious venture, amazed by my own *chutzpah*.

But I was full of curiosity, the essential motivation of the journalist. I wanted to penetrate behind the facades and rhetoric of government, to peer behind the stage at the wires, props and pulleys which somehow kept the show on the road. I wanted to watch how power was really exercised, and to answer the simple questions which had motivated Lenin: 'Who? Whom?' I wanted to pursue what Aneurin Bevan called 'the will-o'-the-wisp of power', to try to find out 'how it was that his life was shaped for him by someone else'. Who was really in charge of the country?

I found many valuable mentors and helpers, but the most precious was Barbara Wootton, an aunt figure from my childhood who was now a prominent Labour intellectual and social scientist and one of the first new life peers. To many of her colleagues she was an intimidating presence, with her haughty gaze and sharp rebukes. 'She has wit, not humour,' said Dora Gaitskell, 'but she's the cleverest woman alive.' But to me she was always generous, and full of insights into the power world. 'Decisions are always taken *somewhere else*,' she explained. Later she was to become a friend of both Sally and myself when we were married. She took great satisfaction from her work as a juvenile magistrate, to which she much later helped to recruit Sally, saying it was the most interesting part of her own career. Barbara always rejected the Conservatives' definition of politics as 'the art of the possible': as a young researcher for trade unions she had campaigned for a minimum wage when most people thought it inconceivable; politics, she insisted, was the art of the *impossible*. She remained a political loner and when she wrote her auto-biography she took her title from the lines of A. E. Housman:

I, a stranger and afraid
In a world I never made

I wrote directly to 200 top people, including the Cabinet, the chairmen of the biggest banks and companies, and leaders in education, science and academia, to ask them for interviews. I was amazed that only three refused: two controversial tycoons, Charles Clore and Isaac Woolfson, and the governor of the Bank of England. Most of them did not want to be left out: usually the more important the person, the sooner he could see me: a junior minister might make a date six weeks ahead, but when I wrote to Harold Macmillan, the prime minister, he asked me for a drink on Thursday.

I developed my own method. I preferred to talk off the record, in a relaxed style without confrontation, to encourage people to talk candidly. I took a few notes discreetly, sometimes scribbling on an envelope, or taking paper from the desk. If my subject became too pompous and cautious I looked bored and sometimes made to leave: he might become suddenly indiscreet as he showed me out to the lift. It was thankfully before the advent of the mass tape recorder, which undermined so much spontaneity, but sometimes I produced a big noisy Grundig machine which my subjects viewed with suspicion. Years later I played back an old tape which began with Hugh Gaitskell saying: 'What a remarkable machine! I've never seen one before.'

I felt vulnerable as a journalist without academic qualifications as a political scientist or historian, but I recalled that some of the historian's most crucial sources were gossip-writers like Pepys or Greville; and I wanted my book to be breezy and informal, like a chatty guidebook to the seats of power, with a fast-moving style like the American journalist John Gunther. I wanted to portray power not in precise constitutional and legal language, but in terms of influences and atmospheres, with all the nuances of confidence, deference and inhibitions which were peculiarly British.

To make the book readable I could not just provide facts, I had to tell stories: the word 'anatomy' was quite misleading. Luckily there were epic stories which lit up the workings of power: the retreat from empire; the attempt to enter the European Community; the battles between insiders and outsiders in finance and banking.

And it was easier for a journalist than for an academic to pick other people's brains. I shamelessly exploited more scholarly friends, including my learned flatmate Ivan Yates, Asa Briggs, the Victorian historian, and my *Observer* colleague William Clark, fresh from No. 10. I took on a research assistant, Virginia Makins, much cleverer than myself, who knew something about the power world through her father, the diplomat Sir Roger Makins. And I found well-placed sources who were still young enough to be sceptical about their own professions, including the bankers Jacob Rothschild and Nicholas Baring, the accountant James Spooner and the MPs Shirley Williams and Dick Hornby. Robin Denniston was my pacer, running alongside the marathon, pointing to themes and connections to weave through the chapters.

My central theme was the 'establishment', the word that had recently been revived by Henry Fairlie, the brilliant but erratic journalist in the *Spectator*, and which he defined in 1955 as 'the whole matrix of official and social relations within which power is exercised'. The word would soon become more loosely used to mean any group of people who excluded newcomers in any profession, like those earlier enemies 'them' or 'the powers that be'. But it had a special resonance in the 1950s and 1960s, when scores of articles and books diagnosed the British malaise with gloomy titles like 'The Stagnant Society', 'Suicide of a Nation' or 'The Chipped White Cups of Dover'. Britain appeared to be ruled by a self-contained interlocked group who seemed resistant to the forces of change, democracy and accountability. The British seemed locked in the past, governed by social rules which protected them against change, like the cartoons of H. M. Bateman, who depicted horrified colonels outraged by an outsider committing a social gaffe: 'the man who smoked before the loyal toast'. Whitehall and the City were full of warnings which defied change: 'It's just not done.' 'It doesn't matter what you know, but who you know.' 'It may seem odd, but it works.'

And in the early 1960s the establishment displayed itself like a pageant. Bankers, dukes and Tory politicians frequented the same country houses and grouse moors, and married into each other's families: many of them could be embraced in a single interlocking network of family trees – which provided a pull-out chart as the centrepiece of my book. They all loved dressing up for their parts and seemed to be taking part in the same old-fashioned play. 'Don't you feel they're all actors who are interchangeable?' Lord Devlin, the wittiest of the law lords, asked me. 'That they're all Gerald du Maurier in the end?' The centres of power looked like stage sets cluttered with period props and furniture. The Rothschilds' dining-room was like a museum, full of trophies and framed letters, with reverential butlers serving vintage claret and Havanas. The foreign secretary, the Earl of Home, still worked behind Palmerston's old desk in a vast drawing-room full of Victorian bric-à-brac. The real facts of government and business were often hard to discern behind the impedimenta. Didn't they get in the way of understanding Britain's changing role, I asked Iain Macleod, the colonial secretary.

'Look at the French,' he retorted; 'it didn't stop their economic miracle.' But I still felt that the grand surroundings created their own atmosphere and distracted the British from facing up to the realities of post-war power.

The British still seemed to be in the shadow of their Victorian inheritance: the Whitehall palazzos, neo-Gothic churches or railway viaducts which I had gaped at as a child seemed to loom over us as reminders of vanished glories. The confident Victorian statesmen, with all their energy and optimism, seemed to be looking down like giants on the post-imperial pygmies, while their ambition and energy seemed to have crossed over the Atlantic, to make the British feel like has-beens. Yet the more the British were losing their power in the world, the more they were fascinated by analysing it. They were still offended by Dean Acheson's words: 'The British have lost an empire and not yet found a role.' But they relished their rituals, titles and pomp like fetishes as substitutes for sex: what Malcolm Muggeridge called the 'pornography of power'. I remembered the warning of my Victorian mentor Walter Bagehot, which I used at the front of the book: 'The characteristic danger of great nations, like the Roman, or the English, which have a long history of continuous creation, is that they may at last fail from not comprehending the great institutions they have created.'

*

At the centre of the pageant was the prime minister, Harold Macmillan, who provided a kind of caricature of the establishment as a network of inter-locking institutions and families. With all his wide powers of patronage he had peopled the government with old Etonians and aristocrats, including a duke, a marquess, four earls and a procession of cousins by marriage from the House of Lords. It was a throwback, not to the pre-war Cabinets of

Baldwin or Chamberlain, but to the Cabinet of Lord Salisbury at the end of the nineteenth century. After the austerity of the post-war Labour government, Macmillan had reinvented the idea of a ruling class of aristocrats and gave others a complex about being excluded from 'the magic circle', as Iain Macleod called this closed world.

It took me some time to realise how carefully Macmillan contrived his persona, for he was a consummate actor-manager who played up his role of Tory grandee, and he could create his own stage and act out his fantasies: being prime minister, he said at a banquet at Oxford, 'makes all those years of Trollope seem worth while'. I had watched him closely while interviewing him in London and following him for the *Observer* on his tour of the Commonwealth, when he exaggerated his Edwardian routine: droopy moustache, drawled vowels, old-Etonian tie and languid gestures. But behind all the stage business he was always the shrewd manipulator, the canny Scots intellectual, and his aristocratic act was largely bogus. He had never liked Eton and never returned to it; he had married the Duke of Devonshire's daughter but he had always been uneasy among the Cavendishes, who made fun of this earnest intellectual who had been cuckolded by the cad Bob Boothby. He had picked up his theatrical style by taking lessons from a stand-up comic in the Crazy Gang who taught him about gestures and timing.

He was a masterly performer. He talked to me in the Cabinet Room with witty monologues and a repertoire of stage tricks – tongue in cheek, leisurely pauses, pulling down eyelids – about his horror of suburbia, his awe of scientists, 'those H. G. Wells people', his admiration for Disraeli, his enjoyment of Homer, as if he was living in a previous century. When thirty years later I went to *A Letter of Resignation*, a play about Macmillan, who was brilliantly impersonated by Edward Fox, with all the corny gestures and phrases, it was hard to believe that the British could ever have been taken in by such an old ham. But in the 1960s Macmillan's audience were part of the show: they wanted to be deceived and reassured among all the humiliations of economic setbacks and imperial retreat. And Macmillan knew how to deceive them.

Behind the stage Macmillan was always a shrewd intellectual and operator who saw Britain's problems quite clearly. He navigated the retreat from empire, while maintaining the style of an imperialist. I was later to see him first hand in action when I accompanied him to South Africa. In Cape Town he was cheered through the streets by the white South Africans from whom he had firmly disassociated himself.

*

I wanted to get behind the theatre of politics, to discover how decisions were really made backstage, inside the bureaucracies of Whitehall. 'What are they all *doing* inside there?' Barbara Wootton said one day as we were walking past one civil service stronghold, looking at the rows of filing-cabinets and desks. 'Nobody will ever know.' I took it as a challenge to follow the trail. Everyone knew that civil servants in Britain wielded a permanent power which was never acknowledged by constitutions or parliamentary debates, and that the frontier between government ministers and their civil servants was becoming more blurred. 'It used to be thought that the minister was chosen by God, and the permanent secretary was just an official,' Rab Butler told me. 'Now they're much more equal.' But how did the mandarins exercise their power, behind the trappings of parliamentary democracy?

Civil servants were still very shadowy figures who cherished their anonymity and were resigned to mockery: 'We shall continue to be grouped with mothers-in-law and Wigan pier', said their ex-head Lord Bridges, 'as one of the recognised objects of ridicule.' It was difficult to discover the real influence that senior civil servants wielded over ministers: their names hardly ever appeared in the newspapers, and it was not until twenty years later that the television series *Yes, Minister*, written by Antony Jay and Jonathan Lynn, brilliantly conveyed the subtle processes by which a permanent secretary prevailed over his political master. But I was determined to explore this crucial interface, where all the hot air of political speeches was converted into practical policies and legislation. And after my experiences in Africa I was convinced that an incorruptible civil service was the most critical element in a democratic system. I found an invaluable guide in the prime minister's principal private secretary, Tim Bligh, who became a close friend: we lunched regularly at Bianchi's restaurant in Soho, sitting at table fifteen, hidden behind a corner. Tim had been a daring wartime skipper of a torpedo boat, and he was still a buccaneer manqué: he loved to describe the power plays and deceptions which lay behind the bland public speeches, and who was plotting with whom. But he never doubted that the civil servants were the real rulers. 'Look at those electric pylons, embedded in deep concrete,' he explained. 'That's the civil service.'

The scientist-novelist C. P. Snow had popularised the 'corridors of power' and romanticised the role of committees, where civil servants thrashed out decisions behind closed doors in their own arcane language, seized, exercised, agitated or embarrassed. 'This is the face of power in a society like ours,' as Snow put it. I spent much time talking off the record to the senior civil servants and permanent secretaries, uncovering the real arguments between ministers and their officials, learning how grand ideas were defeated by the pressures of realities and facts: 'facts that seemed to live in the office', as Walter Bagehot put it, 'so teasing and unceasing they are'. Later I was able to sit in on some committee meetings: I watched the impassive and pulled-in faces of the mandarins, and then leant back in my chair to see their legs under the table, swinging and twitching with frustration – like swans, looking calm above the surface while they paddled frantically under water. It was a lesson in the two faces of politics: the theory and the practice, the extravert and the introvert. However much the civil servants were disliked, they were essential to the business of government.

But I realised that most of the real secrets of the strongholds of Whitehall were evading me; and it was not until forty years later that I learnt more about the true power of the mandarins in the central citadel, the Ministry of Defence. While I was trying to anatomise Britain, it turned out that Harold Macmillan's government was making drastic contingency plans for nuclear war, following the Cuban missile crisis: it was planning for 120 indispensable ministers and officials to retreat to a huge underground bunker-city outside Bath, equipped with the raw tools of power, and was arranging for twelve regional commissioners to run the country in the event of a breakdown of law and order. The high command would be made up of the inner Cabinet, the defence chiefs and intelligence bosses, co-ordinated by the Cabinet secretary, Sir Norman Brook. They would be authorised not by Parliament, but by royal prerogative, directly given by the Queen.[1] Government would be reduced to its basic task of 'the defence of the realm'. It would become the 'cold monster', as Charles de Gaulle called the state – and democracy would go out of the window. It took forty years for diligent scholars like Peter

Hennessy or Richard Aldrich to unearth these secrets of nuclear politics from the archives. The nightmare never happened, and today it appears like science fiction; but the plans revealed all the ultimate ruthlessness and secrecy of the state.

From Whitehall I moved on to business corporations, which were still more obscure and unaccountable. Big companies at that time preserved a strict anonymity: their letters to customers insisted: 'All communications should be directed to the Secretary.' The City pages of the newspapers published dry reports of chairman's statements at annual meetings, describing their steady progress and praising all their colleagues, backed up by respectful commentaries from business journalists. The chairmen, who remained grandly aloof from their staff, saw themselves as the guardians of Britain's national interest rather than as tough commercial competitors, running companies which were proudly patriotic: the British Match Corporation, British Petroleum, the British Aluminium Company. Many were aristocrats, generals or Tory politicians and most of them had some lords on the board. But a few were beginning to feel the winds of competition from America and Europe. The chairman of my father's old company, Imperial Chemical Industries, was a distinguished and charming scientist, Sir Alexander Fleck: but his successor, Paul Chambers, was a tough tax expert who was determined to maximise profits and was widely condemned as a bit of a bounder.

The class divisions in industry had been strengthened rather than weakened by the common purpose of wartime. The officer class had been accustomed to hierarchies giving orders down through the ranks, with unquestioned confidence; and after the war the colonels and captains had moved effortlessly into business, retaining their military perspective. They naturally accepted the concept of 'the two sides of industry': they saw trade union leaders as their sergeant-majors and the workers as troops who must be handled firmly but fairly, but they found it hard to cope with bolshie shop stewards or strikers, who were not tolerated in the army. Like generals their status was measured by the size of their civilian battalions: the extravagant overmanning in British Railways or the Post Office – and even private corporations like ICI – was partly the result of military tradition rather than socialist planning.

When I turned to the financial powers in the square mile of the City of London, I found them still more old fashioned and rigid. The City's central institution, the Bank of England, was intensely secretive and bound by tradition: every evening in the rush hour a troop of guardsmen marched in bearskins from Wellington or Chelsea barracks to guard it against imagined rioters; once a week the discount-brokers arrived in top hats to be told the bank rate. Inside, the governor, Lord Cobbold, presided periodically over his court of directors, who represented the most respectable banks. The style and tone of the City was set by the British merchant banks, still largely dominated by old families like the Barings, the Rothschilds or the Schroeders. The bankers gave long lunches with vintage claret and cigars, and retreated back to their mahogany parlours.

I soon realised that the real masters of money were elsewhere: in insurance companies, pension funds and high-street banks, which commanded billions for loans and investments; most of these leaders were self-made men who had never been to public schools and were not mentioned in *Who's Who*. 'When you are dealing with really big sums of money you find people who *didn't* go to Eton,' said the old Etonian Lord Longford (then the improbable chairman of the National Bank of Ireland). When I sought out the chief investment manager of the biggest insurance company, the Prudential, I found Leslie Brown, a stocky, unpretentious man with a bristly moustache and twinkling eyes, who had come from a Croydon grammar school. His decisions could mean life or death for the industrial corporations in which the Pru invested. The real entrepreneurs who built financial empires were mostly rugged men who had never been to university and were hardly mentioned in the press. I tracked down Harley Drayton, one of the most influential, in a musty office in the City from which he controlled a web of interests across the world. He was a big bucolic man with laced boots and a monocle, whose father was a gardener and who left school at thirteen when he discovered a restless ambition and a sharp eye for figures. 'Some people are born with a bug inside them,' he explained. 'If they are, they can do anything.' He took risks which the old guard would never touch, and when the first commercial television syndicates were launched in 1955 he bought a large share in one of the biggest, Associated Rediffusion – and soon doubled his stake at the bottom of the market by buying out Lord

Rothermere, the chairman of the *Daily Mail*. 'There was quite a lot of wear and tear on the tummy,' he told me. But when the TV advertising began rolling in Drayton was the biggest beneficiary of all.

I was puzzled how few people in the City were seriously devoted to making money. They were caught up in their webs of commissions, mutual agreements and relationships, which were essentially protective, more concerned with what wasn't done than with what might be done. The real drive to make money came from outside these traditional coteries: from Jewish refugees, American intruders or a few upstarts like Drayton, who found new markets and opportunities. 'You have to be an idiot not to make money in England,' said my school friend Paul Hamlyn.

The most formidable intruder in the City was Siegmund Warburg, a refugee from an old Jewish banking family in Hamburg, whom I later saw often: a melancholy man with big soulful eyes who seemed to regard banking as an austere religion, requiring sacrifices and duties. He did what was not done: he operated from a bleak modern office block, gave brisk lunches – sometimes with two sittings – without wine, and recruited unconventional staff who started work early and stayed late, who were motivated by bonuses and internal competition. He was thoroughly un-English: he advised foreign companies, including American and Japanese, and made deals with the strange new currency the Eurodollar. His English competitors regarded him as dangerously unpatriotic, but in a few years he had built up S. G. Warburg & Co. to be the most successful merchant bank in London, the only one which could compete with the American giants.

Throughout the business world ran the deep divisions of class, which were reinforced by the educational divide. The products of the fee-paying public schools and Oxbridge projected a commanding style and social ease which could demoralise cleverer and quieter men and women from the grammar schools. They had the self-confidence which was the key to success, much more than ability; I remembered the graffiti from my naval days: 'Bullshit baffles brains.' The grammar school pupils had long ago penetrated Oxbridge, which provided the main nursery for top jobs, but they were mocked for their gauche and earnest behaviour as part of the 'the meritocracy' – the derogatory term recently coined by the sociologist Michael Young. And the divide was reinforced by the distinction between amateurs and professionals, gentlemen and players. Most Tory Cabinet ministers, judges, barristers, merchant bankers and diplomats were from public schools; most civil servants, solicitors, accountants, industrialists and scientists were from grammar schools. The question of 'background' was thought crucial, and Etonians described grammar school alumni as 'self-invented men'; Macmillan said of Sir Norman Brook: 'He has *no background*.' Language and clothes were part of the class warfare. John Betjeman and Nancy Mitford had popularised the distinction between U and non-U words, which helped to demoralise upstarts, and academics and writers proved the most vulnerable. 'Poets and scholars have one thing in common. They are not gentlemen,' wrote W. H. Auden in 1956. 'The U is that which both, being non-U, with passion worship.'[2]

For myself, I was never sure which side I belonged to. I had been a scholar of an expensive and ancient public school, while my father was a scientist from a Liverpool grammar school. But when I visited country houses I visualised my forebears on the servants' side of the green baize door; and I was outraged by the arrogance and complacency of the public schoolboys towards people with twice their ability.

It was a relief to escape from the class-conscious City of London to the dens of the 'boffins', the scientists and engineers, whom I had enjoyed when I first met them with my father. With their rumpled suits and tousled hair they felt no need to keep up appearances, and they talked with refreshing irreverence about their political or commercial masters. They liked to make fun of their confident predictions: they knew that their researches could blow up all their neat assumptions. But the politicians and mandarins complained that they were not 'house trained' and preferred to keep them at arm's length. And when Macmillan appointed a minister of science he chose Lord Hailsham, a classical scholar with no scientific experience who treated boffins with disdain.

As I reached the end of my pursuit I was all the more struck by the influence of the establishment: Britain was a more tribal country than I had realised. Much of the power in Britain was determined by social networks and assumptions which could override the interests of voters or shareholders and exclude outsiders through a closed system which communicated through nods and winks or raising the eyebrows. As Lord Chandos, the master-operator in Macmillan's establishment, described it, 'somebody would ask: "What do you think of so-and-so for that job?" I would reply: "Mmm," and he wouldn't get it.'

Many potential careers could be sabotaged by those *mmm*s, and that protective network would cost Britain dearly, as it had to compete with aggressive outsiders from North America, Europe or Australasia. Foreigners could make their fortunes by doing what wasn't done and preferring what-you-know to who-you-know. Many rejects from the establishment would eventually get their revenge on the men who had turned them down. I met Norman Collins, a broadcaster and novelist who was turned down as director-general of the BBC: he then joined a trio of conspirators who pushed through the campaign to launch commercial television, which destroyed the BBC's monopoly for ever. George Soros, the brilliant Hungarian financier, felt himself excluded from the City of London; I was to interview him thirty years later, when he had made a billion dollars out of speculating against sterling and brought the pound down.

I never caught up with the will-o'-the-wisp. For it was in the nature of a democracy, as opposed to a dictatorship, that power was disseminated and balanced; and from the top it looked much less clear than from the bottom. 'Power? It's like a Dead Sea fruit,' said Macmillan as prime minister. 'When you achieve it there's nothing there.' To round off my book I sketched a rough map of British institutions – inspired by Asa Briggs – in the form of a necklace of overlapping rings, which would decorate the endpapers and which is reproduced in the front endpapers of this volume (it was drawn by my friend Len Deighton when he had just written his first thriller, *The Ipcress File*). But many of the bigger rings were only tenuously connected – such as corporations with the Treasury, or scientists with industry – and in the middle was a large empty space, for in a plural society like Britain's there was no real central direction. The future of the country depended in the end not on the establishment but on the British people, who were subject to moods and perceptions which no-one could adequately measure.

But the idea of the establishment retained its hold, both on the British public and on ambitious politicians and others who longed to be part of it. Macmillan's 'magic circle' and the surrounding networks of mutual promotion provoked a younger generation of outsiders to consciously develop their own networking systems. Harold Wilson liked to mock the Tory old guard: 'Whatever people say at election,' he told me in 1965, 'the members of the old establishment only have one vote at the end of the day.' But the ministers in his own Cabinet constituted their own kind of establishment, in many respects more alike in education and background than Macmillan's: most were from Oxford and many were academics, while the trades unionists or workers who represented most of the Labour Party's supporters were increasingly weakened. The social revolution which many voters had expected never happened, and the new rulers fitted comfortably in the gaps left by the old. And most people still had the feeling that their lives were being shaped by forces over which they had no control.

But meanwhile British attitudes were changing in ways which were much harder to perceive at the time, through new communications, and the most revolutionary influences came from right outside the political establishment, from the mass media – tabloid newspapers and commercial television. It was a force which did much more than unleash the power of mass marketing: it projected a quite different country of showmen, image-makers and celebrities, bringing in a whole new cast of upstarts from outside the old establishment – from the arenas of pop music or public relations; from Ireland, Scotland or the provinces – with new heroes and role models such as Eamonn Andrews, Jimmy Savile or David Frost. I had a foretaste of the new world when I wrote in 1961:

> The disparate subjects assemble – an archbishop talking to a pop singer, a trade unionist talking to a Tory MP. They troop on and off in an endless cavalcade, all mixed together – professors, jugglers, Cabinet ministers, ventriloquists, dukes, chairmen, comperes and diplomats – all punctuated by quick glimpses of detergents or toothpaste. On the magic screen people who have never met each other before chat away with Christian names, as if they jostled together every day in some inner world of power.

It was soon clear that the political establishment had to pay homage to this new 'celebritocracy'. In 1966 Frost gave a breakfast party to which he invited top people, who nearly all came, including the prime minister, Harold Wilson. But no-one predicted how closely politics would become interlocked with entertainment over the following decades, through the expansion of television; and how much power would flow towards the controllers of the mass media.

I had to write *Anatomy* at speed, to capture the mood of the whole country at a single moment: a quarter of a million words in fifteen months, alternating interviewing with writing. As I lost myself in the maze I felt more disoriented and isolated, like a loose ball bearing tossed up and down by mechanical cogs, and despaired of giving the book any shape or unity. As I saw the end in sight I was exhilarated with adrenalin, but I felt I was preparing a bomb which could go off anywhere – probably in my face. In my mind I wrote imaginary hostile reviews from contemptuous critics: ' "This meretricious, misleading work" – Hugh Trevor-Roper'; ' "He completely fails to understand the establishment" – Henry Fairlie'.

Just before *Anatomy of Britain* was launched in July 1962 I escaped to South Africa, avoiding any interviews or TV appearances. But my editor, Robin Denniston, soon wrote with extraordinary news about the book's reception, from both right and left, including praise from Trevor-Roper and Bernard Levin. Only Fairlie dismissed it: 'Whatever induced Mr Sampson to write so fatuously misleading a book?' The shop window of Hatchards was filled with copies of *Anatomy*, adorned with bowler hats and umbrellas. It would remain a best-seller for week after week, and sold more copies in the second year than the first.

I was lucky with the timing of the book because it came out just before the full triumph of television. Its success gave me many entries into the power world which I had tried to describe. Left-wing friends saw the book as a dissection of the ruling class, while conservative careerists saw it as a route map to the top, or a guide to getting a gong: 'If I refuse a CBE can I still get a knighthood?' I was invited to lunches and dinners by financiers, property-developers or social climbers who wanted to be in the index as members of the establishment. I was welcomed by brash tycoons like Robert Maxwell who spelt out their achievements, expecting them to appear verbatim in the next printing. I was pursued by public-relations men on behalf of their clients. I was flattered by political hostesses such as Ann Fleming or Pamela Berry who took me up to provoke their lunch guests – who in turn looked at me as if I had a gun in my pocket.

Where on earth did I belong here? Was I a fly on the wall which had dropped on to the table, or a butler who had joined the guests? The sociologist Michael Young reviewed the book in the *Observer* under the heading 'Sir Anthony Pendennis', suggesting I had been seduced by the world I was describing. But it was Michael who became Lord Young. I learnt more about the nuances of power and ambition from my occasional excursions into the world of chandeliers and banquets, and I found friendly spirits who shared my own curiosity, but the view was clearer from outside, and I came back to the journalist's old dilemma: those who tell don't know, and those who know don't tell.

The success of *Anatomy* brought me in touch with hundreds of new acquaintances who had their own interests, who shared my curiosity, who wanted to put me right, or who wanted to be in the index. I learnt a lot from them: it was a tantalising feature of writing books about contemporary life that you discovered many of the answers after they came out. But I learnt most from the people who came from the underworld of power, who had seen its impact on ordinary lives.

One of them was Christine Keeler, the young call girl who became suddenly famous in 1963 when she had an affair with the Tory minister John Profumo, who saw her swimming in the nude at Cliveden, the Astors' grand country house, and whose other lovers included the Russian spy Yevgeny Ivanov and a West Indian gangster. She played her role in history by helping to bring down the Macmillan government, but she had been cast aside in the subsequent recriminations.

Christine asked to meet me through a mutual friend to discuss the possibility of writing her memoirs. I was taken by her casual elegance, an exotic creature who had strayed into the stiff English world. Soon afterwards she married a young businessman, and invited me and my wife Sally to dinner in their bijou house in Seymour Walk, Chelsea, where she had a young baby, called Seymour after the street. She was an entertaining hostess, full of gossip and speculation about men. When we asked her back to dinner, she soon captivated the other guests, who included the poet Al Alvarez and his Canadian wife.

It wasn't long before I heard that Christine's marriage had broken up. But some time later, when we were quietly celebrating New Year's Eve at home, the front doorbell rang, and outside was an old South African friend with the familiar figure of Christine. They joined us for champagne, and Christine was in sparkling form: after she left my mother-in-law asked: 'Who *was* that charming woman?' and could hardly believe the answer. Our friend, a generous bachelor, had tried to look after Christine and had lent her his Mayfair flat, but he was 'not my type', as she later explained; she found life a continuing struggle, while yearning to be back in the great world. I saw Christine more as a victim of British hypocrisy and exploitation than as a villain: to anyone interested in how Britain works, Christine had thrown a light.

*

I had written *Anatomy* primarily for school-leavers or young graduates who wanted to understand the strange world they were entering, like me a decade earlier, and I soon realised I had succeeded in that. 'I have had to tell boys that we too have read *Anatomy*,' said Robert Birley, the head master of Eton, as he noticed exam papers cribbed from it. But I was more gratified to find it taken seriously by academics themselves: when I later met a distinguished young economist he said, to my surprise: 'I must thank you for getting me my first-class degree.' I felt vindicated in my view of the role of journalist, as a bridge between difficult subjects and the plain reader.

I had achieved what I had intended at that lunchtime at El Vino's three years before, to find an alternative career. With the royalties I bought a big house in Notting Hill and a small one in Walberswick, near my mother's cottage. But writing a best-seller, as Graham Greene said, is a chastening experience: the more the book sold, the more I felt exposed. I felt acute withdrawal symptoms and thankfully returned to the *Observer*, to write a column and return to the camaraderie of fellow-journalists. But I was still bitten by my bug, to pursue my own curiosities about the world of power; and I was committed to the lonelier but more rewarding career as a book-writer.

5

The other Africa

While I followed the labyrinths of power in London I was still constantly drawn back to Africa, where the issues and conflicts seemed simpler and more fundamental – throbbing like a ground bass of horns and drums below the intricate descants of Britain. And my contacts with blacks gave me vivid glimpses of the receiving end, showing how those political decisions really looked at the grass roots. It was a confusing contrast. One day in London I was invited for a drink by a Scottish clergyman who had read *Anatomy*. 'How do you reconcile your baroque interest in power', he asked, 'with your radical interest in Africa?' But the study of power was only interesting in so far as it affected the powerless.

I sought out Africa-in-London, which I welcomed as an escape route from conventional drawing-rooms and the domestication of heavily married friends. I was refreshed by the growing community of multiracial exiles with a more bohemian lifestyle. I saw a new kind of Britain through the eyes of visiting *Drum* friends: Zeke Mphahlele stayed in my London flat and was shocked by the British attitude to old people; Todd Matshikiza lived with his wife in Kilburn and played the piano at the Colony Club, and came with his family to stay in Walberswick. I glimpsed the underside of Britain's prosperity and the British colour bar. James Phillips, a prominent Coloured activist and singer from Johannesburg, found a job as a garment worker in London, but for a long time could not find a landlord who would admit non-whites. When I took Bloke Modisane, my old *Drum* friend, to my local Chelsea pub, the Queen's Elm, a big man brushed past him saying: 'You ought to take a trip to the West Indies – I'm told it's a very pleasant place.' I had new insights into other cities too. In Paris I spent time with Gerard Sekoto, the South African painter from Sophiatown, who frequented bars on the Left Bank; in New York I spent a day in Harlem with the *Drum* exile Nat Nakasa.

I also made lifelong friendships with English people I had met in Africa, where like me they had found an extra dimension and shared my indignation against white racism. As the political scene worsened in southern Africa, more white exiles arrived in London, at first feeling lost and diminished. In Africa they had been big fishes in small pools who had seemed larger than life, as they took bold decisions which affected whole communities; but back in Britain they were small fishes in big pools, involved in intricate compromises and committees. Yet they often brought with them a much clearer vision of the real choices and values than their English counterparts, and a greater courage and sense of purpose as they took politics back to first principles. Many white South Africans, whether conservative or liberal, would rapidly achieve important positions in Britain; but those who had been most involved in the struggle would always feel displaced and torn between the two continents.

I felt especially close to Trevor Huddleston, who had played such a heroic role in Johannesburg but was abruptly recalled to Britain in 1955 by his superior, Father Raymond Raynes. He soon became famous in Britain after writing his best-seller *Naught for Your Comfort* (which I had encouraged him to write), but he desperately missed Africa. I felt all the contrast when I visited him over a cold January weekend in Mirfield, the bleak monastery near Leeds which was the headquarters of his Community of the Resurrection. It was a forbidding Victorian building with brown and mauve walls, alongside the gaunt chapel which the monks called the 'powerhouse of prayer', where they gathered as regularly as workers in a factory. There were notices saying 'No Talking Before Tierce', and at breakfast we silently ate thick slices of bread and margarine. It was a world away from the sunny cloister in Johannesburg, and I realised the gulf between myself as an atheist and the monks who believed in God.

Trevor had first enjoyed his new-found fame in England, with an element of vanity: 'I can draw bigger crowds than MPs.' But he soon tired of repeating the same sentiments about the beloved country he had left. He was depressed by British materialism and resented the discipline of the Church of England: 'It's the main cross I have to bear.' He longed to return to the straightforward challenges of Africa: 'I pray every night to go back.'

Why had he been recalled? On my first night in Mirfield Father Raynes explained to me over the course of three hours, with his penetrating blue eyes, how he had spent fifteen anguished months deciding. Africans had petitioned him to let Trevor stay, but he had 'shot his bolt' and was in danger of putting others in trouble. The community's vow of obedience had made it easier for Trevor to come back, he insisted, because it let his superior take the blame; and Trevor with all his sorrow was inwardly relieved after all the strain and frustration in Johannesburg. But I still believed that he should have stayed, not so much because he needed Africa as because it needed him: he was one of a tiny group of whites – apart from the communists – with whom blacks identified, and he symbolised the commitment of Western Christians to the cause of liberation.

The exiles from Africa brought a passionate urgency to the political scene and a welcome release from British inhibitions. Doris Lessing, the left-wing novelist, had arrived from Rhodesia, like a magnificent panther from the veld, leaping across walls and fences, with her mixture of beauty and directness. Soon after I first met her she rang up to ask to look through my copies of the South African paper *New Age*. Later I took her to see a John Osborne play and we came back for cold chicken at my flat. Doris brought a passionate African freshness to both politics and her whole life, but she retained a realism about Africa's future. One evening at dinner with Johnny Dankworth she had a classic argument with the young Kenyan revolutionary Abu Mayanja. 'When I'm home secretary and prime minister I don't want to have to ban the *New Statesman*,' said Abu. 'Can't we agree *now* on what the rules are? African justice will be different from British justice.' But Doris replied: 'No, I won't agree. I *know* that white dictatorship will be succeeded by black dictatorship, and that you'll treat people just as badly as we did, and I'll attack you just as fiercely. No, not quite so fiercely, because I prefer Africans.'

Nadine Gordimer, who often came to London with her husband, Reinhold Cassirer, had an almost opposite presence – taut, intellectual and precise – and I was struck that she and Doris wrote in such different styles, though they liked and admired each other. Nadine wrote with a cerebral intensity and sharp observation, Doris with a natural instinctive flow, as if following her own feminine stream of consciousness. They had both been first stimulated by the frontiers of Africa, and had then ranged further afield.

Doris had settled to live in West Hampstead, and wrote increasingly about London or mysticism, while Nadine's life became increasingly international: she spent time in New York and the south of France, and built up a network of intellectual friendships. She loved the English countryside as well as London, and gave me new insights into my own country. But she became increasingly committed to the black South African struggle and remained firmly based in Johannesburg. Both women had gained a dimension from their African background and they expressed all the richness and understanding that came from the interaction between the two continents.

I had tried to convey my own experience of that interaction when I wrote my book called *Drum*, encouraged by Nadine and by my old friend Robin Denniston, who edited it for Collins. It was written in a raw, jerky style, but it was enlivened by the dialogues I had scribbled down in shebeens, which let blacks tell their own stories. On the Sunday morning after it was published in July 1956 I woke from a nightmare about Elspeth Huxley reviewing it as 'naïve and misleading'. I rushed downstairs to find that Huxley had indeed reviewed it, in the *Sunday Times*, but very generously as 'crisp, clear and revealing', while other reviewers welcomed a new view of the black world.

After the publication of *Drum* I was drawn further into the lobbying, protests and arguments which were raging through London, as the government tried to decide the future of Britain's African colonies. While at the *Observer* I was drawn into conferences and committees, and became involved in the Africa Bureau, which David Astor had founded with his mentor Michael Scott to give the liberation movements a platform and a voice. I joined the committee of the newly formed Institute of Race Relations, set up by Philip Mason; but I soon protested that it included no black people, and resigned. In the campaigns against apartheid I often found myself awkwardly sharing platforms with academics, politicians and missionaries: I was relieved that they had never seen copies of *Drum* magazine with its cover girls and gangsters' memoirs printed on cheap newsprint. But the blacks of Soweto, I reflected, had more political relevance than the romanticised tribes imagined by some of my fellow-crusaders.

I became more interested in South African history, in tracing how Britain had allowed the tragic confrontation to develop after the Boer War; how

Lord Milner, the British high commissioner, had rebuilt South Africa with the help of his 'Kindergarten' of young Oxford men; and how he had betrayed the blacks when he gave white South Africans their independence in the South Africa Act of 1909. I was all the more curious having known some of the 'children' of the Kindergarten, including Patrick Duncan, in Johannesburg. After the *Drum* book was published I was amazed to receive a letter of congratulation in shaky handwriting signed by Lady Milner, who explained how her husband Alfred had always regretted ignoring the natives. Soon afterwards she invited me to lunch: in her nineties she was a wonderful flashback to an imperial heyday, wearing a huge black hat which made her look like a pirate queen, and excavating her nose with her handkerchief. 'I remember sitting between Neville Chamberlain and Geoffrey Dawson the day they took the vote from the Cape natives,' she said. ' "You really must do something for the poor natives," I said to Neville. Do you know he hadn't even *heard* of it?' The consequences of that betrayal were now all too clear in South Africa, as the blacks were left at the mercy of the Afrikaners.

But reading and talking about South Africa was no substitute for being there. I still missed the intense and vibrant society of black Johannesburg and the circle of black friends with whom I felt at home, who brought to life all the dry abstractions about franchises, human rights and civil liberties. I felt impelled to return whenever I could, and over eight years I watched how the apartheid government inexorably clamped down on the black opposition.

*

My first chance to return came only two years after I had come back to London, while still working on the *Observer* and before starting *Anatomy*. In 1956 the Pretoria government arrested 155 opposition leaders, including prominent blacks such as Albert Luthuli, the president of the ANC, and Nelson Mandela. As the government prepared to charge them with treason I decided to write a book on the ensuing trial and flew back to Johannesburg for a month. When I arrived, on a cold wet day, I couldn't remember why I'd wanted to come back to this bleak city with its harsh skyscrapers, tense atmosphere, treeless streets and stark street names – Gold Street, Nugget Street, Diagonal Street. In Soweto the box houses looked grimmer than ever, now overshadowed by giant hoardings advertising cigarettes or soap. But as soon as I was in a shebeen with *Drum* friends, listening to a calypso in my honour, I remembered what I had been missing in London: the vitality, the creativity, the direct human values. 'I can understand, grasp and *feel* this country', I wrote, 'as I can never grasp England with all its trusts, lobbying, electoral pressures and remote political shadows. Here I know what I stand for.'

White Johannesburgers seemed still more distant from the blacks. The newspapers featured human-interest stories about businessmen helping black 'piccanins', alongside reports of black convicts being beaten. White liberals continued to offer the ANC friendly advice, but they still did not listen to it. I called on Harry Oppenheimer, the powerful liberal business-man who had also been at Christ Church; he was welcoming and courteous but seemed little interested in Mandela and his friends. He was impatient with a one-day strike which had paralysed industry 'for the sake of a gesture' and found the ANC 'immoderate' and hard to contact. 'Those Oppenheimer people can't be blamed for not knowing,' said Joe Matthews, a young ANC activist; 'they never meet any Africans except their chauffeur or their lift boy.'

For my old *Drum* friends the future was now much bleaker as the government clamped down and they argued with anguish as to whether to emigrate or become more committed to politics. The most heroic of them, Henry Nxumalo, who had investigated so many horrors of apartheid, had been found stabbed in a gutter in Soweto, supposedly murdered by a crook he was about to expose. But the others were all feeling the political strains. 'I can understand why the whites behave as they do,' said Arthur Maimane, 'but when I think about it I get so angry that I can't write about it.' Soon afterwards he left for Ghana, then for London. 'There's going to be one hell of an explosion,' said Bloke Modisane. 'There'll be only two camps, black and white. That's why I'm clearing out.' He escaped to Rhodesia soon afterwards. 'They've got the needle and it goes in bloody rough: it *hurts*, man,' said Todd Matshikiza, who later went to London. 'The time will come when the people will only see black,' said Woody, who would soon disappear underground. 'The people are looking for a Hitler to tell them what to do.' 'Life is more dark now,' said young David Sibeko, who manned the telephone: two years later he had joined the Pan African Congress and was plotting to assassinate the prime minister, Dr Hendrik Verwoerd. 'They say that Africa looks like a question mark,' said Can Themba, chewing a pin through his lop-sided mouth. 'But I keep on *telling* those fellows, it looks much more like a gun.'

Talking to the suspects at the treason trial, who included friends, I did not realise how seriously they were committed. One of them, the prominent white communist Ruth First, gave a party which seemed as carefree as ever, full of comrades of all colours drinking and jiving, with a CIA man among the guests. The Indian communist Dr Yusuf Dadoo looked more like a smooth socialite than a serious revolutionary and his colleague Dr Monty Naicker was asleep in a corner, looking like a Buddha. The whites still seemed to be showing off their revolutionary spirit – 'peacocking' as the blacks called it. Only occasionally did someone betray their real fear: 'You can hang for treason,' the young black activist Peter Nthite said, with his cigarette in the corner of his mouth. 'I often wonder how we will be able to save our white comrades when the time comes.'

The black leaders were still reluctant to close the doors on the white world. Albert Luthuli, the Christian chief who had given up his chieftaincy to lead the struggle, discussed the problems of maintaining resistance, screwing up his face with anguish: 'Old people grow *soft*.' Visiting Mandela in his neat box house in Soweto, I wondered how far he was prepared to sacrifice his whole career as a promising lawyer: there was imbuia furniture and china mermaids on the mantelpiece, below pictures of Stalin and Lenin – and also Luthuli. But young militants were already talking about burning the passes on which the apartheid system depended. 'Once you attack the actual instruments of white supremacy', said the communist journalist Govan Mbeki, father of Thabo Mbeki, 'there will be a bit of shooting – a lot of shooting.'

The treason trials achieved their objective of putting most of the ANC leaders out of action. They continued off and on for three years – which made my book *The Treason Cage* rather inconclusive when it came out in 1958.

*

Taking time off from researching *Anatomy*, I had a unique opportunity to observe British policy-making at first hand when I followed Harold

Macmillan on his tour of Africa in 1960, the year when the whole continent seemed in flux. It was the first tour of Africa by a serving British prime minister, and I heard a private running commentary from Macmillan at each stage of the trip. He had a simplified view of Africa: it was, he explained, like a lazy hippo which had been suddenly prodded. He was worried that Africans were not ready for the freedom which was coming so fast, but colonial officials had persuaded him that to delay independence for twenty years would only cause more bitterness and bloodshed without teaching Africans any more about exercising power.[1] He saw the intransigence of the apartheid government as a serious obstacle to peace, and he planned to end his tour with a speech in South Africa.

Macmillan gave a New Year's Eve party in Downing Street just before he left, where he talked with apparent candour. The *Observer* had just published a letter from Albert Luthuli, Alan Paton and others warning him to say nothing in South Africa that could be construed as supporting apartheid; and he assured me that he agreed completely with the letter. I did not believe that he would dare criticise Hendrik Verwoerd while he was his guest; but his private secretary, Tim Bligh, kept assuring me through the tour that the speech would include paragraphs which would clearly dissociate Britain from apartheid. 'They're still in,' he promised me as we travelled down the continent, 'they're still in.'

Macmillan was soon exposed to all the problems of the emerging black nationalism. He began in Ghana, where President Kwame Nkrumah was already flexing his muscles without bothering much about democracy: he seemed to follow the revised precept 'power is delightful; absolute power is absolutely delightful'. Macmillan seemed to enjoy the laughing exuberant 'Showboy' who set off his own languid Edwardian style like a music hall turn. He reckoned that Ghana was already moving towards a one-party system, and that Nkrumah would soon emerge as a dictator; but he took a long historical view and recalled how gradually Britain had emerged from Tudor tyranny in the seventeenth century.[2] He went on to Nigeria, the huge territory which was moving towards independence; he was worried by the viability of the new nation whose borders had been so casually drawn, but he liked the sense of fun and merriment of 'these happy folk'.[3] He flew down to Rhodesia, where he was confronted by furious white settlers who rightly suspected that he was preparing to sell them out by accepting majority rule. He was fiercely confronted by Sir Roy Welensky, the prime minister of the Central African Federation, a rugged ex-boxer who would become increasingly intransigent over the next three years; but Macmillan would outmanoeuvre him in the end. 'It is too simple a reading of history', he told Welensky in 1962, 'to think you can exercise control simply by the use of power.'[4]

But in South Africa Macmillan had to confront a much more deeply entrenched white minority, over which Britain had much less influence. He had little respect for the Afrikaner ministers, and was amazed by their incompetence. 'They can't do anything properly, can't even get a car in time,' his eccentric private secretary John Wyndham complained to me. 'All they could do was the Great Trek, and what was that? Anyone can get onto a fucking ox wagon and fuck off to the horizon.' But Macmillan knew he was facing determined nationalists who could threaten the peace of all Africa, and he had prepared his bombshell with scrupulous care. In Parliament in Cape Town I heard him deliver the finest speech of his career; he was so nervous (I discovered much later) that he vomited in the lavatory beforehand.[5] He first flattered the Afrikaners as the pioneers of 'the first of the African nationalisms', and then warned them that a 'wind of change' was blowing through Africa, and emphatically dissociated Britain from apartheid doctrines. It was so courteous that the Afrikaner MPs were at first reassured, until the London papers explained that it marked a fundamental shift in British policy.

It had long repercussions in black Africa. In South Africa Macmillan met no black leaders, not wanting to further offend his Afrikaner hosts, and my *Drum* friends thought he should not have come. But Luthuli thought the speech gave the African people 'some inspiration and hope' and Mandela thought it was 'terrific'. Nearly forty years later Mandela, speaking in Westminster Hall, would recall Macmillan's courage in confronting 'a stubborn and race-blind white oligarchy', and would refer to the Johannesburg newspaper cartoon which showed Macmillan reciting:

> O pardon me, thou bleeding piece of earth,
> That I am meek and gentle with these butchers.

Macmillan's wind of change soon appeared an understatement. Later that year the Belgian government precipitately granted independence to the Belgian Congo, which erupted into a hideous civil war, alarming white settlers everywhere in Africa and leading to chaos from which the independent Zaire would never recover. Macmillan had to explain that his wind of change had not meant 'a howling tempest which would blow away the whole of the new developing civilisation'.

*

The Western structures in Africa were gradually crumbling, and the imperatives of the continent were reasserting themselves. After following Macmillan's journey, I travelled to Tanzania, just emerging into independence, to visit Trevor Huddleston, who had been appointed Bishop of Masasi, one of the poorest regions of Africa. In the Tanzanian capital, Dar es Salaam, I stayed at the Hotel Splendide with damp rooms, rubber mats on the stone floors, in a stifling heat like a Turkish bath in which nothing seemed to matter. A few white drunks sat at the bar, and the city seemed to be already flaking: my taxi was stuck in a motionless traffic jam, and then ran out of petrol. I flew down the coast, in an ancient Dakota which hopped from one port to the next, as far as Lindi, a dead-alive port which was closing down; there were a row of thatched shops and coconut palms along the desolate beach, and a white visitor was greeted with amazement. I hitched a lift in a Chevrolet van with a stuttering Greek contractor who was longing to get back to Greece: he drove me 90 miles along a dirt track full of potholes, perilous bridges and subsided tarmac, with jackals running across the road, passing little villages of thatch and mud with families sitting outside round fires. At last we reached the settlement of Masasi: we turned into a track with high grass all round it, up a hill to find a long grey stone cathedral with a steep thatched house above it, with bright bougainvillea against the grey stone, and mango trees like in children's picture books. After a hoot on the horn the tall white figure of Trevor Huddleston appeared, astonished but welcoming.

Trevor took me into his plain house to drink bourbon and talk about old friends, in an atmosphere of peace which obliterated all the restlessness of the journey. He talked candidly about his problems as a missionary: how the region was still bedevilled by old rivalries with Roman Catholics; how he could exploit his fame to raise money but must resist its temptations; how he had learnt to be practical, not picturesque, and build houses with brick walls and tin roofs rather than mud huts with thatches. He still desperately missed Johannesburg, but he heard himself repeating old clichés about South Africa which had no meaning; and it was important to *never go back*. Trevor seemed to fit completely into this community, animating it with his quiet authority, talking Swahili with the children on the porch as naturally as if he had been brought up to it. After two days I had abandoned all my suspicions of missionaries. When I took off from the airstrip in a tiny Piper Apache, I watched Trevor waving goodbye, surrounded by a small group of children in front of the little airport hut. Here at least were some obvious achievements in Africa, providing education, healthy food and a sense of purpose.

One vivid glimpse of how Africa was reasserting itself occurred when I arrived at the little port of Mtwara, looking across the Indian Ocean, with dhows, buoys, bright blue sea and pink sunset. I recalled the name of Mtwara from a bizarre episode in Britain's colonial policy: it had been developed in the late 1940s as the port for the great groundnuts scheme by the Labour government, in conjunction with Unilever, which had spent huge sums clearing the bush to plant groundnuts which could be exported to Britain to relieve the food shortage. The contractors had built a whole inland town in colonial style, with broad avenues and spacious houses for British officials. But the scheme had been a fiasco: it was run by incompetent ex-officers who knew nothing about the terrain; the bulldozers that were used to pull down the great baobab trees broke while the trees remained standing. After a few months they abandoned the whole project and the bush reclaimed the land, and invaded the houses. Mtwara itself had been planned as the port at the end of a single-track line, but the railway had never been properly used and was now interrupted by lions and leopards. In 1962 part of it had been washed away by floods, and the rails were being sold off for scrap. Mtwara was a ghost town with a crumbling station, antique carriages abandoned in a siding, and a derelict dock. There were wide streets called Broadway, Bank Street or Coronation Square, but few houses had been built, and only an old post office with a red tin roof bore witness of past ambitions. It was a poignant reminder of how Europeans could blunder into

Africa, and how quickly the bush could reassert itself. Evelyn Waugh had visited the place as a tourist a few years before, and had written: 'If the Groundnuts Scheme had been conceived and executed by natives, everyone would point to it as incontrovertible evidence that they were unfit to manage their own affairs.' It was the resistance of Africa, not of Africans, which had brought the white man's great project to disaster.

*

Events in South Africa were overtaken by a more serious crisis in March 1960, two months after Macmillan made the speech about the winds of change. Black protesters refused to carry passes and gathered at police stations to be arrested. At Sharpeville the police opened fire on a crowd of 10,000 people and shot sixty-seven dead, precipitating a wave of furious protesters and pass-burners.

I flew back to South Africa to cover the crisis for the *Observer*. It was one of those weird interims in history, so hard for any journalist to analyse, when the whole power system seemed to shake, and anything could happen. For a few days the two rival black parties, the African National Congress and the Pan Africanist Congress, were competing in militancy. The ANC organised a one-day strike and their leaders, including Albert Luthuli and Nelson Mandela, publicly burnt their passes. 'Only a truly mass organisation could co-ordinate such activities,' Mandela told me in Soweto. 'We'll have them roasted,' said the ANC leader Duma Nokwe in Soweto. 'The country is in a pre-rev—' – he stopped himself from saying 'revolutionary' – 'in the state before major changes take place.'[6]

In Cape Town the PAC organised a general strike and a mass march on the city. The revolutionary spirit seemed to have seeped everywhere and the *Drum* writers were infected. 'It's the people they say don't exist who have hit them over the head,' said one of them. On the state-controlled radio a black employee had smuggled an old radical song onto the airwaves: 'Wake up, my people, be united. The fault is with us.' Once more there was a Shakespearean echo:

> The fault, dear Brutus, is not in our stars,
> But in ourselves, that we are underlings.

The mood of expectation reached a climax on 9 April, when a white farmer shot and wounded Hendrik Verwoerd at an agricultural fair. The government seemed genuinely paralysed and uncertain: ten days later one minister, Paul Sauer, explained that Sharpeville had closed the old book of South African history and that the country must reconsider race relations 'seriously and honestly'.

But by the end of April the prospects of reform, let alone revolution, had evaporated. Verwoerd rapidly recovered and took charge decisively. The police fought back more brutally, arresting all defiers. Blacks who had burnt their passes found that they could not draw a pension or withdraw their savings, and queued up meekly to reapply. The Afrikaner government was clearly far more determined to hold on to power than any British colonial government further north. 'This isn't *it*,' said Can Themba. 'People say that the wind of change has turned into a hurricane or a whirlwind. It never seems to occur to them that it might be only a breeze.'

*

I could not return to Africa for two years, while I was writing *Anatomy*, but just before it was published in 1962 I escaped with relief to Johannesburg. The political scene was much grimmer. The ANC and the PAC had been banned, and the press could not even mention them. The government had just passed a new Sabotage Bill, which prescribed the death penalty even for minor offences. The police, after training abroad, had become more efficient and systematic: they wasted less time on harassing ordinary blacks and concentrated on serious interrogation of political suspects.

The days of 'peacocking' had ended. The ANC had abandoned passive resistance and was committed to the armed struggle. 'People are facing an outright military build-up,' Walter Sisulu, the former ANC secretary, told me in his hiding-place. 'The talk of non-violence is an anachronism.' The PAC was preparing for a much more ruthless grass-roots struggle: 'Essentially the struggle's here; the world won't help,' its leader, Zeph Mothopeng, told me in Soweto. 'The world backs the winning horse.' And the white horse was winning.

The British government under Harold Macmillan was still worried about the repercussions of apartheid but it needed to maintain trade with South

Africa and dreaded offending Hendrik Verwoerd. I went to see the well-polished British ambassador, Sir John Maud. He was preoccupied with ingratiating himself with the Afrikaner government and invited no blacks to his parties. As one white professor remarked, 'with Maud you have to take the smooth with the smooth'.

It is always frustrating for a journalist to be in the midst of an impending crisis and be surrounded by secrecy; I felt for the first time what it was like to live in a police state. What I did not know was that the ANC leaders were plotting a revolutionary coup in a hideout in Rivonia, just outside Johannesburg, and that Nelson Mandela was receiving military training in Ethiopia. A few days after I left, Mandela returned to the country clandestinely, visited his fellow-revolutionaries in Johannesburg, and was caught and arrested on the road from Durban. By that time I was back in London.

*

Two years later I made a last tour of Africa, which revealed how rapidly it was moving away from European influences. *Anatomy* had given me an extra calling-card: one day in London a despatch rider delivered a message elegantly inscribed in Amharic, with a translation opposite, beginning: 'We have read with pleasure your book *Anatomy of Britain* . . .' It went on to invite me to visit Ethiopia and was signed 'Haile Selassie, Emperor'. I first took it to be a practical joke but it turned out to be perfectly real.

I soon had an opportunity to take up the invitation. The *Observer* asked me to follow the Chinese prime minister, Zhou Enlai, who was making a journey through Africa, which was seen as a dangerous escalation of the Cold War: the Chinese were seeking to outbid the Soviets by actively supporting black revolutionaries, and Zhou would soon announce that 'revolutionary prospects are excellent throughout the African continent'.[7] I began pursuing him without much success: I was fascinated watching this shrewd old Marxist with his darting eyes, but I never uncovered any African–Chinese plots.

Instead, my journey gave me some close personal insights into the insecurity of the new African rulers.

My first glimpse was in Ghana, where Kwame Nkrumah had been in power for seven years, increasingly corrupted by business dealings and surrounded by enemies, imaginary and real: an assassin had just tried to kill him. When Zhou arrived Nkrumah was holed up in his castle, but eventually the journalists heard that he was giving a party there, and three of us tried to gatecrash it. We arrived at the gateway in an imposing limousine, but the guards stopped us, took our names and sent us back to our hotel. The next day a black policeman came to the hotel and took me to headquarters for questioning. I realised that I was under arrest. But the policeman was courteous and while we waited he offered me a book by J. B. Priestley, while he took another for himself, which looked familiar: it was *Anatomy of Britain*. I asked him if he recognised the author's name: he looked down, roared with laughter and exclaimed: 'It's you!' I felt reassured, but I still had to spend the night in a dank prison cell reeking of stale urine, which I shared with a Nigerian 'money-doubler'. (The Nigerians' genius for fraud was already exerting itself.) The next morning I was taken to my hotel room, which was searched; but soon a senior official arrived to apologise and let me go. I owed my release, I soon discovered, to an American businessman who had bribed his way into Nkrumah's favour, who interceded on behalf of the journalists; but I was in no state to be choosy about my benefactor. Ghana was already on the way to becoming a police state in which journalists were expendable, and Nkrumah's 'African personality' was showing a less attractive face. Two years later he would be overthrown by army plotters who had only contempt for intellectual theories about democracy.[8]

From west Africa I flew to Ethiopia to take up my invitation from the emperor. The capital, Addis Ababa, looked from the air like a fairyland city sparkling in the sunshine, surrounded by blue mountains. The Ethiopians were celebrating the Coptic Epiphany and the race track was packed with people dancing, playing polo and acting a traditional play in mime. Back on the ground, though, I could see that the city was a jumble of primitive mud dwellings with only a few solid buildings: the imperial palace dominated the centre rather as King Charles I's banqueting hall in Whitehall must have loomed above Jacobean London. The people were poor but full of dignity; with their fine triangular faces, sharp eyes and long noses they looked like aristocrats, wearing white robes and jodhpurs. They were proud of their continuous history as a nation which had defied colonisation.

When I visited the British ambassador, Sir John Russell – an appropriate aristocrat who kept polo ponies in the grand diplomatic compound – he explained why the emperor was interested in *Anatomy*: he had in mind to transform his kingdom into a British-type constitutional monarchy, complete with parliament, permanent secretaries and independent judges, and *Anatomy* was to be his guidebook. I was irreverently reminded of a Dr Dolittle story in which the local chieftain decides to start a postal service and put up pillar boxes round the country, not realising that they needed postmen to distribute the letters. But I was flattered that my book should have such influence.

I waited for the emperor in his palace, surrounded by petitioners hoping to gain favours while courtiers revelled in their power. Eventually I was shown into the Throne Room, where the tiny monarch sat between his two pet dogs. He complimented me on my book, explained his admiration for British democracy, and arranged for me to meet his family. I spent some time with the Crown Prince – a shy man who was clearly nervous about his future – and the emperor's grandson, Alex Desta, an enthusiastic old Harrovian with whom I made a trip to the hills. The mountain kingdom was an obvious anachronism, an ancient absolute monarchy surrounded by revolutionary republics. But the emperor was a shrewd old fox who had exploited the Cold War brilliantly to attract aid from all sides, and he was a father figure to visiting African nationalists, including Nelson Mandela, while Ethiopia had apparently avoided the bitter racial and tribal conflicts of the rest of Africa.

It proved a tragic illusion. The emperor was hopelessly out of touch with his impoverished people, and his moves towards democracy were too little and too late. He waged extravagant wars – internally with Eritrea and with neighbouring Somalia – which were exacerbated by cold war rivalries. The monarchy collapsed in 1974: the 82-year-old emperor was deposed and confined to an army barracks where he died a year later. Most of his family were murdered and the country was taken over by a Marxist dictator, Mengistu Haile Mariam, whose brutal regime, the Derg, became one of the nastiest in Africa.

But in April 1964 the Ethiopian monarchy looked much less seriously threatened than its neighbouring young republics, many of which faced mutinies soon after becoming independent. The mutinies had been set off by a revolution in Zanzibar, the beautiful island on the east coast which the British had hastily made independent the year before, under a young Arab sultan who dominated the African majority. Now the sultan had been abruptly overthrown by a swaggering 25-year-old Ugandan, John Okello, who seized control over the radio and promoted himself to field-marshal. Zanzibar was the first of the coups by African soldiers, who seized power crudely, down the barrels of their guns. I flew to the island to find an ugly racial melodrama: the Arabs were under siege, draping white flags from their windows, fearfully watching black soldiers pulling old Arabs through the streets by their beards; while white women at the English club sat talking on the verandah. I was taken to see Field-Marshal Okello, who protested fiercely about lies in the press, with glaring eyes and a gun on his belt, and I flew out as soon as I could.

The mutinies on the mainland began shortly afterwards with next-door Tanganyika, which had become independent two years earlier. Its president, Julius Nyerere, a peace-loving idealist, was totally unprepared for trouble, and when I arrived in the capital he had disappeared into hiding. Then to my surprise I was invited to the presidential palace for a talk with him. It was a strange and moving insight into the basic problems of power. Nyerere talked with disarming candour like a Shakespearean king (he had once translated *Julius Caesar* into Swahili) and discussed what lay behind the mutiny: 'In matters of violence,' he said, 'Tanganyika has been a virgin. In advanced countries it is a kind of miracle that soldiers take orders from a civilian.' The revolt was a warning that he could not afford to be too British: 'African countries are not left enough. I am too Western: socialism is essential for us, and China has a lot to teach us.' He sounded like a philosopher-king, but he soon proved his pragmatism: he had asked the British for support and an aircraft-carrier was already anchored in the bay. He quickly established a union with Zanzibar, to make a single country, Tanzania, and defused the wild leadership on the island. It was not for nothing that he would remain president for twenty years.

I flew across the border into Kenya, which had also faced mutineers only a few weeks after becoming independent. Black Kenya presented a dramatic contrast from the old white colony: only a few years earlier I had heard the swashbuckling settlers at the New Stanley bar reviling Jomo Kenyatta as the evil genius behind the terrorist rebellion of the Mau Mau, and rejoicing that he was in jail. Now the same settlers were talking about the 'grand old man' who had become president. Kenyatta did not hesitate to ask Britain for troops to quell the mutiny. But the challenge to his leadership made him less tolerant of any opposition, and he was already moving towards a single-party system.

Uganda, the fourth of the independent ex-British colonies in east Africa, was less seriously threatened by mutiny, but it was already heading for a more brutal autocracy. I was invited to see Milton Obote, the young prime minister, in his lakeside lodge: a flamboyant populist with long hair, flourishing a decorated walking stick. He harangued me about the advantages of a single party: 'Tell me, which African country had a two-party system before the European came?' But he had no concept of alternative democratic systems: two years later he would arrest all his opponents in his Cabinet, abrogate the constitution and appoint a thug, Idi Amin, as military commander. Finally in 1971, while Obote was at a Commonwealth conference, Amin seized power in a coup and instituted the bloodiest dictatorship of all.

And on the borders of Uganda I had a preview of a wider tragedy that was beginning to spread through east Africa. In neighbouring Rwanda the proud ruling tribe, the Tutsis, had been ruthlessly ousted by their former subjects, the Hutus, and 20,000 Tutsi refugees had fled into Uganda. I drove down to the frontier to find the refugees camped in the Oruchinga valley. The scene, as with so many African catastrophes, had an outward Biblical beauty: the tall Tutsis maintained a calm dignity as if they were suffering only a temporary exodus in their tents, and planned to regain their power in Rwanda. In fact they had been disinherited and uprooted, and were now pathetically dependent on emergency aid administered by an English schoolboy and a Red Cross nurse. But their predicament proved minor compared to the massacres and reprisals which would devastate the whole region in the 1990s.

After this extended trip, I returned briefly to South Africa in June 1964, at the end of Nelson Mandela's long second trial, when he and his colleagues were charged with conspiring to overthrow the state. The atmosphere was still bleaker after two years of oppression. The police were more professional and ruthless, with the help of detentions, torture and more systematic intelligence which they had learnt in Israel and the United States. White Johannesburg was booming with the help of massive foreign investment:

Barclays Bank and ICI proclaimed their support with shining new business palaces, and the blacks showed little outward sign of resistance except for a few scrawled slogans, such as 'Apartheid Means War'. One night I drove to a shebeen in Soweto with two old *Drum* colleagues, but no blacks now dared discuss politics. On the way back we were stopped by two cars filled with armed Afrikaner thugs in plain clothes, who questioned us threateningly. When I showed my press card they told me to go: I insisted that they must release my black colleagues, but in the meantime the Afrikaners had taken their names and addresses. I was ashamed to feel physically scared when they had much more to fear. I fell into the trap which any correspondent must dread: leaving his informants in danger while he escapes scot free. The might of the pen was feeble when confronted with the full power of the police.

I had a last glimpse of the power of the state when I went to Pretoria to observe the trial. The Supreme Court was packed with armed police who watched the spectators like hawks and took down all names. I sat on the press bench watching the prisoners being led up from the cells under the court. The familiar faces of Walter Sisulu, the Indian activist Ahmed Kathrada and Mandela, which I had seen so relaxed in their homes, now looked drawn and austere in their prison clothes: they were all facing a possible death sentence. Then Mandela looked back at the courtroom, recognised me, smiled and pointed me out to his colleagues. Instinctively I responded with the ANC clenched-fist salute. Immediately an Afrikaner policeman rushed up and beckoned me out of my seat. He questioned me for ten minutes about how I knew the accused and what I was signalling to him, before I was allowed back, to the visible enjoyment of the prisoners.

When the trial was adjourned I was approached by one of the defence lawyers, George Bizos, a stocky, bushy-haired Greek barrister who later became a close friend. He told me that Mandela was now asking me to advise him about the long speech he had prepared, with an eye on international opinion. So I spent an extraordinary evening in the lawyers' room alongside the court with the defence team, including Bizos, Arthur Chaskalson, Joel Joffe and Bram Fischer, the dedicated Afrikaner communist who led the defence. They showed me Mandela's long draft speech, which he had prepared in his own hand. I was engrossed by his moving testimony of his political development: how his tribal elders had first made him aware of African injustices, how he had widened his horizons and embraced the multiracial struggle with the help of communist allies, and how he had been compelled to begin the armed struggle when passive resistance was suppressed by the violence of the state. I made a few suggestions about the style and presentation, which were mostly ignored: probably rightly, for the text as it emerged was one of the historic speeches of the twentieth century.* I would always feel privileged to have been minimally involved in it, and to have worked briefly with these dedicated lawyers who would all become friends; for the first time I appreciated the law as the ultimate safeguard against autocracy.

The end of the trial on 12 June 1964 was my last sight of Mandela for twenty-six years, and my last glimpse of black South Africans before they entered a long age of darkness and repression. For the *Drum* writers the future was much bleaker as apartheid increasingly bore down on their lives, and most of them came to tragic ends, cut short by violence, unhappy exile or drink. Todd Matshikiza was driven into exile, first in London then in Zambia, where he drank heavily and died prematurely. Can Themba became increasingly frustrated and alcoholic, was fired from *Drum* and died from a heart attack in Swaziland. Bob Gosani and Casey Motsisi both also drank heavily and died young in Johannesburg. Perhaps the most tragic exile was Nat Nakasa, the talented young *Drum* writer who escaped to America, with a fellowship at Harvard, where he felt desperately isolated. In December 1964 I spent a happy Sunday in New York touring Harlem with him and the next month he wrote to me in London gleefully reporting that the *New York Times* were publishing a piece about Harlem. But a few weeks later he threw himself out of a high window in Manhattan.

In South Africa the nature of the power was still unresolved and the future

---

* It was such an odd experience that in later years I wondered whether I had not romanticised it. So I was reassured forty years later, when I was writing Mandela's authorised biography, to come across the manuscript of the memoir he had written on Robben Island in 1975, in which he described the incident: 'The British author and reporter for the London *Observer* Tony Sampson was in court one day as we came in. He was previously editor of *Drum* in South Africa and was well known to most of us. When we greeted him he responded with the clenched-fist salute. He was immediately called out rudely by the Security branch and warned. He was also in contact with defence lawyers and made valuabe suggestions to them.'

less predictable. In military terms the apartheid government had an overwhelming superiority and was building up its formidable arsenal and intelligence system, to suppress any likely black revolt; while the British and American governments, worried by communism and needing precious minerals, were not prepared to impose sanctions. Mandela and his ANC colleagues were serving life sentences on Robben Island while the remaining political leaders had gone into exile, trying ineffectively to organise guerrilla warfare or sabotage. In the early period of their imprisonment the black leaders expected to be freed within five years; but the five was extended to ten, fifteen, twenty; and the end of apartheid was still out of sight.

But military force was not always the decisive kind of power, as the British had painfully learnt through their retreat from empire. The power of ideas – of nationalism, liberation and freedom, however illusory – had proved stronger than armies all through Asia; and in Africa the clamour for independence had rapidly made colonies ungovernable. In South Africa the Afrikaners had a much stronger will to rule than the British further north, and much greater military resources; while the black opposition was incompetent and now hardly visible. But I had been convinced of the spirit and resilience of black resistance in the demos and shebeens in Johannesburg; and blacks were all the more determined to achieve their freedom when they saw the martyrdom of their leaders in prison. Two rival ideologies were reinforcing their confidence, each promising its own version of equality: communism and Christianity. It was the first which most alarmed South Africa's rulers, but it was Christianity which would prove the more potent in the longer run.

*

Returning to London from South Africa in 1964, I remained haunted by the images of the embattled African rulers: the proud emperor dreaming of a constitutional democracy, the gun-slinging young field-marshal, the philosopher-king reflecting about armies and mutineers. They were as disconnected as trailers for epic movies, but they were all part of the same developing story of the bewildered continent. The upheavals were already shattering the more naïve British hopes of the New Africa; and the *Observer*, the 'Black Man's Friend', would often be blamed for not criticising the new dictators more candidly. Was Africa condemned to replay the past horrors of Europe, from the Wars of the Roses to the Thirty Years War, before it could find its own way to establish secure, well-managed democracies? That was not the whole story, however. African states were at the mercy of the geopolitical forces of the Cold War, which most observers at the time, including myself, could only dimly understand. The Soviets and the Chinese were competing to provide modern weaponry far more deadly than assegais or pangas; the Americans and Europeans were soon offering financial and military support to any corrupt ruler who proved himself sufficiently anti-communist, so that he might build up his own police state and fill his coffers with the proceeds. The original greed of the white colonisers, to grab the continent's mineral wealth, had been superseded by the greed of Africa's own rulers, encouraged by foreign companies and governments.

What had we really left behind us in Africa, after this sudden power shift? Certainly parliamentary democracy already looked irrelevant in most countries, as presidents from Nkrumah to Obote depicted any opposition as treachery, locked up their judges and tightened their hold with their police and armies. In many parts of Africa it was easy to answer Lenin's 'Who? Whom?': 'Who' was in the government and 'Whom' was in jail or in exile.

The British, after all their constitutions and rhetoric, had retreated hastily without leaving any serious interval to prepare for the democratic process. Colonial governors had been swiftly succeeded by presidents who took over their powers. And already the new black ministers were accumulating private fortunes, which cut them off still further from their indigent populations.

It took time for the scope and consequences of corruption in Africa to become clearer. The big Western corporations which exploited the minerals and agriculture had set a pattern which spread from one new black government to the next, from Ghana and Nigeria to Kenya and Uganda. The company bosses could safeguard their interests and bypass the bureaucracies by bribing the new rulers directly, and the most dynamic entrepreneurs, like Tiny Rowland of Lonrho, established private networks by putting key government officials in each country on their payroll. And as the Cold War extended, the governments in Washington and Moscow escalated the corruption by exporting armaments and funds to support rival rulers, leaving them with fat commissions. African presidents enjoyed the perquisites and privileges of power, with their seats at the United Nations and their secret bank accounts in Switzerland; but much of the real power was exercised outside the continent, by the governments and corporations which were their paymasters. For the great majority of impoverished Africans, the concept of independence was a hollow sham.

Of course in the mid-1960s the future of Africa was still very unclear, and I saw it through a glass, darkly. Most of the British arguments were based on political preconceptions, and each side found what it wanted to find. On my travels I spent some time arguing with conservative friends such as Peregrine Worsthorne, who always maintained that the blacks were not fit to rule anyway, and often found themselves vindicated. But they offered no real alternative: no British government would be prepared to delay independence for very long, given the financial and military costs; and the UN did not have the mandate or the resources to act as peace-keeper, even in Congo, where it was most needed. Since the first disappointments in Ghana I had not shared the optimism of the left about socialism in the independent black states, while I had seen enough of the Cold War to realise how both sides were corrupting and militarising their client states. But after my experiences in Soweto and Sophiatown, and my glimpses of life in the townships of black Africa, I still felt a confidence in the sheer resilience of the Africans and their ability to improvise their own societies and human relationships, with their own creativity and humour – if only they could be given a chance.

6

'Only connect'

Since my earliest memories, I have always felt different. I was very conscious of being left-handed and felt that there was something different about my whole family. Years later I would realise how many interesting writers I met, from John le Carré to Michael Holroyd to Victor Pritchett, had emerged from embarrassing and insecure family backgrounds which detached them from the ordered world and gave a spur to their own creativity.

South Africa, working on *Drum*, seemed to provide a perfect escape, but I soon began to feel a stranger in a strange land. *Drum* gave me confidence as a journalist, and at the *Observer* I had felt fulfilled, but sometimes I felt that I was a social spy between two camps. The writing of *Anatomy of Britain* and its success made me a 'real' journalist and fulfilled the ambitions I had set myself, but there was some sense of emptiness once it had been completed. I found that the chance to revisit southern Africa whenever possible provided the release from some of the claustrophobia I felt at home.

*

I may have learnt something about the workings of power in Britain and Africa but I was not learning much about myself. Many novelists had depicted Africa as a journey into the subconscious, the Dark Continent where visitors lose themselves in order to find themselves. 'We carry within us the wonders we seek without us,' wrote Sir Thomas Browne three centuries ago: 'there is all Africa and her prodigies within us.' But I found the real Africa full of contradictions. I owed much to black friends who had shown me different values and ideas about living; but that had only seemed to widen the divisions in my own life. In my travels I was not finding myself but escaping.

It was a familiar journalists' disease, I realised. Each time I returned from abroad I felt more subject to the alienation which afflicted so many roving foreign correspondents as they were exposed to harrowing experiences which superseded one another, disconnected and confused, soon remembered only through detached highlights. Those heroic people on the spot, enduring unforgettable experiences, faded into blurred faces and names which you could scarcely remember if they made contact a few months later.

I had seen enough of foreign correspondents to notice the insecurities and worries that lay behind their confident despatches, as the youthful adventures gave way to middle-aged doubts. The intrepid heroes of Fleet Street in the 1950s, such as Sefton Delmer or René MacColl – before television outdated them – would venture to a new crisis-spot every week to proudly proclaim: 'I was there!' But most of them had private confusions behind their public personas, and vulnerable egos. Even my friend and mentor James Cameron, who talked as well as he wrote, was racked with self-doubt: 'Each time I sit in front of a typewriter', he said later, 'I feel terrified of being found out.' The better they wrote, the more uncertain they seemed in themselves.

The most admired British reporter in Africa was James Morris, famous as the first journalist to climb Everest, who had been my contemporary at Christ Church, when he was already ahead of the rest of us, married and living outside Oxford. I envied his enterprise and independence as he reported new scenes with an exotic vocabulary and irreverent candour: he wrote a comic report about the pomposity of independent Ghana's first parliament, with its black-robed speaker with his mace and rulebook, with a scepticism which proved prophetic. Later I envied him further when I saw him in Venice, where he was living on the Grand Canal and writing a travel book which became a classic: he took me out on his motor boat, navigating the narrow canals through the back side of the city, showing me the garbage-collectors or undertakers as if he was a born Venetian. But when I met him again in London I noticed a difference: his body lither, his skin more delicate and softer, while his writing style had become still more rarefied. Two years later my agent, Michael Sissons, told me that James had invited him to lunch at a club, where he could not be found until a woman came up and said: 'I think you're looking for me': the intrepid correspondent had been transformed with the help of hormones into the matronly Jan Morris, who

1. AS's father, Michael Sampson,
as a young man.

2. AS's mother, Phyllis Seward, as a
nurse during the First World War.

3. AS's parents' wedding,
17 March 1923.

4. With his parents, 1926.

5. In front of Downing College, Cambridge, c.1928,
where his grandfather was master.

6. AS (*left*) with his sister, Dorothy, and his brother, John,
on holiday at Swanage, 1936. (Helen Muspratt)

7. AS (*far right*) on holiday in Suffolk with his mother (*second right*) and sister (*middle*), c.1938.

8. In a school production of *Henry IV, Part 2* as the Archbishop of York, 1943. (Fox Photos Ltd)

9. Oliver Tambo (*left*) and Nelson Mandela, ambitious young lawyers in the 1950s.

10. Jim Bailey, co-founder of *Drum*, at his desk in the magazine's office. (Schadeberg Images)

11. The editor of *Drum* at his desk. (Schadeberg Images)

Four of the people who made *Drum* famous. (Schadeberg Images)

12. Henry Nxumalo.

13. Jürgen Schadeberg.

14. Can Themba.

15. Todd Matshikiza.

16. The *Drum* office in Johannesburg. (Schadeberg Images)

17. Father Trevor Huddleston, a close friend of *Drum*. (Schadeberg Images)

18. David Astor, proprietor and editor of the *Observer*.

19. Promoting *The New Anatomy of Britain* in 1965 at a Hodder & Stoughton sales conference, with Robin Denniston, AS's publisher and friend since schooldays.

20. Norland Cottages, Walberswick. AS wrote his first Anatomy at No. 8, his mother's cottage.

21. In the garden of Valley Farm, Walberswick, early 1970s.

was planning a book about his (or her) sex change, published as *Conundrum*. Had his uncertain sexual identity always been the secret of his restlessness and adventurous style?

Of course most journalists were torn between their home lives and their professional excitements, and many felt fulfilled by reporting wars and disasters which submerged their own doubts. But most of my contemporaries were now more-or-less married and had outgrown their restlessness, while I felt more deeply divided. Creative bursts alternated with destructiveness, with the familiar depressive symptoms. In my mid-thirties the success of *Anatomy* had brought me financial security and independence, but that only increased my sense of isolation. As I returned to an empty flat from endless parties or hectic interviewing, I felt I knew everyone but no-one. I had been lucky with sympathetic and generous girlfriends, who often stayed the night; but affairs fizzled out in a pattern of rejection and dread of commitment. I still felt lured by an adolescent fantasy life of *femmes fatales*, like Orpheus in the underworld; and I was left with more guilt than fulfilment, 'an expense of spirit in a waste of shame'. I knew there was a much deeper inhibition, but I had found no-one who could help me resolve it. I was searching for something which I would never find. I could only feel stabilised by writing, like a top that wobbles as it stops spinning, or a boat which rocks at anchor but steadies under full sail.

Was I escaping from some kind of god? I kept remembering Francis Thompson's line: 'I fled Him, down the labyrinthine ways | Of my own mind'.[1] I had been impressed by the role of Christianity in Africa, and I found some reassurance among Christians such as Trevor Huddleston, who had experienced his own conflicts between Africa and Britain. But I could never share his faith and discipline, and I realised that my own instinct was not so much religious as 'oceanic', as Freud called it – a longing for something vast and eternal. I found more truth in poetry than in scriptures.

I eventually reluctantly turned to psychologists, a common resort within the *Observer*. The first two I tried sounded less stable than I was, obsessed with their own theories. But the third was a more promising man – I will call him Dr Venables – who had a quizzical smile and an intellectual curiosity. He was himself a part-time author and had read *Anatomy*: he asked me why I had not mentioned doctors in it. He listened sympathetically to my own worries

111

and dubious interpretations, saying little but occasionally questioning me about Africa, journalism or my parents, with a humorous touch. At the end he told me that a full psychoanalysis could probably resolve my tensions, but at the cost of creativity, which he did not recommend. Instead he proposed a few consultations, eased by injections of Methadrine, culminating in a dose of lysergic acid or LSD (at that time legal) under his supervision. The key was to bring my different lives together. 'I see no reason', Venables said, 'why you should not have a permanent relationship within a year.' I was astonished and sceptical, but curious, so I agreed. After a few quite enjoyable sessions with Methadrine which induced free association and opened up my perceptions, I found myself spending an extraordinary night in a London hospital, which took me on a journey which was stranger than anything I had experienced in Africa.

I drank a small glass of tasteless liquid in the evening. For an hour nothing happened. Then very suddenly I lost control of myself, giggling helplessly, swirling down and down with a corkscrew motion through a kind of whirlpool into the centre of the world, or the womb. It was like the beginning of *Alice in Wonderland*. I was in the room yet out of it, coming back repeatedly, still aware of my surroundings, the pillow, the doctor, the hospital. I writhed on the bed, twisted and contorted, compelled to turn round and round in an endless spiral. My arms were pulled towards my ankles, but with no peace, as I tried to pull myself up. I cried out to the doctor as I writhed and gripped the pillow.

Then I began to have vivid visions. I was descending into what looked like the inside of hell. It was agonising, but beautiful, like (I recognised immediately) the paintings of William Blake or Francis Bacon, filled with lumps of raw tormented flesh. There were forks with four or five prongs, prodding twisted bodies including mine. Long flattened hands flapped and groped like gloves without fingers inside them. There was a long channel looking very like an intestine, full of water with dirty little minnows or worms nibbling away inside. The tips of my toes kept turning up and down in tension, like a baby's. I said to the doctor: 'Now I understand that awkwardness at parties, that twisting of the legs, that uneasy walk.' I felt a strain in my stomach and instantly made the simple connection between indigestion and nervous strain. There seemed no difference between physical and psychological awareness: I thought I was inside Dante's Inferno, and pompously told the doctor: 'I'm part of the suffering of the world.' My restlessness acquired a new dignity. I was desperately trying to tug all the disparate bits into the middle, like a painter or a writer trying to contract his imagination onto a single canvas or sheet of paper.

I went on down and down like Hampstead Underground station. Eventually after an hour I felt exhausted and told the doctor: 'I think I've had enough. I'd like to go to sleep.' I added in a matter-of-fact way: 'I've been down to hell.' He said: 'All right. You'll come up tomorrow.' He injected me with a sedative, and I soon felt drowsy, thinking it was all over. The writhing and restlessness gradually diminished, and perhaps I slept for a time.

Then came more reassuring adventures. I began to see intense, bright scenes of dazzling beauty which seemed like elaborate pageants representing stages in the world's history, depicted as sharply as Coleridge's *Kubla Khan*. I was not just watching them, but enveloped in them and their powerful atmosphere. There were Arabs riding a long caravan of camels across a steely white desert, reciting guttural romantic poems against the harsh background, with wild animals roaming around them like films of big game. There was a drunken Elizabethan orgy, like something out of Rabelais, in a huge pink palace, with exquisite turrets and minarets: in the gardens elegant couples were strolling across lawns which went down to a river; but beneath them was an underworld of dung and stink and violence. There was a display of enchanting couples skating over frozen lakes and rivers like a Dutch painting, bright with a cold beauty, but with mud and slime and potential disaster lurking underneath the ice. There were witty conversations in an eighteenth-century London salon. There were processions of persecuted refugees in South Africa, both African and Afrikaner. There was a sophisticated modern party with pretty women talking lightly in a big airy apartment filled with Klee paintings and mobiles hanging from the ceiling. The scenes were in rough historical sequence, but they each seemed to belong to all centuries at once. I had been told how children as they grew up had to experience all preceding centuries from dinosaurs to atom bombs before they began living in the present; and now this seemed to be happening, as I felt myself reincarnated through the ages, like Virginia Woolf's Orlando.

It seemed like a literal journey from the gates of hell: beneath each radiant scene lurked a red inferno full of licking flames, pursuing demons and furies. The palaces and spires and songs seemed to have been forged from the fire, inseparable from it. It was a journey through art and religion, with nothing commonplace or mathematical. The colours and atmospheres came straight from paintings: the ice-cold blue skies from Cima da Conegliano; the dangerous rocks from behind Leonardo's *Virgin of the Rocks* (the relationship was suddenly obvious); the macabre and agonised settings of Brueghel, Memling or Bacon, or the sunny peace of Klee and Derain. They all seemed interconnected, peace and elegance inseparable from squalor and brutality.

I was enthralled by the visions as they went on through the night, but I was also quite conscious of the details of the hospital room around me: I suddenly noticed precisely the 'Aseptor Flushable Urinal Cover' that was by the window. I was able to scribble notes as it happened, writing in big rounded letters on scraps of paper. I could even stumble into the corridor to ring up a friend, to describe the extraordinary scenes. I was intercepted by the duty doctor, who told me to go back to bed: 'You've had enough sedative to knock out a horse.' 'You're just the person from Porlock,' I retorted, and he replied: 'It must be interesting for you, being a writer.' But gradually the visions subsided, my energy ran out and I relapsed into a contented sleep. In the morning I woke feeling surprisingly fresh, to discuss the experience with Dr Venables. He was thoroughly encouraged. Was it always so reassuring, I asked him. 'No. One of my patients was a priest who had very bad visions: he saw God getting smaller and smaller and eventually disappearing.'

The memory of that night has never left me. The adventure seemed more real than anything I had experienced in the material world. It provided what I expected least from a drug – a sense of truth and clarity, as if I were emerging from darkness into a clear universe without contradictions. I was lonely but not alarmed, because I seemed at one with it. It seemed like the world of Jung, with ancient myths pervading the collective subconscious. I would never again experience the fear of death and non-being which had haunted me since childhood.

*

For some weeks I was exhilarated and light headed, as if a great weight had been lifted, leaving me with a physical sense of oneness in my breathing and body, the back of my head connected to the pit of my stomach. It did not last long. I was soon back with the same contradictions, as if I were working my way back through adolescence and adulthood. But I still felt more unified, more confident of my own personality, more open to other people. I was once again caught up in the whirl of events: I reported the frenzied Tory party conference in Blackpool in October 1963, when Harold Macmillan resigned and four rivals competed for the premiership. But I felt more self-possessed and I had never written so easily.

In this new mood of hope I got to know Sally Bentlif, a young Oxford graduate who worked at the A. D. Peters literary agency, which looked after my books. We shared interests and friends, and gradually, almost imperceptibly, our two lives came closer. She had a habit of closing her eyes while awake, which I took as a challenge to stimulate her, while she was determined to make me laugh, and to see the funny side of the political world: she was never impressed by grandees or great occasions and had a sharp eye for pomposity and line-shooting. Sally sought out unusual characters and eccentrics and had a special gift of friendship. She moved into my flat and appeared to accept all my shortcomings. I felt a sense of togetherness which I had never known before, as if a combination lock had opened up a different world from where the dark shapes of the underworld had retreated. I realised how two people can stabilise each other, and wondered how I could ever have lived alone for so long, or could do so again. For the first time I could see a long road opening up ahead, with twists and turns but without roadblocks. When we went on holiday together I realised we could be mutually self-sufficient, and that there need be nothing constricting about sharing two lives.

We were married in 1965 after living together for a year. I was afraid it would spoil things, being Mr and Mrs, but I soon felt freer than I had been as a bachelor, as I was liberated from the burden of having to decide how to please myself – an impossible person to please. We had a daughter, Katie, exactly nine months later and a son, Paul, two years after that; we lived in Ladbroke Grove and spent long family holidays in Suffolk and in France and Italy, where Sally's languages opened up new friendships. I found new outlets for aggression in gardening and we shared an obsession with operas by Mozart and by Wagner, who brought his own resolution of atavistic emotions and myths. We enjoyed a private life which kept the public world at a distance, with a range of friends including many who had little interest in power politics, and with a richness of life to which this book can scarcely do justice.

I still guarded my own private writer's world, with surges of creativity and destruction. I still had moods of depression, particularly when submerged in a book, when old demons emerged from their caverns, which put a strain on the family. Once a year I went back to see Dr Venables, who was always reassuring and encouraging, insisting that the conflicts were part of the creative process and that the two sides would not, and should not, join. After twenty years the consultations stopped when he retired, and I asked him whether he had learnt anything from the experiences of myself or other patients. He smiled enigmatically: 'We've ventured into areas where people haven't ventured before. But I still don't understand it.' I never tried the experiment again.

I was still driven by my own bug of curiosity to try to understand the workings of power in the world, which was rapidly changing around me: over the next three decades I wrote a book every two years, including some arduous research. I took countless long flights in jumbo jets, arriving in bleak L-shaped hotel rooms, isolated and jetlagged. With each book I tried to understand strange new corporate tribes and became fascinated by new heroes, villains and conspiracies. I spent too long away from home, but was always fortified by the awareness of a home base. The pulls between home and abroad, between roots and rootlessness, seemed less my own problem and more part of the predicament of the wider world. And I felt the more challenged to try to connect up the dehumanised world of power politics and business with the human condition.

7

Young Europeans

I still felt claustrophobic in Britain. Each time I flew back from Africa, landing at overcrowded Heathrow and driving past the dingy terraces of west London, I was reminded how little was changing in the old country; and the wide world seemed to contract into parish politics and post-war nostalgia. My researches for *Anatomy* had left me more impatient with the insularity and complacency of Britain, with its tribes and class system.

I escaped whenever I could to the continent, which was being transformed by successive 'economic miracles'. It seemed most miraculous in Germany, which I had last seen so desolated during my service in the navy and ruined by the war from which I thought it would never recover. Most English people in London were still hostile to anything German and thought it unpatriotic to buy a Volkswagen or a Mercedes. I got to know a brilliant young Anglophile German, Ted Sommer, with an impeccable anti-Nazi history, who worked for a time for the *Observer*; but when I took him to a party he was assailed by the Australian journalist Jill Neville: 'How can you bring yourself to come to an English party?' When I revisited Germany I still felt a frisson in crossing into the ex-enemy country, with all the associations of wartime broadcasts. The signposts saying '*Nach Deutschland*' still looked ominous, and the signs on the autobahns such as '*Anschluss*', '*Verboten*', '*Achtung*', '*Ordnung*' all evoked memories of Nazis and jackboots. But in Hamburg I was amazed by the transformation a decade after I had last seen it, just after the war. The bombed-out port was being rapidly rebuilt with brand-new shipyards and cranes which made London's dockland look antique. The rubble had given way to rows of neat houses and spectacular office blocks. The hotels had bathrooms with hot water which gushed out from the taps. The dowdy *Frauen* were giving way to glamorous *Fräulein*. When I stopped to ask the way in faltering German I was answered in impeccable English. The journalists at the weekly paper *Die Zeit*, for which I wrote articles, were passionately interested in Britain and took the *Observer* as their model. Everyone was talking about the future of Europe, while the British went on watching war movies, arguing about the empire and congratulating themselves on the special connection with America.

All western Europe was taking off into high growth rates and optimism. The French and Italians were turning out Renaults and Fiats which were much more elegant and reliable than Morris Minors. The restaurants and cafes were full of delicacies and espresso machines which had not reached England. All the old stories from my schooldays about incompetent and lazy Latins were turned upside down as British workers kept striking and could not compete: even the beloved British motorbike became extinct. What was wrong with the British?

I was convinced that we had to come closer to Europe, to escape from our insular attitudes: from the nostalgia, the class system and the complacency. I was excited when in the mid-1950s the French and Germans began planning a common market to open up free trade and establish a political union between the former enemies, and invited Britain to join and help make the rules. And I was exasperated when the Conservative government and its diplomats turned down the chance, thinking it would not work.

After the European Economic Community was formed in 1956, and the European economies raced ahead, Harold Macmillan began to realise the mistake. He saw the new community as a way out from Britain's protection and industrial strife, to stimulate competition and enterprise: 'It is a cold shower we enter,' he warned, 'not a Turkish bath'. But he prepared the way very cautiously, and he would not accept that joining Europe involved loosening other ties. 'We are the point at which three circles intersect – Europe, America and the Commonwealth,' he told me in 1961; 'making our ties with Europe closer and stronger doesn't mean weakening the others.' He thought he could make a new nuclear agreement with America, for Polaris missiles, without jeopardising his European relations. But the French president, Charles de Gaulle, saw Britain as a 'Trojan horse' which would strengthen American domination and subvert European solidarity; and in 1962 he slammed the door into Europe. I heard the news in Brussels, which filled me with gloom; but I felt hope for the future when the minister for

Europe, Edward Heath, delivered a remarkable speech which made clear that he was committed to trying again.

And I was inspired by Jean Monnet, the father of the European Community (though not of the Common Market),[1] who was a new kind of hero. I first met him in Paris, in his faded apartment on Avenue Foch: a spruce little man with a neat moustache and a questioning smile, who spoke in clipped sentences, always logical, repeating: 'It's all quite simple.' He had an ordered mind, but he worked in chaotic surroundings: 'Order and invention don't go together.' I began to understand why the first chapter in the Bible has creation and chaos in consecutive sentences.

I saw Monnet quite often in the early 1960s, whether in Paris, or at the Hyde Park Hotel in London. I was fascinated by his optimistic view of the world and how it could gradually be changed. He admired the British and wanted them to join the European system in order to democratise and stabilise it, but he was exasperated by their insularity. 'The British had persisted in the illusion of their power,' he wrote later, 'long after the nations of continental Europe had realised they were no longer a match for the modern world.'[2]

He sounded very Gallic and reminded me of Hercule Poirot, Agatha Christie's Belgian detective. But he was more transatlantic than that: 'He is not a Frenchman in hock to the Americans,' de Gaulle snidely remarked; 'he is a great American.' He had begun as a brandy salesmen for the family firm in Canada, and later become a banker in California; he had come to admire America during the First World War, when he was co-ordinating arms-buying for the allies. In the Second World War he became convinced that Britain and France must co-operate closely: he even drafted a plan for a union between the two countries in 1940, and persuaded both de Gaulle and Winston Churchill to propose it – too late.[3] But he retained close American links: after the war the Ford Foundation financed him and he enjoyed easy access to top people in Washington.

I was convinced by Monnet's philosophy; he was convinced that Europe's future depended on overcoming nationalisms and that France must collaborate closely with Germany to ensure that they should never fight again. When faced with an insuperable problem you must 'change the context'. Western Europe, confronted with communist ideology, must be given new hope in democratic institutions: 'You can only get people to do things if you can offer them hope . . . Hope is all the communists have to offer, and they have done well with it.' New institutions could gradually create new loyalties, through the process of *engrenage* or intermeshing. 'Human nature does not change, but when nations and men accept the same rules and the same institutions to make sure they are applied, their behaviour towards each other changes.'[4] You could 'make Europe' through common institutions which would lead to an 'ever-closer union'.

Monnet never held elective office and always chose his own assignments: 'I've never had a job I didn't ask for.' In the 1950s he was put in charge of the French national plan, which made him realise that a single nation was not big enough to allow successful planning. He liked to quote the words of the American banker-diplomat Dwight Morrow: 'There are two kinds of people: those who want to *be someone* and those who want to *do something*. There's less competition among the second.'[5] He preferred to do something, operating behind the scenes, influencing politicians and allowing them the glory. 'You can change the world,' he said, 'provided you don't take credit for it.'[6]

But when Britain was denied entry into the EEC in 1962, Monnet faced his first major setback; and when I heard de Gaulle give a press conference in the gilded ballroom of the Élysée Palace, I realised the full power of his nationalistic mystique. The two eloquent Frenchmen provided a classic confrontation between two concepts of power: one rallying his people behind the nation state with appeals to their pride; the other patiently building up new relationships and institutions to establish new loyalties and contexts. Monnet refused to be discouraged by de Gaulle's emphatic rejection: 'We are off the *autostrada*', he told me in February 1963, 'but the process of change will go on. De Gaulle cannot stop it.' And the next year he said: 'Our countries have begun to delegate part of their national sovereignty to common institutions.' But by 1965 de Gaulle had precipitated a crisis among the six members, and I found Monnet for the first time deeply pessimistic, exasperated that 'the voice of a united Europe has remained silent'.[7]

After writing *Anatomy* I was widening my own horizons. I felt the context of British politics was too narrow, as so many of the roads led off the map. I was more exasperated by Britain's insularity and convinced that she must connect up with the continent. I was encouraged when early in 1967 Harold Wilson, the Labour prime minister, announced he would make a new application to join the Common Market. I decided to write a book about the emerging shape of Europe, to describe the emerging power structure of the European Community, and to test how far Monnet's structures and ideas were really 'making Europe'.

Anatomy had provided me with useful contacts: it had been translated into several European languages, and readers made me realise how much they still looked to Britain as a model of democracy, though the Anglophilia often took strange forms: when the book came out I saw my face on the front page of the scandal sheet *France Dimanche*, under the headline 'The man who made the Queen cry'. I began my travelling across the continent for six months with Sally and our lively year-old daughter Katie, staying in flats, driving from northern Germany to southern Italy, and then to France. I talked to politicians, businessmen and academics; but I wanted above all to feel the mood of ordinary Europeans from my new perspective as a family man.

We could not find much common European awareness. We began in Germany, in a flat in the capital, Bonn; but it still seemed a sleepy provincial town, with its level crossings along the railway and its ferries across the Rhine. Our neighbours were reproving *Hausfrauen* who swept the pavements outside their front gardens and disapproved of an extravert child. I felt oppressed by the suburban complacency, and I suffered from back pains. I was more stimulated by German industrialists in their shiny new office blocks in Düsseldorf, who relished the continental marketplace, and by young German idealists who embraced the European idea as a liberation from the Nazi past. But the German politicians at their stiff gatherings in Bonn showed little sign of French *joie de vivre* or Italian *brio*, and were becoming more engrossed in their national problems. The European idea was already fading.

When we crossed the Alps, Italy still seemed to belong to a different continent half-way to Africa: my back pains disappeared in the sun and relaxation, and restaurants and hotels welcomed a toddler as a guest of honour. The Milanese were exuberantly cosmopolitan – much more welcoming to the English than the Germans were – and swept us into parties and conferences where everyone was talking about Europe. But it was hard to connect the enthusiastic ideas to any practical policies, particularly on the left. The socialist millionaires discussed a Marxist Europe with their courts of writers and artists, in luxurious country houses. We were charmed over lunch by the mega-rich publisher Giangiacomo Feltrinelli in his elegant Villa Deati: he was a lean and passionate communist with a long comic moustache who talked about his friends Castro, Guevara and Régis Debray with fire in his eyes. But his Marxism seemed to have more to do with his fascist mother than with the real problems of contemporary Europe.

Talking to Italian politicians, engrossed in parliamentary intrigue and rhetoric, I could not understand how Italy could become so prosperous without a continuous government, until I realised the full role of its real rulers, the companies and families who overrode all changes. The heads of the big corporations like Eni, Pirelli or Olivetti continued their expansion unaffected by the shifts from left to right, with a much clearer view of the continent. The most powerful of them, the chairman of Fiat, Gianni Agnelli, with his fine leonine head, talked like a modernised prince about the comedy of Italian politics: he contributed to all the parties and was scarcely affected by the changing coalitions: to him the politicians were merely temporary obstacles in the way of the industrialists' grand design.

When we ended up in France, which we both knew much better – Sally was fluent in French – we settled with relief into a picturesque flat on the Left Bank and relished the Parisian lifestyle, which revolved round families and food. We were welcomed by Anglophiles who retained an old-world romance with Britain, and were enriched by our French friendships, as we have been ever since, as we kept on crossing the Channel.

But it was the contrasts which attracted both sides, whether in eating, driving, filmgoing or attitudes to NATO, which the French even spelt backwards. And I became more aware of the benefits as well as the dangers of the French state: the decisive planning of transport, education and health; the intelligence of the master-engineers and senior civil servants. When I toured the state-owned Renault car factories and saw the workers enjoying the paternal welfare – including tempting canteen lunches, up-to-date equipment and long holidays – I felt ashamed by the gimcrack conditions and class divisions of BMC factories.

After these glimpses of national contrasts I could not believe that continental politicians or technocrats were 'making Europe' in any social sense. At the endless conferences and colloquia about European unity I was more struck by the differences, as each speaker dwelt on their national problem: 'take the case of *my* country'. In the formal discussions they would sound very *communautaire*, talking about modalities, harmonisation and *engrenage*; but in coffee breaks they clustered with their countrymen in their own language. The interpreters were the realists in this Tower of Babel, sitting frowning in their glass boxes as they translated high-flown Latin rhetoric into a few concise words of English; but they were developing their own bleak Eurospeak of Germanised long abstract nouns, which provided the lowest common denominator of unity.

The six countries of the EEC still shared an energy and optimism in contrast to the pessimism of Britain – or to their own gloom twenty years before. As western Europe went on booming manufactures were streaming across frontiers. German Volkswagens rolled into France and Italy; Italian Ignis refrigerators flooded into Germany; French farmers exported camembert and claret. The *autostrade*, filling-stations, supermarkets and airports proclaimed the new Europe of machines, food and drink. Shopping-streets and phone directories were full of names like Eurocomfort, Euromatic, Euromusic, Eurofoam, Eurolabor. The Eurovision Song Contest thrived on TV, and trans-Europe expresses linked the capitals. But their mechanical unity was not enough to inspire young idealists.

The view was still bleaker from Brussels, the headquarters of the 'Eurocrats' who ran the European Commission, the bureaucracy of the Common Market. Its first president, Walter Hallstein, a dedicated German law professor, explained to me how it had been created by a small group of convinced Europeans; but the unity had only been achieved, he said, by two external events – first the Suez crisis and then the Hungarian uprising and its brutal suppression by the Soviets, which compelled European politicians to unify against common threats. But the EEC was like a bicycle, Hallstein liked to explain: you either rode on or fell off; now the external threats had receded and it was visibly wobbling, while President de Gaulle was vetoing further progress and boycotting the commission, 'this embryonic technocracy'.[8] The Eurocrats persevered and took the long view. 'We are in the same process the Americans went through 200 years ago,' said Hallstein's successor, the quiet Belgian Jean Rey. 'We may have our quarrels between federalists and nationalists, but we are moving towards unity.' But two centuries was a long time, and I could not believe in a federal Europe on the American pattern. I was depressed by the lack of democratic debate and supervision over this self-enclosed bureaucracy, with its legalistic language. When I listened to the European Parliament in Strasbourg I heard the MPs fiercely criticising the commission's accounts; but they dared not vote for the ultimate sanctions, of sacking the whole commission.

Brussels itself was a depressing advertisement for the New Europe. It had been a symbol of bourgeois commercialism ever since Belgium became a nation in 1830, after a revolution which broke out in the opera house (itself known as Le Théâtre de la Monnaie). Leon Trotsky had coined the word 'Belgianisation' to mean the abandoning of national responsibility in favour of commercial values.[9] Its banking families, 'the great vegetables', had established their fortunes with little countervailing power, and its royal palace and grandiose banks had been financed by the profits from forced labour in Congo. Now Brussels was more than ever the city of Mammon, the headquarters for many multinational corporations as well as the bureaucracy of the Common Market; and it represented a soulless and materialist new Europe. It seemed to fulfil the prediction of the French philosopher Henri de Saint-Simon, the prophet of the technocrats: 'The government of people will be replaced by the administration of things.'[10]

Now the commission, without a proper parliament to control it, was administering things, rather than people, pressing the continent into one mould. In Brussels they joked that the EEC was meant to combine the best qualities of each nation: German efficiency, Italian elegance, French cuisine and British continuity; but what if it ended up with Italian efficiency, German elegance, British cuisine and French continuity? Nevertheless, I still believed that the European nations needed to escape from their own nationalisms and to be more mixed up with each other, whether to increase their economic potential, to stimulate their creativity, or to provide political stability.

I was keenly aware of national differences, and particularly of the special character of Englishness, which I felt much more clearly from abroad, more clearly than in Africa. I was more impressed by the qualities of British democracy, with all its muddles and compromises, and its ability to stabilise the more volatile politics of the continent. After talking to romantic Italian intellectuals or narrow-minded German industrialists I became more aware of the benefits of British realism and social conscience. But I still felt that Britain needed the stimulation and challenge of European competition to disrupt the complacency and protection which had exasperated me when I wrote *Anatomy*; and I believed that the entry of Britain into Europe would give strengths to both sides, as Jean Monnet had hoped. Yet when I went back to London, the British seemed no closer to the continent. I played a game of asking British Europhiles to name ten living Germans: few could get beyond seven or eight, while they could rattle off a hundred Americans.

I was becoming more doubtful whether Harold Wilson and his negotiators really wanted to get into the Common Market: when *Le Monde* commissioned me to write three articles making the British case, I asked the Foreign Office to brief me about the arguments, but our diplomats seemed obsessed by their hatred for de Gaulle and to be nurturing centuries-old rivalries with the French diplomats. And de Gaulle anyway soon removed the choice. In October he again imposed his veto on Britain's entering Europe. A few days afterwards he gave his explanations at a press conference in the Élysée Palace, surrounded by damask and chandeliers: with his tall melancholy presence and beak-like nose he dominated the great hall like an eighteenth-century monarch, invoking all the past glory of France. I felt all the continuity of French nationalism and the difficulty of replacing it with a European loyalty.

*

My book was looking as shapeless as a blancmange, and I blamed it on Europe's own lack of unity: *The New Europeans* was the most difficult book to construct, and I realised I should have been writing six books, not one. I could not imagine Europe emerging as an economic and political power to compete with America: in so far as it was being unified, it was by American rather than European influences.

But while I was despairing of finding a shape, a sudden political explosion threw a harsh new light on all Europe's institutions, sparking off the same ideas. In the spring of 1968 angry students all over western Europe challenged their governments with an impatient urgency that mocked the slow modalities of the bureaucrats who were 'making Europe'. The students had no experience of war; they took peace and European unity for granted; and they were prosperous and secure; but they could not stand the materialism of the New Europe. They were hemmed in by the complacency of their parents' generation, who had been preoccupied with their bourgeois structures; and at their overcrowded universities they confronted authoritarian professors who lectured at them *ex cathedra*. They were certainly influenced by the American student rebellions which had been set off by the Vietnam War: they borrowed their techniques and language of sit-ins, teach-ins, demos and showdowns, and protested against 'manipulation' or 'repressive tolerance'. But their spirit was essentially European: they harked back to the earlier revolutions of 1789, 1848 or 1870. I found them less like practical politicians than like latter-day Romantics, reasserting their personal freedom and imagination against the rigidities of the state.

It began in Germany, where the materialism was most stifling: after our brief encounters in Bonn with nosey and fussy neighbours, I had some sympathy. The student rebels all saw themselves as Europeans, but I found them very German, efficiently organised through their movement, the SDS. 'We are in the methodical tradition,' I was told by their engaging president, Karl-Dietrich Wolff, who was the son of a judge.[11] Their hero was Rudi Dutschke, a fierce-looking leader with rolling eyes, a thatch of black hair and an American wife, who was nearly killed by an assassin; but his looks concealed a basic moderation and dislike of violence. A few sounded more extreme: in Hamburg I met the editor of a tabloid-style magazine, *Konkret*, with his attractive wife, Ulrike Meinhof, who were campaigning for sexual as well as political freedom; but the magazine seemed surreal, and I could not take Ulrike seriously.

The German students railed against the German chancellor, Kurt-Georg Kiesinger, a former Nazi, and against the ex-Nazis of their parents' generation. They effectively undermined the hierarchical universities, where tenured professors exploited their privileges, forcing them to share their power and adapt their courses. But they never achieved a wider political power. They hoped to ally themselves with the workers, like all student revolutionaries; but the workers never shared their contempt for material comforts. The students still had an adolescent idealism which did not connect with the political realities; and they were surprisingly uninterested in the plight of their fellow-students on the other side of the Iron Curtain, in the communist East. In the end they were more interested in liberating themselves than other people.

But when the German rebellion crossed into France it had further-reaching consequences. A German-Jewish student in Paris, Daniel Cohn-Bendit, became the most eloquent spokesman: 'Danny the Red' was a stocky redhead with a podgy face who looked like a mother's boy, but he made fiery speeches in three languages which demolished his opponents – most notably the French Communist Party, which he denounced as obsolete and hopelessly conservative. Above all he could cheekily defy the French universities and demoralise the professors at the Sorbonne: when he and his colleagues were summoned by the disciplinary committee, they walked in singing 'The Internationale'. The showdown set off a week of furious protest when the students took control of the Sorbonne and turned it upside down. They stuck up vivid posters with defiant slogans: 'It is forbidden to forbid'; 'Take dreams for reality'; 'Make love and begin again'; 'Imagination has seized power'.

Had imagination really seized power? Returning to Paris I found the city transformed and rejuvenated. The students were brilliantly re-enacting all the rituals of earlier revolutions, putting up barricades, pulling up paving-stones and waving huge red flags. The Sorbonne was packed with moving bodies wearing beards, jeans and leather jackets, while in the grand amphitheatre radical students engaged in a permanent debate on the revolution. The venerable Odéon theatre carried a banner: '*L'Odéon est ouvert*', while inside the students conducted passionate debates about political power.

The students seemed to be unifying Europe in their own way as they spread their ideas between the capitals as they did in 1848 or 1870 – far more rapidly than the European Commission in Brussels. Their style was emphatically French, but they were much more European minded than traditional French politicians: when *L'Humanité*, the French communist paper, attacked Cohn-Bendit as a German Jew, the students coined the slogan 'We are all German Jews'. After all my bleak conversations about growth rates or harmonisation with German businessmen or Brussels technocrats I felt that Europe was at least being humanised with flair and imagination.

In May 1968 the students seemed to hold the future of France in their hands. For a few days their revolt was actually supported by the Renault car workers, who occupied their factory on the outskirts of Paris. It was an odd spectacle: as the two groups, students and workers, paraded outside the factory they seemed to have changed sides: the workers in smart suits looked much more bourgeois than the students with black leather jackets and long hair. Soon workers all over France were persuaded to declare a general strike, which the Communist Party was reluctantly compelled to support. France seemed to be in a genuinely revolutionary condition, as de Gaulle's government appeared to abdicate and agreed to the wage hikes which the workers demanded.

It was a weird interim. For two weeks the government was silent and power in France seemed totally volatile, as I remembered South Africa after Sharpeville eight years earlier. Then de Gaulle consulted the army, recovered his nerve and declared a general election. The voters were decisive. 'Before half-past four France had been the equivalent of Cuba,' wrote de Gaulle's biographer Jean Lacouture. 'At four thirty-five, she was practically back to the restoration of Louis XVIII.'[12] The French middle classes took fright and rallied behind de Gaulle; the students were hopelessly divided, and their occupations soon degenerated into chaos and squalor. The police moved in to clear the Sorbonne, the government reimposed discipline and the workers returned to their factories and their bourgeois aspirations. The wage increases set off a wave of inflation, for which the French public blamed the students. 'We should have realised that for the workers, the car is a fetish,' Cohn-Bendit admitted. 'Our action went ahead of our theory.'[13]

Imagination had not really seized power: it was a revolt of ideas and language, without practical policies or structures. The slogans advertised Che Guevara or Mao Zedong and protested against global oppression and poverty, but the students showed little interest in oppression closer to home, in the shack towns of Paris or the workers' ghettos behind the Iron Curtain.

And as in 1848 or 1870 the outburst of anarchy provoked an authoritarian reaction. The power of ideas dissolved in the face of serious political power.

Most British observers saw the continental revolt as thoroughly foreign and absurd. When Cohn-Bendit visited the London School of Economics at the peak of his fame most of the British students seemed unmoved by his fiery rhetoric. A few new universities, such as Essex and Warwick, were besieged by angry undergraduates demanding more relevant courses and protesting against capitalist pressures, but most saw student power in terms of fees and conditions at their unions. Christ Church, my old Oxford college, was shocked when a scholar recited a Latin grace before dinner which turned into a protest against the food: it upset the dean for three weeks. The British remained sceptical as always about the power of ideas. But for myself, I had to admire the continental students for bringing a more human dimension to the New Europe, and for contesting the power of money and bureaucracy. And at least they gave some shape to my book.

The New Europeans was published late in 1968, when British curiosity in the continent was waning. It did not have much impact on British politicians or diplomats: they were preoccupied with the United States or Rhodesia and were much less interested in a book which did not mention them in the index. But it sold well in America and was translated into many languages, which extended my continental contacts. And it had most impact in Sweden, which was outside the EEC but was much more internationally minded than its six members and was the home of major multinationals which had interests across the continent. When I visited Sweden frequently afterwards I came to realise that industrialists and traders were integrating Europe more forcefully than politicians or bureaucrats.

*

I would often be tantalised by finding my best contacts just *after* I had published a book; and just after *The New Europeans* came out I had an opportunity for a much closer insight into the psychology of continental students. I had a visit from Bernard Cassen, an energetic young left-wing lecturer and master-fixer at the Sorbonne whom I had first met after I wrote *Anatomy*. Would I like to teach at a new university in Paris? He explained that the new minister for education, Edgar Faure, was trying to placate the student rebels by rapidly expanding higher education, and was building a prefab university, to be put up in three months, in the Bois de Vincennes. It would develop new teaching methods, including language laboratories, and would bring in English lecturers to teach in their own language. Could I join it? I had to say yes.

I was soon commuting every fortnight to Paris, to find myself in the midst of an educational maelstrom. Vincennes had attracted a cluster of French intellectuals, including Pierre Dommergues and Hélène Cixous, and lively English and American visiting lecturers including John Wain, Edna O'Brien and the experimental novelist Christine Brooke-Rose. But more important, it provided a crash course in French politics, for it soon became a hotbed of revolutionary students of every shade of red – *gauchistes*, *anarchistes*, *maoïstes*, *guévaristes*. It was a confusing melee. They were all competing to attack their main enemy, the French Communist Party, which they condemned as bourgeois, reactionary and revisionist. Most of them were fiercely anti-American, and one of the courses I taught was 'American Imperialism'. But most of the students came from prosperous and bourgeois backgrounds, and many of them picked up slogans and arguments from summer vacations in California. Their rhetoric was all about revolution, but few of them were real proletarians. 'There's one rough rule about students here,' a French colleague told me: 'the richer the lefter.' Many of the *gauchiste* men looked suitably ferocious, with unkempt hair, stubble chins and dirty jeans, while the women wore thick studded belts and boots under their jeans and had burning eyes like La Pasionaria. But the fiercest debaters, I noticed, were expensively dressed in cashmere pullovers or tight leather trousers; later they would drive off in sports cars – not to their own pads, I soon learnt, but to their parents' apartments, where they remained dependent on their bourgeois mothers and fathers, while angrily resenting them. Their lives were very different from those of British students, who lived away from home, surviving on their grants, and were forced to grow up in the adult world. Here in Vincennes much of the fierce protest was really directed more against parents than against the state; and the rich kids were really protesting against their own privileges. 'Ah, Vincennes,' said one taxi-driver who took me out there. 'It's not a political problem, it's a psychological problem.'

Every fortnight I found the demonstrations and debates continually escalating: they were so theatrical that I thought a movie camera must be whirring behind them. The students kept on organising strikes, ranging from stay-aways (*grèves passives*) to militant protests (*grèves actives*), which began to escalate to disrupting classes and even assaulting incorrect teachers. The prefab corridors accumulated posters with slogans: '*Gadget, cache-toi*', '*Salle d'Amour*', '*Transformons les classes en love-ins sauvages*'. The tensions rose as the *gauchistes* became more furious with the communists, the 'revisos' who were betraying the revolution. They reached a climax when the students were expected to vote for the new joint councils which were part of the government's plans for participation. The *gauchistes* were determined to prevent them and turned out in battle gear with tin helmets and goggles, to prevent the voting, and climbed onto the roofs to construct battlements with upturned tables, to defend the university against the police. It was like a scene from Lindsay Anderson's film *If. . .*, which was showing in Paris at the time. But the communists had organised a more serious army of real horny-handed workers recruited from factories, who barged into Vincennes, tore down obscene posters and confiscated truncheons and mortars. They stood outside the voting-rooms, looking with contempt at the theatrical *gauchistes*, who eventually retreated in fury while the moderates voted for participation.[14] It was a caricature of the turnabout in French politics: the communists were now the true conservatives, the toughest opponents of any revolution.

But the students at Vincennes were never as revolutionary as they looked. With all their talk of *contestation* they left most of their rhetoric behind when they entered the classroom: when they did contest in my classes, they did so politely and in English. 'You see, the classroom is still sacrosanct in France,' explained a French co-teacher. 'They could never shout back at the professors like the Americans.' The students still worked harder than their British counterparts: in the evenings the language laboratories were full of frowning faces listening intently through their earphones. Even in the midst of a battle, a student rushed up to me with her essay, just on time. After my two years at Vincennes I became more impressed by the discipline of the French educational system and the dedication of the teachers. The French governments after 1968 were expanding their higher education much more rapidly and systematically than the British.

In the decade after 1968 most of the students' revolts across Europe fizzled out. The next generation gladly embraced the consumer society which their predecessors had contested: they happily wore T-shirts advertising mass products and competed to join multinational companies. Many of the student leaders became successful businessmen; only a few, like Daniel Cohn-Bendit, developed from rebels into serious politicians.

Small fanatical groups continued the rebellion with more extreme methods. In Germany Ulrike Meinhof, whom I had met in Hamburg, co-founded the notorious Baader-Meinhof gang, which bombed army bases and kidnapped politicians; she was imprisoned in 1972 and hanged herself in her cell four years later. In Italy the Red Brigades turned to sabotage and terrorism, while in March 1971 Giangiacomo Feltrinelli, the Marxist millionaire, was found dead under an electricity pylon outside Milan which he was trying to blow up. Some factory workers continued to strike against the oppression of their bosses: in the Fiat factory in Turin workers went on the rampage, burning the cars they had just been assembling. But when Europe faced a recession after 1973 workers were more concerned with keeping their jobs. Most Europeans looked back on the rebels of 1968, the '*soixant-huitards*', as dangerous romantics and fantasists who served only to provoke right-wing reactions.

That was not the whole story as I read it. The student revolts, for all their half-baked ideas, represented a protest against the dehumanisation of the New Europe which politicians and corporations had to take seriously. When I revisited the Fiat factories in Turin many years after the revolt I found a much more humanised company: the PR department was peopled with former student rebels, and the chairman, Gianni Agnelli, explained how drastically Fiat had adapted factory conditions to placate its workers. When I addressed a meeting of company chairmen in Sweden in August 1969 they were worried about missing the brightest recruits, and trying to co-opt student rebels: Volvo soon took the lead in devising more humane systems for assembling its cars. Even in Britain Shell, the most internationalised company, organised seminars with young radicals to convince them that they had common interests. Thirty years later its personnel director complained that it had missed out by not recruiting student rebels: 'We were too arrogant, and didn't understand the attitude shift. We didn't just lose the oddballs, we lost some of the clever mainstream graduates. We're suffering the results now.'[15]

*

Many veteran Europeans believed that the students' revolt had been necessary, as a counterweight to the deadly materialism of the New Europe. 'The cause for which they had fought still remained,' said Jean Monnet afterwards. 'It was the cause of humanity. And I believe that we have still not adequately responded, either before or after that salutary warning.'[16] The students may have breathed some young life into the mechanical Europe, but they were not interested in democratising the bureaucratic structures of Brussels or the national capitals. And the new institutions of the EEC were increasingly preoccupied with harmonising and regulating, cut off from their own people without an effective European parliament to connect them to the voters. Monnet's grand vision of European unity was beginning to fade into history.

Yet in much business life Europe *was* coming closer together. As I was to find out in research into my books on ITT, the oil companies and where money really lay, I came to value this earlier chance to study the multinational corporations which were extending through the continent, and 'making Europe' in a much more practical and supranational sense than the bureaucrats in Brussels. The giant companies such as Unilever and Shell, IBM and ITT, were crossing over frontiers and cross-posting their managers as if those frontiers were dissolving. They sent German managers to Italy, French to Britain, British to Germany. They used English as their business language while the European Commission endlessly interpreted between French, German and Italian. Their top managers forgot national rivalries in their common preoccupation with growth and profit. And they were far more efficient than national governments: their theme song, said the economist Andrew Shonfield, was 'Anything You Can Do, We Can Do Better'.

Most of them were not specifically European in spirit or ownership; they were American. But the Americans in Europe, I noticed, had much more confidence in the unity of the continent than most Europeans. From their English-speaking enclaves, their Hilton hotels and offices with bilingual secretaries, they were much less worried than the Europeans about national sensitivities and differences. As they flew casually between the capitals – 'if it's Tuesday, it must be Brussels' – they saw Europe as just another land mass, like America. 'They talk about Europe as if it really existed,' said Gianni Agnelli of Fiat. 'They come out with concepts like "the southern European market", which I never thought about before.'[17] Did Europeans need Americans, I wondered, to give them a sense of their own continent? 'You Europeans decide that you have got to get together,' complained an American publisher, 'and what do you do? You fly off to New York to talk about it.' Perhaps Europeans could only unite through their links with America. It was not the kind of unity that the founders of the EEC had in mind, but they had to face it.

Soon after *The New Europeans* was published IBM invited me to give a lecture at the Ritz in Paris. I put forward my argument that the multinationals were taking over much of the role of integrating Europe rather more effectively than the EEC. I noticed with embarrassment that Jean Monnet himself was sitting opposite; but when I finished he passed me a note saying that he agreed with everything I had said. Soon afterwards I decided to pursue my quest further, to find out who exerted the real power over Europe. I had to learn more about the workings of these mysterious organisms, the multinational corporations.

8

The boss from Hell

The bright signs of Ford, Fiat, IBM or ITT shone out from the skyscrapers all over Europe, and some of the multinational headquarters, like the Shell Centre in London, dwarfed the national parliaments. Big companies were more permanent and continuous than young nations: many were celebrating centenaries. They were the masters of new technologies which were transforming the lives of ordinary people and constantly influencing governments: Unilever, they said in Brussels, was the seventh member of the Common Market.

But the public knew far less about the chairmen and managers of these companies than they knew about politicians or generals, and the corporations were a lot more opaque and less accountable than governments. I had been curious about big companies since my childhood, when I visited my father in the ICI palace on the Thames: I was awed by the tall nickel doors at the entrance and by the big office where my father seemed so much more confident than at home. But I had become warier of corporate power when I came across the great mining companies in Africa which occupied whole territories and made their own deals with apartheid governments; and I was alarmed by the accounts of how apparently ordinary managers in corporations like Krupp or Thyssen had willingly joined Hitler's war machine and employed slave labour. I wondered how far British companies like ICI could have been corrupted to become accomplices of evil.

As a journalist I was surprised by the lack of information about how these corporations really worked. There were not many exciting histories or biographies of businessmen to compare with the endless accounts of political battles. Only a few novelists, for example Trollope, Thomas Mann and Wodehouse, had attempted to describe the lives and intrigues inside business offices. Yet these were the background to daily life for many of their readers;

and the decisions which were made in the boardrooms were increasingly affecting the world around them. After my travels in Europe I wanted to follow the trail of power, to find out more about these mysterious organisms.

In 1972 I noticed that one of the biggest companies, ITT, was repeatedly hitting the headlines with its apparent abuses of corporate power, like a rogue elephant trampling on the undergrowth. I soon discovered that the International Telephone and Telegraph Corporation, as it was first called, was an unusual maverick. It had been set up in the Caribbean in 1920 by Sosthenes Behn, a Danish-French entrepreneur, to buy up telephone systems in Latin America and Europe. The company languished after the Second World War, but since 1959 it had been dominated by a dynamic president, Harold Geneen, who was determined to widen its scope by buying other international businesses, and to control them with rigorous accounting. Geneen acquired a ragbag of companies from all areas of business, from Sheraton Hotels and Avis car hire to the house-builders Levitt & Sons and Hostess Cakes, which all seemed worthy workaday concerns but which became part of an increasingly visible political juggernaut.

ITT was a new phenomenon, a multinational conglomerate which could run anything anywhere. To many executives 'the Geneen machine' provided a model of dynamic and rational management which could exert constant pressure on performance and profits. But Geneen was impatient of any government that got in his way, particularly of American anti-trust laws; and his ruthless lobbying and pressurising in America was attracting the interest of many politicians and journalists, and antagonising more conventional corporations which saw ITT as a dangerous disrupter.

By 1972 ITT had burst into the news with two scandals which both revealed the company's determination to undermine governments. First, a memo was leaked from its chief lobbyist, Dita Beard, which clearly implied that Geneen had pledged support for the Republican convention in San Diego before Nixon's re-election that year, just when he was trying to prevent an anti-trust suit. Second, a set of leaked documents was published showing how ITT executives in Chile had conspired in 1970 to prevent the election of the Marxist president Salvador Allende – who by now was in the process of nationalising the Chilean telephone company, in which ITT had a majority stake – by undermining the Chilean economy, in collusion with the CIA. The two scandals seemed to bear out the worst suspicions about ITT's supranational power and Geneen's determination to bludgeon governments into submission.

Pursuing these clues, I decided to explore the wider ramifications of the ITT empire and to try to write a book about it, as an extreme case of multinational power. I began in Brussels, the home of so many European multinationals, where ITT was preparing to occupy a 24-storey skyscraper as its European headquarters, appropriately dwarfing the buildings of the European Commission. As an author and journalist, I was fortunate to be invited as the only 'outsider' to ITT's annual barbecue, which was held in a marquee in the garden of the 'executive mansion', draped with blue-and-white ITT bunting. The senior managers had flown in from all over the world and were queuing up for their steaks and sweet corn from the charcoal grill, still with the dazed, sleepwalking look of jetlagged travellers: the American contingent kept their watches on New York time. But the European managers – whether Swedish, Greek or even French – were hard to distinguish from the Americans as they all sat together: they all spoke the same hearty English, joshed, shoulder-punched and joked with one another. They seemed much more cosmopolitan and interchangeable than the staff of the European Commission: their corporate loyalty seemed to override any national status. As we sat down to dinner I noticed an owlish figure in a neat dark suit whom I recognised as Geneen, and at the end of the meal Mike Bergerac, the young Frenchman who had recently become president of ITT Europe, made a jokey speech in praise of him. He said the boss had recently been spotted watching cricket at Lord's, and presented Geneen with a cricket bat, stumps and pads: the executives rocked with laughter and Geneen grinned like an imp. Then Geneen replied with a rallying speech about ITT's rising profits and how the recent scandals had provided 'terrific publicity'. 'I want you to know that I'm having a lot of fun,' he concluded, 'and I want you to have fun too.' There was a roar of applause; but the tense faces did not suggest fun.

Later I was introduced to Geneen in the emptying marquee. He was welcoming to an English writer: he had been born in London, he said, and loved revisiting it; he admired the British though they gave up their empire too hastily and should have supported Ian Smith in Rhodesia. Back in 1962, he had warned that Americans might soon have to move into Arab countries to protect their oil supplies. He talked passionately, eyes twinkling, fingers touching his nose, grinning, as if he were weaving a spell, like Rumpelstiltskin turning thread to gold; while his vice-presidents nodded and laughed in sync. He had 400,000 employees across the world, he explained, and only businessmen could create jobs: of course they had to lobby governments to protect their workers. Why didn't Washington back them up instead of wasting time on trust-busting? As for liberal newspapermen, what did *they* know about making jobs? I interrupted him: 'Perhaps *I'm* a liberal newspaperman.' He laughed in disbelief. As we parted amicably I felt I was leaving a mission station embattled against a benighted world of backward tribes. Or was it a pirate ship, flying the skull and crossbones?

Geneen was clearly not just a master-accountant but also a control freak: 'I want no surprises' was his recurring maxim. He needed to exert his power in person: 'It's not enough to see the accounts,' he told me; 'you must see the face of the man who presents them.' The next day I saw how he enforced his discipline, when I managed to sneak into the back of the monthly meeting of senior executives. It was a scene of filmic melodrama. A hundred top executives sat round a huge horseshoe table: the curtains were drawn and the lights were dimmed. In the centre, swivelling on his rocking-chair, sat Geneen, like the spider in the middle of the web. A big screen flashed the crucial monthly results for each of ITT's subsidiaries, while the low voice of a controller on the microphone emphasised the salient facts. A bright sharp arrow pointed to the most significant figure, like an extension of Geneen's own finger, lingering much longer when it denoted a loss. Sometimes Geneen's voice would intervene: Why was the target not reached? Why is the inventory so high? 'We're already looking into that, Mr Geneen.' He would nod, or reprove, and the arrow would move on. Nearly all the managers looked strained and anxious in the face of this corporate inquisition: one senior manager had recently fainted before a meeting, I was told, and another had got blind drunk for two days afterwards. It was a dazzling display of one man's command over an intricate global empire – far more complex than any emperor or tsar in the past had attempted – ranging from dog food to radios, from face creams to telephones, all controlled through the tight reins of money. But was it workable and was it worth the human sacrifice?

I was haunted by this image as I investigated the truth behind the ITT scandals. I began in New York, the heart of ITT's empire, where I first saw their chief banker, André Meyer, the legendary head of Lazard Frères, with an introduction from a London friend. Meyer was a wizened nut of a man, a legendary French-Jewish financial brain who had enriched many American multimillionaires. He was friendly and discreet, giving only one tantalising clue at the end: 'It's terrible what governments ask corporations to do.' His partner, Felix Rohatyn, was more forthcoming. He would later become a financial statesman who would rescue New York City from bankruptcy and go on to be US ambassador to Paris; but he was then leading a bohemian life with a glamorous French photographer, driving a small Toyota and wearing a shabby raincoat. He was making big profits for Lazard by arranging ITT's acquisitions and he was fascinated by Geneen, but he had some misgivings about his methods and he dropped some more clues.

I followed the trails through America and Europe, trying to get the feel of the ITT business style, staying at Sheraton hotels and hiring Avis cars, visiting the ITT offices and meeting their executives. They all showed signs of tension: Geneen believed in paying them rather more than they were worth and then stretching them to the limit, keeping them on the move, making them put their corporate loyalty before their family. They told me stories of broken marriages, drunks and even suicides. One ex-ITT man who had just resigned explained: 'I decided to rejoin the human race.' A few executives would talk candidly, or assumed I was one of them: once a melancholy man walked into the elevator in the ITT headquarters, having just left a PR meeting, and sadly muttered a line from *Paradise Lost*: 'to make the worse appear the better reason'.

As I rushed from jumbos to hire cars to hotels, I began to share the neuroses of this new nomadic species. Uprooted from London and my family I realised how displacement increases dependence. The airports themselves were always disorientating nowhere places: everyone looked lost; the flutterboards proclaimed every airport but their own; tickets ended with the word Void; the passengers watched the baggage carousels as anxiously as refugees without property. Compared with this the plane itself offered a strange kind of home, providing the same music, uniforms and patter about your comfort and safety: the bedroom and the office contracted into the suitcase and the briefcase. 'What's your address?' I asked one businessman, who replied: 'Just 747.'

One airline executive had designed his own drawing-room to look like the front of a jumbo, with curved walls, reclining seats and portholes, to make him feel relaxed. But in this strange limbo it was easy to develop doubts about your identity. On one delayed flight from London I arrived jetlagged in a Washington hotel to unpack the suitcase and find it full of lingerie. I rang the airline in a fury, to be stopped short by an equally furious official: 'Do you know whose bag you've got? It's Sheila Graham's.' I remembered having met that dominating woman, the former mistress of F. Scott Fitzgerald, on a Californian talk show and took some pleasure in imagining her confronting a case containing creased trousers and shabby shoes.

Above the clouds, peering down at coastlines and suburbs, the new nomads could easily feel superior to earthbound people trapped in settled lives and local customs; as they strode off the plane with briefcases and spare suits slung across the shoulder, they looked like evangelists for some new cult. But the more they were uprooted from their own families and homes, the more dependent they became on their corporate boss.

I had to stop myself becoming obsessed by my lonely pursuit of ITT. I felt like Captain Ahab pursuing the white whale Moby Dick, disappearing and suddenly spouting water: 'There she blows!' It was hard to avoid the paranoia which afflicts so many investigative reporters; when I rang one Washington regulator who had battled with ITT he was not reassuring: 'You're staying at the Sheraton? They'll tap your phone!' The ordinariness of the ITT empire, with its hotel clerks, hire car agents or insurance salesmen, made the abuse of corporate power seem much more threatening, as Geneen and his colleagues tried to subject governments to his will.

Was any counter-power strong enough to stand up to this relentless machine? America in that post-Vietnam time was full of zealous investigators of the misdeeds of big business. I owed much to the radical young lawyers known as 'Nader's raiders' and to journalists such as Larry Stern and Morton Mintz of the *Washington Post*, Brit Hume of ABC television or Eileen Shanahan of the *New York Times*, who had all crossed ITT's path. Some of the investigators sounded more like gumshoes than journalists, single-mindedly obsessed with their quarry, but the best were masterful in piecing together the evidence. Their patron saint was the veteran Izzy Stone, who had first started his paper *I. F. Stone's Weekly* at the time of Joe McCarthy. He was a scholar as much as a journalist: I eventually tracked him down – a small wrinkled man with bright eyes behind pebble glasses – in a library, teaching himself ancient Greek and talking about Socrates. He explained to me that his main sources were the green and grey volumes of Congressional hearings, which contained nuggets of gold that revealed all the lies of government. And back in 1971 he had written his own commentary on a historic report on conglomerates, including ITT, which summed up my own fears: 'In the pages of this study, the young can see the morals and mores which mould our economy and threaten to some day remould our politics. For as corporate concentration grows, the threat of a corporate state grows with it.'

Back in Washington I regained some of my confidence in American democracy as I watched it in action. The evidence that ITT had tried to subvert the government of Chile prodded the Senate Foreign Relations Committee into action and they formed a subcommittee to investigate multinational corporations, armed with powers to subpoena officials. The chairman of the sub-committee was Frank Church, a clever populist from Idaho who was suspicious of all big business; he chose a persistent and radical lawyer, Jerome (Jerry) Levinson, as his chief counsel – who in turn picked a team of eager young investigators. They had assembled a mass of documents and interviews to prepare for their hearings, and when I walked into their offices I entered a journalists' dream. 'You might like to look through those files in the corner,' said one investigator.

The files turned out to be a treasure trove: a detailed record of ITT's links with enemy countries in the Second World War, including telephone transcripts, which had only recently been declassified. They revealed how Sosthenes Behn had met with Hitler and Goering to ensure that he retained ownership of ITT's German subsidiary, which bought a share in the Focke-Wulf bomber company just before the war; how his Latin American companies co-operated with Nazi networks; and how at the end of the war ITT obtained compensation for factories which Focke-Wulf bombers had destroyed. Everyone knew that the Nazis had exploited and compromised American companies to use their technology, but as I spent days poring over

141

the ITT documents I pieced together a picture of how a multinational company in wartime could show no real loyalty to anyone, appearing one moment thoroughly German, and the next impeccably American. ITT had grown up as a corporation with no real base and no conscience, and it had effectively buried the memory so that hardly any current managers knew about it. As I hid my notes I felt like an assassin with a bomb in his pocket.

But Senator Church's sub-committee was preoccupied with the more recent allegations about ITT's intervention in Chile. Leaked memoranda implied that the company had sought to stop the election of President Allende and that Geneen had offered the CIA $1 million to help bring him down – which seemed the more credible because an ex-director of the CIA, John McCone, had become a director of ITT. In March 1973 the senators began their hearings, armed with their subpoena powers. They summoned McCone, who admitted that he had discussed bringing down Allende with his indirect successor at the CIA Dick Helms, and also with Henry Kissinger; but he insisted that the $1 million was merely for constructive housing projects. But then the actual CIA agent involved, William Broe, came to testify – an unprecedented event – and admitted that Geneen had offered a substantial sum to be channelled through the CIA to support the opposition to Allende. Broe had rejected it but had come back with his own plans for economic disruption.

Finally the senators summoned Geneen himself. It was a unique confrontation between the two powers, Congress and business. In a back room beforehand I listened to the staff anxiously preparing questions which might at last extract the truth. Geneen appeared in the hearing-room flanked by two attorneys and a bodyguard, occasionally grinning at his colleagues: only he knew the full story, but he seemed more than ever like some genie who had made everyone write things down while he evaporated into the air. When the senators pressed their questions he explained calmly that he had met Broe in the Sheraton Carlton Hotel, and that on two occasions had offered funds to stop Allende coming to power. He admitted that he might have been ill advised, but he believed in hard-line policies and was shocked by the government's weakness: now the hearings themselves were damaging America's interests.

Having elicited these secrets Senator Church backed down from further attacks and focused on the CIA: 'We are just left wondering who they report to or who they take their orders from.' And he gave a warning: 'The wider the distance between these big businesses and the CIA, the better for all concerned.'[1] (Church would later conduct historic hearings about the CIA which revealed some of their dirtiest tricks.) The Senate staff still thought Geneen was lying, but two years later he sounded more convincing when he told an interviewer how he had lobbied in Washington for CIA action. He had told everyone:

> 'Don't you think we ought to get together and come up with a plan and we'll put money in it?' But we got nothing done. Nothing. Later on we learnt they did have a plan for Chile, but didn't even tell us about it, a plan not too different from what we were suggesting.[2]

The senators could never prove that Geneen had bribed President Nixon's administration to drop an anti-trust case by subsidising the Republican convention. But the value of a scandal to a journalist lies not just in the outcome, but in the light it sheds on all parts of an opaque institution, and Senator Church's sub-committee had provided me with a unique collection of memos, interviews and testimony. They showed in detail how a ruthless and irresponsible corporation can pressurise governments and media to impose its own policies and maximise its profits. In a state of white heat I finished the book, which was serialised in the *Observer* and *New York* magazine and published in Britain and the United States in the summer of 1973 under the title *The Sovereign State*.

The timebomb was more explosive than I had ever imagined. The book became a best-seller in both countries and was translated into fifteen languages. In America it became a mass paperback with a lurid jacket, displayed in airports alongside bodice-rippers and romances. The ITT managers tried hard to abort or discredit it: they sent a team of lawyers to Europe while the company's PR chief, Ned Gerrity, tried to find dirt to discredit me. They could not believe that the book was the work of an individual without a corporate sponsor, and suspected it was masterminded by their rival IBM. They produced a thirty-page rebuttal and kept lobbying the media; but their tactics were so clumsy that they later featured in a manual on public relations, as an example of how not to do it. In the prevailing mood of distrust they could make little headway. Robert Sobel produced an authorised history of ITT nine years later, which described how, 'not since Ida Tarbell wrote her sensational muckraking work *A History of the Standard Oil Company*, seven years earlier in much the same form, had the appearance of an attack on a large corporation been so fortuitously timed or generated so much interest'. Earlier in his book, discussing *The Sovereign State*, Sobel said:

> Biased and riddled with exaggerations, it nonetheless was a vivid indictment of ITT and its leaders, and it firmly implanted the picture of a heartless, corrupt, and thoroughly amoral entity headed by a veritable automaton. This barrage of unfavourable publicity created a siege mentality at headquarters and in the field, an attitude that wouldn't be dissipated as long as Geneen remained in command and traces of which remain to this day.[3]

Geneen hung on as chairman, while the 'scandal discount' still depressed ITT's shares, and analysts criticised his overstretched empire. In 1977 he was forced to agree to a new chief executive, Lyman Hamilton, who began selling off ITT subsidiaries, to Geneen's fury. Two years later he engineered Hamilton's downfall and his replacement by Rand Araskog, a cold and efficient Swedish-American; but Araskog too began to dismantle many of the components, after Geneen finally retired as chairman in 1980. Geneen set up his own business and wrote a book, *Managing*, in 1984, but it did not deal with his problems with ITT: 'Wide areas of ITT's development,' complained the *Economist*, 'captured in Mr Anthony Sampson's *The Sovereign State*, are unmentioned, unexplored or undeveloped.'

By the 1980s the image of ITT as a model for managerial efficiency and profits was rapidly fading. The fashion was now for 'de-conglomeratisation', and ITT's components were reckoned to be worth more outside the corporation than inside it, while it had missed out on the rapid growth of telecommunications, which had been its original business. By 1995 it was a collapsed house of cards: it had offloaded, completely or partially, 250 companies; it had bought Madison Square Garden and the casino Caesar's World; it had split into three separate companies. The edifice which Geneen had built up at such human cost was now in pieces, and the only beneficiaries were the bankers and lawyers who earned fees first from acquiring companies, then from divesting them. Geneen had introduced rigorous management methods to some incompetent companies, it was true; but by ignoring the human factor and ruling through fear he had produced an unworkable empire. He went down in history as an ogre: after he died in 1997 the *Wall Street Journal* called him a workaholic and *Time* magazine chose him as one of its 'bosses from Hell'.[4]

But its influence over foreign policy had more sinister consequences and a longer time frame. We will never know how far ITT influenced the CIA in plotting to destabilise President Allende's regime: but over the next thirty years the consequences became grimly apparent. In September 1973, only six months after Geneen had testified, a military coup led by General Augusto Pinochet seized power and Allende shot himself inside the presidential palace. Pinochet swiftly imposed a brutal regime, including assassins and torturers, to extirpate all opposition from Allende's supporters. Allende's ambassador to the United States, Orlando Letelier, was arrested and deported to a concentration camp on an island near Antarctica. Later, after strong international pressure, he was allowed to return to Washington as an academic, where he campaigned against Pinochet; but when he was driving to work one day in September 1976 a bomb exploded in his car, killing him outright – a crime which the FBI traced to the top of Chile's military regime.

How far did Washington support Pinochet's coup and condone his subsequent policies? Henry Kissinger, who was then secretary of state, insisted in his memoirs that 'we had no dealings at any point with military plotters' and that Washington merely funded opposition newspapers and parties. But he admitted that 'it would be idle to deny that we felt a sense of relief at Allende's collapse'.[5] While the round-up of civilians caused him anguish, he said, he preferred 'quiet diplomacy' to confrontation with Pinochet's regime. But twenty-five years later secret Washington documents revealed details about Kissinger's meeting with Pinochet in Chile in June 1976, after the revelations about torture had caused a furore in America: in private Kissinger told Pinochet that much of the criticism was hypocritical and said: 'We wish your government well.'

The role of ITT in plotting for the Pinochet coup in 1973, and in subsequent events, remains partly hidden. It was operating in one of the many grey areas of history when secret understandings between like-minded people have influenced crucial events with nods, winks and unstated agreements. But it was clear from the published documents that Geneen was keen to destabilise the previous regime, to influence American foreign diplomacy and to bypass democratic governments. And Pinochet's coming to power suited ITT interests very well.

For most of the 1970s the multinational corporations remained bogeys for much of the media, both in America and Europe, who saw them as secretly influencing government policies. Dominating tycoons became favourite villains in movies such as *Network*, written by Paddy Chayefsky, who acknowledged a debt to my book. But by the 1980s the political attacks on multinationals petered out under the governments of Reagan and Thatcher. Congress largely ceased to investigate them and the media became more anxious about offending their advertisers. The sunlight faded and the clouds once again closed in. With booming share prices and technological wonders the corporate bosses were idolised rather than demonised, as wealth-creators and national heroes, like generals in wartime. The idea that corporations should influence government policies was less shocking. During the American presidential elections of 2000 both candidates were dependent on corporate funding, and George W. Bush's Cabinet was dominated by rich former business executives, effectively representing 'America Inc.'. As the columnist William Pfaff wrote, 'corporate money determines national policy and even foreign policy'.[6]

But I remained convinced that the big corporations must be made accountable as their power increased. And in the twenty-first century the public in America and Europe was again becoming more concerned about multinationals as the global marketplace gave more scope for uncontrolled profit-making and new villains like the tobacco and the pharmaceutical companies, which were visibly exploiting the developing world. Scandals over Enron, WorldCom and Hollinger were later to cause more harm to business reputation than had ITT, but the question refused to go away: who was really running the world?

9

Nixon's America

Pursuing my trails through Europe or Africa I saw signposts everywhere pointing to America as the ultimate repository of political and financial power. I realised I must try to grapple with the realities of American politics.

I had first been thrilled by New York in 1958 when I spent two months there for the *Observer*, just before starting research on *Anatomy*. Escaping from the austerity of London, only four years after the end of food-rationing, I found a fantasy city which belonged to the movies. I stayed in the same hotel as my colleague Philip Toynbee (who had only just been unbanned as a pre-war communist) and we exchanged notes every breakfast about how Manhattan lived up to our filmic expectations: the shop front of Tiffany's, the traffic lights flashing *Don't Walk*, the wisecracking barmen and the drinkers slumped along the bars, the short-skirted girl skaters at the Rockefeller Plaza – we knew them all from movieland. Luckily there were New Yorkers who had reciprocal fantasies about Englishmen with Oxford accents, from films about wartime heroes; for English visitors, with strictly rationed dollars, had to be licensed spongers. It was a heady welcome: I was whisked to parties full of film stars, wooed and lunched by many in the media. I was introduced to the *New Yorker* by James Thurber, shown round the German bars of 86th Street by Joe Liebling, escorted to Harlem by Langston Hughes; I shared free drinks with diplomats in the Delegates' Lounge of the brand-new United Nations building, which still glowed with global idealism.

It was an extraordinary vision after the drabness of post-war London, to realise how far Britain had slipped from being the centre of the world. Viewed from New York, Britain seemed like a third-world country dependent on American beneficence and secondhand ideas. I was prepared for the materialist wonders, which I knew from films, but not for the creative and intellectual vigour which made London seem so provincial and antiquated: the daring novels, the punchy columnists and the explosion of pop art seemed to have escaped from any European legacy into a future where anything could happen.

I loved the electric air and hype: Manhattan was like a huge ocean liner anchored off the coast, with its passengers exhilarated by shipboard romances and the sea air. I admired the inventiveness and creativity in this great marketplace, which seemed so exuberant after drab London: the glories of Prexy's, the 'hamburger with the college education', the splendour of the Seagram Building. The consumer was king, able to get anything at any time: on my last evening I was drinking with American friends until the small hours and wanted to spend my last few dollars. They suggested I order a turkey from the delicatessen, and ten minutes later it arrived miraculously at the door.

Over the next fifteen years I went back to Manhattan whenever I could, for book launches, research and reporting, returning to London with new ideas and enthusiasms. Britain was coming closer to America in material terms, as supermarkets, motorways and skyscrapers crossed the Atlantic, while British politicians from left and right looked to Washington for solutions: when I met the Labour intellectual Anthony Crosland at a New York party he seemed much more in his element than in any London left-wing set. After Vietnam I was more worried about Britain's dependence on American foreign policy, but I had not experienced the full anguish of liberals in Washington as they faced the traumas of that war or Watergate.

*

I wanted to try to understand it from the inside, and in 1973 I had a promising opportunity to observe the American power scene at close quarters, when the *Observer* asked me to be its Washington correspondent, in the midst of the Watergate crisis. With Sally and our two children, now aged seven and five, I embarked on the elegant French liner the SS *France* for a magical voyage to New York, with delicious meals, courteous service and new movies every night. It would turn out to be one of the last voyages of the *France* to New York: a few months later the mounting oil price made passenger liners uneconomic, although they were to stage a remarkable recovery thirty years on. But in 1973 the *France* still evoked the golden age of transatlantic leisure, and we enjoyed the company of lively academics including Harry Pitt, the Oxford historian of America, and Lionel and Diana Trilling, the New York intellectuals. Lionel warned me that American history was harder to understand than British history because of the lack of public opinion and connections between its parts, and as we approached Manhattan I realised that he anticipated his return with some dread. But I was still excited by the prospect of observing Nixon's America at first hand, and my book on ITT had just become a best-seller in America.

I soon experienced a severe anti-climax. We arrived in Washington in August to be soaked in a muggy heat which physically depressed me. I had felt quite welcome as an in-and-out observer but now as a resident correspondent I was surrounded by seriously worried Americans in a national crisis who had little interest in British inhabitants. We rented a house in Georgetown, which looked superficially like a prettier Chelsea, with picturesque old houses along charming streets; but it soon seemed like a façade concealing the harsh realities of Washington, a company town preoccupied with the single all-demanding industry of politics. The city centre had been devastated and downgraded after the riots of the 1960s: my office was only three blocks from the White House but it was surrounded by sleazy bars and strip joints, and I looked out on birds nesting in the forsaken bedrooms of the empty shell of the once-grand Willard Hotel (which would be sumptuously restored ten years later).

The city's social life seemed bleakly functional. Washington, I realised, was a hello-goodbye place, full of newcomers and strangers desperately trying to pick up any contacts and find ways to storm the central citadel. Politicians' wives were left in the suburbs while their husbands spent evenings plotting in a male-dominated world, while women on Capitol Hill were dismissed as 'the third sex', too busy with their careers for social or sexual activities. Parties were designed for advancement rather than enjoyment, as politicians pressed the flesh and worked the room to extend their support. The parties seemed strangely limited in representing the diverse American people: in my year in Washington I never met socially any black Americans, though they made up more than half the city's population, though they frequented bars and restaurants next door to my office; the black middle class nearly all lived in Washington's north-east quadrant, a quite different place from the north-west, where Georgetown is located. The only blacks I met were visiting South Africans, and the unofficial segregation seemed almost as complete as apartheid.

The more professionalised the politicians' social life, the more they were vulnerable to fixers and lobbyists who could create livelier scenes to bring people together. Once I was invited to a party in Georgetown by a Dr Julian Knox, who claimed to know me, and out of curiosity I went. I soon realised that I had never met him, and neither had the other guests, who all compared notes. Dr Knox turned out to be an exuberant Hungarian who sounded so like Gatsby that I expected him to call me 'sport'; he was quickly extending his own network and he clearly had a great future in Washington. Diplomats were too busy establishing political footholds to maintain wider interests: the most entertaining host was the Iranian ambassador, Ardeshir Zahedi, who dispensed caviar and champagne with much flattery and a clowning playboy style. He was very close to the Shah, and as the oil crisis developed we were supposed to disapprove of Iran, but it was hard to say no to his parties, which provided the only light relief in the city, or to refuse the jars of Iranian caviar that arrived on our doorstep.

I had to remind myself that we were living in the centre of the free world, where power was no joke. Votes and decisions on Capitol Hill were deadly serious: they could deploy armies, finance huge projects, make and break foreign rulers, and there was no room for British frivolity or mockery. Would London have been like this a century earlier, I wondered, when Lord Palmerston or Lord Salisbury were ruling half the world and the British were committed to their imperial mission? The comparison was impossible, for the workings of democratic power on Capitol Hill were much more complex and impersonal than the bargains and deals between a handful of rich Victorian aristocrats. The endless battles between the White House and Congress, the horse-dealing for votes and budgets or the bargains between senators in the committees were parts of an intricate system of levers, motors and brakes which left little room for sentiment or eccentricity. It was a city of strangers: the senators' offices, full of eager young aides and emblems and flags from their home states, were more like embassies of foreign powers than the offices of individual representatives. Power was being exercised not as a development from an ancient society and monarchy, but as a calculated process within a constitutional framework which in turn was dictated not by people but by the laws of the written constitution.

We felt ourselves thoroughly European, despite our many American friendships and contacts. We longed for street life, irony and humour and a few decadent English eccentrics or drunks to leaven the relentless and sober political talk. And we felt even more European as the Nixon administration became more resentful of European governments, which they saw as craven in their dependence on Arabs in the Middle East, culminating in a 'Hate Europe' week, reminiscent of 'freedom fries' and 'cheese-eating surrender monkeys' in the build-up to the Iraq War, thirty years on. I found myself looking on the Italians, the French and even the Germans with a new sympathy as we exchanged ironic thoughts about Americans like naughty schoolboys. We shared our grouses with a few British colleagues like Peter Jenkins and Polly Toynbee, but with some unease, for, as Polly put it, 'what we really dislike about Washington is the democracy'. Was this how British democracy would end up?

It was the restlessness of the Americans that seemed the greatest contrast with the Europeans, as they all moved in or out, or on and on. Had the gods laid a curse on them, by allowing them so much empty space while making them forever nomads, detached from any territory or the cultures that go with it? Yet this mobility was their greatest economic strength, allowing them to constantly embrace new industries and concepts, and to leave the past behind them.

I had expected that Europeans might still have some influence in Washington, as elder statesmen with a sense of history. I remembered Harold Macmillan's wartime advice to his British colleagues about the Americans: 'We are the Greeks in their Roman Empire; we have to change their minds without them realising it.' But these new Romans had little use for Greeks, and the much-vaunted special relationship with Britain was looking rather less special as the post-war alliance receded, though it was to stage a remarkable recovery under George W. Bush and Tony Blair. The fitful news from London in the *Washington Post* was hidden at the back of the paper among the lingerie ads; and few American journalists were thrilled to meet a correspondent for the *Observer*.

Some Americans in Washington shared feelings with the British and felt pulled between two continents. There were Rhodes scholars in Congress like John Brademas, Paul Sarbanes or Les Aspin who felt nostalgia for Oxford; there were world-minded journalists like Joe Kraft who hankered after Europe; there were ex-ambassadors like Averell Harriman and David Bruce and their wives with grand British friends. And I had good friends at the *Washington Post*, which kept up its courageous opposition to the prevailing presidential power. On a bad day, when I felt ground down by the conformity of Washington, I would revive my spirits by wandering round the *Post*'s huge newsroom – soon to be made famous in the film *All the President's Men* – acquiring a new insight from the executive editor, Ben Bradlee, discovering a new corporate scandal from Morton Mintz, picking up a new Watergate lead from Bob Woodward, or escaping for a drink with Larry Stern, the rebellious investigator who was always hospitable to English visitors. (After he died prematurely I became a trustee of the annual Stern fellowship, which commemorated his tradition by allowing British journalists to spend a few months working at the *Post*.) But these broad-minded Americans were constantly frustrated by the relentless pressures from the White House, where President Nixon could still conceal the truth.

Katharine Graham, the *Post*'s chairman, was a remarkable person. When her alcoholic husband Philip finally committed suicide, she had to take over the family newspapers, about which she knew almost nothing, and to master a media world where she was ill at ease and felt patronised by male colleagues. But she gradually found a new social confidence through male friends like Truman Capote; and she was determined to impose her will on the newspapers and increase profits with the help of well-picked advisers including Warren Buffett, the 'Wizard of Omaha'. Graham soon intervened to improve the editorial quality of the *Post*: she appointed Bradlee as executive editor, a stylish and dynamic *Newsweek* journalist with whom she soon worked closely. She stood by him when he wanted to publish the secret Pentagon papers about the origins of the Vietnam War, against massive opposition from Nixon; and soon afterwards she backed his investigation into Watergate, resisting all the pressures from Nixon and his colleagues, including her friend Henry Kissinger. The unique partnership of editor and owner, respecting each other from very different viewpoints, established the

Post for the first time as a major national force and a formidable rival to the *New York Times*.

*

As President Nixon remained embattled over Watergate and the threat of impeachment, Washington found itself in a state of siege, and the political atmosphere became more tense and touchy. Europeans could observe it as an exciting melodrama, but the Americans were in the midst of a searing and alarming ordeal which threatened their democracy and left no room for jokes or irony. We were watching a family tragedy from which we were excluded. It was a battle for political life and death which could end in catastrophe; and Nixon revealed the naked face of power almost as dramatically as an African dictator defending himself against a *coup d'état*.

And Henry Kissinger, Nixon's secretary of state, emerged as the grand master of realpolitik, playing his intricate game of global chess, the reincarnation of his nineteenth-century European heroes, Metternich and Bismarck. I had already read his book *A World Restored*, which revealed all his admiration for the European concert of powers; and when I met him he appeared as a modernised Metternich, with all the skills to manipulate politicians and the press with flattery and deception: 'Not the real Anthony Sampson?' he asked me. He built up his own myth as 'Henry the K': the guttural bespectacled professor had improbably become a sex symbol, for in the dehumanised atmosphere of Washington power was an aphrodisiac. Kissinger revelled in the exercise of personal power, alternately bullying and cajoling Americans and Europeans, Arabs and Israelis.

With all the ruthless manipulation of power, would the great American constitution really work? The Europeans watched the workings of the separation of powers with wonder, as successive special investigators sought to subpoena evidence against the president. Sally and I listened to Judge John Sirica in his courtroom, encased in his black robes like a great vulture, probing relentlessly into the president's missing tapes; we watched the anxious congressmen initiating the committee to impeach the president. They seemed to be acting out the constitution as a living lesson in history, as they tried to interpret the wishes of the founding fathers: Jefferson and Madison were still stalking the streets. But they also provided extraordinary flashbacks into British history, with Nixon playing the role of a monarch and Democratic congressmen playing anxious regicides. The Oxford historian Hugh Trevor-Roper compared Nixon to Charles I, and Congress had to look back to the eighteenth century and the trial of Warren Hastings for precedents and definitions of impeachment. The word 'impeachment' still carried a special dread, as a threat to the continuity of the presidency.

The squalor behind Nixon's exercise of power became more evident as presidential tapes were recovered which revealed how systematically he conspired with his henchmen H. R. Haldeman and John Ehrlichman to mislead the public, with a flood of 'expletives deleted', intriguing against the 'shits' and 'bastards' and prepared to 'fuck the lira': the pornography of power. But Nixon could still exploit the full majesty and panoply of the presidency with monarchic surroundings which could overawe his critics; and he could always commandeer the TV screens to present his latest lies without dissent. Just when those lies looked like finally catching up with him I went to a press conference inside the White House, where I thought tough American journalists would at last nail him. At close quarters the splendour of the great room looked as hollow as a stage set, the cameramen roped off, the chandeliers outshone by the floodlights and scaffolding holding up the temporary curtains. Nixon looked wan and exhausted, his face thick with make-up. But the TV cameras could still make him look like a president, and the formality and pomp still demoralised the journalists, in total contrast to the press conferences of British prime ministers, where little respect is shown for the elected leader. Nixon could call on his friends to ask sympathetic questions while his enemies were silenced. I was standing next to the feisty reporter Eileen Shanahan, a fellow-crusader against ITT, who whispered to me: 'Now you can see why you're lucky to have a monarchy, which separates the pomp from the politicians.' The pursuit of Nixon remained a spectator sport: as a journalist I felt increasingly helpless, condemned to be part of the pack, who knew as little as I did.

It was not just journalists and foreigners who felt excluded from the truth. One day I had a letter from the chairman of the Republican National Committee, who said he had heard about me from my brother-in-law in Texas; could I 'stop by' for a chat? It was signed by someone I had not heard of: George Bush. I duly stopped by on Capitol Hill, to be welcomed by a charming, modest-sounding man with a sophisticated East Coast style. He wanted, to my surprise, to explain what a horrible job he had taken over (the US ambassador to the UN): he was thoroughly isolated, he never knew what his president was up to or how far he was lying, and he had to wait for each public statement by Nixon before he tried to justify it. No-one trusted anyone else. He was disarmingly candid, but he seemed too weak and helpless in his exposed position to do anything about it, and I thought he would not survive in politics. Sixteen years later he was president of the United States.

As Nixon became more vulnerable and the impeachment process gathered momentum, Washington became more worried about the succession. His vice-president, Spiro Agnew, was visibly incompetent, and evoked special fears before he was forced to resign for receiving bribes. But his successor, Gerald Ford, was not much more promising: he seemed to justify Lyndon Johnson's crack that he couldn't walk and chew gum at the same time. I interviewed him on a plane trip: he deplored America's lack of interest in Europe, talked warmly about Britain and distanced himself from some of Nixon's statements; but he showed no signs of independent views, and seemed keener to explain how many lengths he swam in his pool. He seemed a purely physical politician, with no worries: he said he had never had a headache in his life. I was baffled by the slow Midwestern style: did it conceal shrewd thinking or no thinking at all? I could not imagine him ever wielding serious power. The American journalists who followed him on the plane were very dismissive: when he delayed disembarking one of them said: 'He's got to take the gum out of his mouth first.'[1]

I spent a frustrating year of Nixon-watching in Washington, and I was relieved to take a long family holiday away from it. We ended up on the beautiful island of Martha's Vineyard, where we rented a house on the beach from a Harvard professor. It was an idyllic place which we revisited often, before the island was discovered by presidents and tycoons: the children bathed from the empty beaches and caught fish in the ponds, while we were entwined in the gossip of writers and philosophers from New York. I felt myself back in the fantasy world of fifteen years earlier, again basking in American hospitality, removed from the harsh realities of power and democracy. Martha's Vineyard may have been a haven of privilege, with its

155

miles of private beaches protected from the populace; but that was not a British responsibility. With our New Yorker friends we watched the latest news from the impeachment committee, but worries about Washington were washed away by the sea and the wine.

Then suddenly the plot of the long thriller in Washington was unravelled. Nixon was forced to release another tape which finally proved his complicity in deception. Congress turned against him, he was isolated and he resigned. I flew back to Washington to cover the abrupt shift of power, only to find that Nixon had taken off in a helicopter for his Californian retreat. The siege was lifted. With a group of journalists I was escorted round the rooms of the White House, where portraits of Nixon were already being removed, and we saw sitting in the Oval Office the dull but reassuring shape of Gerald Ford, uttering appropriate platitudes. The relief was palpable; after all the nightmares about impeachment one president had quietly succeeded another, and the White House was open to daylight. It was a sudden anti-climax for obsessive investigatory journalists who had been pursuing Nixon like a pack of hounds, whose fox had vanished. But the constitution had worked, and American democracy had triumphed.

It had been a weird and disconcerting year in Washington, watching the lies multiply, the distrust spread, the confrontations build up. It was the more puzzling because the original offence of Watergate, the bungled petty burglary, had been the cause of disproportionate cover-ups and lies; but the discovery of the burglary had provided the pretext and opportunity to avenge much more serious grievances: the escalation of the Vietnam War and the ignominious retreat, the intolerance of dissent at home, and the authoritarian attitudes within the White House. As with Harold Macmillan's mishandling of Christine Keeler or Bill Clinton's affair with Monica Lewinsky, the first concealment became the flashpoint to light up much deeper concerns and problems. But in the end I was filled with admiration for the self-correcting machinery of the American constitution and its laws. The truth came out, and Washington could start again. 'Watergate is just what was needed to cleanse the system,' I had been told a year before by Thomas Corcoran, the old crony of Franklin Roosevelt who had been a prosecutor in the Teapot Dome scandal in the 1920s. It sounded unlikely then, but now it seemed convincing.

I was still relieved to leave Washington. Over the next thirty years I would return once or twice a year to the United States, often with Sally and the family on relaxed holidays. In researching my books I would experience many very different Americas which appeared to have little connection with one another: the surreal America of Hollywood; the corporate America of oil companies in Texas, arms companies in California or Microsoft in Seattle; the academic America of Harvard or Stanford; the radical America of crusaders against apartheid in New York. They were each linked to global networks, with separate views of the world, and I found them more revealing and stimulating than the political America of Washington.

Back in London we soon found that almost half our friends were Americans, who brought their own refreshing energy and directness to Europe, while sharing most of our values and concerns. How could we generalise about being anti-or pro-American? For holidays we were always pulled between the two continents, while each was borrowing more from the other: McDonald's sprouted in remote French towns while Manhattan became a showplace for European companies.

But as the United States kept re-creating itself, under Carter, Reagan or Bush, I understood it less and felt more instinctively European. The more Americans kept recharging themselves, moving on to new industries and new centres, the further their lifestyles and attitudes seemed to diverge from Europeans'. Their work ethic seemed to get stronger as their affluence increased, while the Europeans became more insistent on leisure, longer holidays and weekends. Americans became more punitive towards crime, and more states brought back the death penalty – which no western European country practised. And American Puritanism was re-emerging in a new form with a strict political correctness which was at odds with European tolerance; I suggested that signs should be put up at John F. Kennedy airport saying: 'You are now entering the United States. No smoking, no flirting, no irony.' Religion and morality were to dominate much of the country, becoming an increasing factor in political and presidential primaries and elections.

Nevertheless, I remained full of admiration and some envy for American energy and confidence, and I was often reminded of Tocqueville's assessment:

> Democracy does not confer the most skilful kind of government upon the
> people, but it produces that which the most skilful governments are frequently
> unable to awaken, namely, an all-pervasive and restless activity, a super-
> abundant force, and an energy which is inseparable from it, and which may,
> under favourable circumstances, beget the most amazing benefits.

But I was becoming more worried about the crudity and changeability of
American foreign policy, more aware of Tocqueville's belief that diplomacy
is not compatible with democracy. And I became more concerned about
American policies towards the developing world, as I saw more of the
consequences in Africa or the Middle East. Washington seemed to put every
country into the same matrix of the Cold War, while commercial interests
overrode long-term relationships and security. After 9/11, major problems
were to emerge over foreign policy at the time of the Iraq War and the
resistance to the 'axis of evil'.

10

The power of oil

After my pursuit of the ITT scandal, and as my time in Washington came to an end, I continued my interest in trying to understand further the power of international companies. Then suddenly the world was overwhelmed by a global emergency which laid bare the biggest corporations of all: the energy crisis of 1973.

Almost no-one had expected the sudden collision of oil and politics. On 6 October 1973 Egypt and Syria prepared to cross the Suez Canal and invade Israeli-occupied territory. The next day, by coincidence, the biggest oil companies met in Vienna to negotiate the oil price with the producing countries of OPEC. The countries wanted to put up the price by a dollar, to $5 a barrel. The companies refused and negotiations broke down. The Western public was too excited by the war to notice, and even the *Financial Times* tucked the news away on page 13. But a week later the military war was abruptly mixed up with an oil war. The OPEC countries met again in Kuwait, without the companies, and put up the price unilaterally to $5.12. The Arab members – including the key member, Saudi Arabia – were now inflamed by the war with Israel. They decided to cut back their oil production by 5 per cent and then embargoed all oil to the United States.

The Israelis were winning the military war, recrossing the canal and nearly reaching Damascus. But the Arabs were embarking on an economic war, and their cutbacks and embargo immediately caused panic-buying of oil which pushed up the price still further. In December the OPEC powers met once more, this time in Tehran, where they decided to redouble the price to $11.65, thus almost quadrupling it within two months. The Western world was being held to ransom by oil. The oil companies proved powerless to prevent the producers escalating the price; the real oil powers were now nation states which few people had heard of. The West took some time to realise how much their world had changed: over the next years the huge transfer of wealth would induce economic crises, inflation and recessions, which would bring down governments and bankrupt corporations.

Everyone now turned on the oil companies which were blamed for creating the crisis. I had long been curious about the political role of the oilmen, while I had been researching my Anatomies; and in Britain they enjoyed a special prestige. The executives of BP and Shell talked like master-diplomats who were dedicated to the public interest, far removed from sordid commerce; they lived as grandly as ambassadors and earned much more. In London Shell's new stone skyscraper dwarfed the Houses of Parliament, symbolising its supranational status, and its directors talked like global statesmen. 'The dogs may bark', the princely president, John Loudon, told me in 1961, 'but the caravan moves on'. The oil cartel of the big companies, 'the Seven Sisters', was not much questioned. (The seven were Esso, Shell, BP, Mobil, Chevron, Gulf Oil and Texaco, as they were then called.) In Rome I once lunched with Enrico Mattei, the maverick entrepreneur who had challenged the Sisters by making deals with the Soviet oil-producers; but soon afterwards he was killed in an air crash, which most Italians were convinced – without evidence – was contrived by the Sisters. In America the big oil companies had come under periodic attacks ever since John D. Rockefeller had created his Standard Oil monopoly. But all Western governments and consumers had been content to leave their oil supplies in the hands of the cartel so long as they delivered oil regularly and cheaply.

But now in 1973 the price had rocketed, the oil was in short supply and the Seven Sisters had been taken over by foreign potentates, 'six sheikhs and a shah' (BP had originally been the Anglo-Persian Oil Company). The companies were powerless to prevent this extreme transfer of power: they found themselves in the unenviable position of having to execute the Arab embargo, to ration the countries who had supported Israel. The shortage enraged the consumers. American car-owners, who had taken for granted unlimited cheap fuel, had to line up for hours to fill up with more expensive gasoline. Meanwhile the oil companies showed record profits. They became the ideal scapegoats for the fury of consumers, and their role was examined as never before.

It was Senator Frank Church, whom I had got to know during the ITT investigations, who first gave me the idea of writing a book about the oil companies. He had generously asked me to introduce him at a big lunch in Washington, and he began his own speech by saying: 'Now I'm going to tell Tony the subject of his next book: the oil companies.' I listened engrossed while he dramatically described the relationship between governments and the companies and how they had conspired to determine world events. Soon afterwards Church and his sub-committee began hearings to investigate the role of the oil companies in conducting American foreign policy. It was an irresistible opportunity to write a book which could be backed by subpoenaed testimony and documents which revealed the secret diplomacy of oil.

Senator Church launched his new crusade with panache. 'We must re-examine the premise that what's good for the oil companies is good for the US,' he said in Iowa in December 1973. The next month he opened his sub-committee's hearings with the warning: 'We are dealing with corporate entities which have many of the characteristics of nations.' His chief counsel, Jerry Levinson, and his investigators uncovered a long trail of subpoenaed documents, which they guided me through, uncovering how successive governments in Washington had secretly connived with the oil cartel to ensure cheap oil from the Middle East. They had divided and ruled the competing producing countries, pitting Iran against Saudi Arabia, Iran against Iraq, to prevent them uniting against the West. It suited Washington to let the oil companies pursue their own relationships with the Arab producing countries while the State Department supported Israel – thus separating the contradictory foreign policies. Now the oil crisis had brought the two policies into collision and the secret dealings into the open.

Armed with this detailed evidence, I set off on a journey through the Middle East in early 1975 to add flesh and blood to the skeleton of facts. It was a thrilling insight into contemporary history: I felt like a historian of the Napoleonic wars who had suddenly been able to interview Wellington; the balance of world power had apparently been overturned as abruptly as after Waterloo. The circular stage had rotated to reveal an unfamiliar cast of characters: the confident corporate chairmen and ambassadors had trooped offstage, replaced by an exotic group of potentates facing the lights in white robes and burnooses, dispensing their new-found billions with casual ease, while Western Cabinet ministers and tycoons were allowed walk-on parts as messengers and petitioners who were (as the new chairman of Shell, Sir Frank McFadzean, complained) 'waiting to kiss the hem of every passing galabea'.

I stopped in Switzerland to interview the star performer, the Shah of Iran, who was holding court at the Suvretta House hotel in St Moritz, where European ministers were waiting nervously to plead for special oil supplies. It was a Ruritanian comic-opera setting: the Shah arrived in his suite straight from the slopes in his skiing-suit, surrounded by his bodyguards and courtiers in fancy dress. He was a surprisingly slight figure, tense but talkative, and he explained candidly how he saw his oil power in psychological terms. He had been brought up in fear of the Seven Sisters, 'the oil kings' as they were called in Iran. 'There was still that mystical power and the magic behind the names of those big countries. People were just clicking their heels to the orders of the oil company'. When OPEC was first formed, he said, 'we were just walking in the mist'. But now he sounded quite confident of his new-found power: he had saved the airline Pan Am and invested in Krupp. He condemned the decadence of the West and explained that in terms of military power there was no difference between Iran and the western European nations. As I left clutching my tape recorder he said: 'Now you've got quite a bit of history in that magic box of yours.'

I flew on to Tehran, the Shah's capital, which seemed to have seized up with the glut of money: luxury cars jammed the streets and glittering half-equipped hotels had shot up from unpaved streets and stinking gutters. Inside them were bevies of Western bankers and adventurers packed three in a room, waiting to sell weapons or buy oil, while Western ambassadors were competing to suck up to the Shah with rival arms deals, as I was later to investigate in my next book (see Chapter 11). From there I flew to Beirut, the booming playground of the Arab world, where the shops were sparkling with gold jewellery and Western investors wooed Arab partners in the luxury of the St George Hotel. I continued to Kuwait, whose citizens were being flattered and pursued by diplomats and bankers as never before; the British ambassador explained he was now primarily an arms salesman. 'We thought we were pygmies facing giants,' said Abdlatif al-Hamad, the master-banker who would soon become minister of finance; 'then suddenly we found that the giants were ordinary human beings. The Rock of Gibraltar was made of papier mâché.'

I ended up in Saudi Arabia, where I waited to see the young oil minister Sheikh Ahmed Yamani, a commoner hired by the princes, who was now the most sought after of all the new players. He kept chairmen waiting for days in his anteroom, while he dictated messages to three male secretaries from his enormous desk. When I eventually saw him he sounded completely at ease in his role, talking softly and confidently about Western follies. 'We know that oil is a weapon, and nothing can take it away from us,' he assured me. 'We don't want to use it, but we will have to if America again helps Israel in a war.' He felt no awe about the Saudis' new power. 'The real power is to curb yourself from using power as you desire . . . we're fed up with money; what we're interested in is stability.' As for the Western attempts to form their own counter-cartel, the International Energy Agency, it was like the fable of Suleiman, the old man who leant on a stick: when the stick was eaten by ants and collapsed, Suleiman fell with it, and everyone realised that he was dead.

All through the Middle East the Western envoys had been demoralised by the new money power as they found old relationships comically reversed. Patronising diplomats and bankers had been transformed into anxious petitioners, effusively greeting anyone in a white robe who they hoped might give them some access to a sheikh. I watched the proud panjandrum of British banking Sir Kenneth Keith wait half a day for an audience with Yamani, his aide explaining: 'He's a very important man in his own country' – while eccentric old British Arabophiles went through before him.

The transfer of power was still more dramatic in the old world of Vienna, where OPEC had its headquarters in a small office block which had been ignored for years. In December 1974, a year after the oil price had quadrupled, the world's journalists converged for OPEC's annual meeting. They expected that the oil-producers would be divided and that the Saudis would give into American pressure to reduce the price, and Yamani assured them: 'It has to go down, it has to go down.' But it still went up and each member blamed the others for being intransigent; it was like Agatha Christie's *Murder on the Orient Express*: the crime turned out to have been committed by everyone. The Europeans bowed down before the new power: that evening Abderrahman Khène, the Algerian secretary-general of OPEC, gave a banquet for 400 guests, including the Austrian chancellor, Bruno Kreisky, in the ornate Palais Schwarzenberg, where Western businessmen slipped between the Arab tables to help them spend their money.

The colossal shift of wealth had defied all the projections of economists, planners and political scientists. Only six years earlier the famous futurologist Herman Kahn had written his book *The Year 2000* without mentioning either oil or Saudi Arabia. Now the calculations of Western treasuries depended on this greasy currency. In 1974 Western growth rates fell to zero, OPEC took $80 billion out of the world economy, inflation leapt up, corporations sank into debt, New York City faced bankruptcy. The whole capitalist system seemed in pawn to the OPEC powers: the Shah bought shares of Pan Am and Krupp, while, Libya's Colonel Muammar Gaddafi bought part of Fiat. Historians looked for precedents for this enrichment, like Spain in the fifteenth century, with its gold and silver from South America. None had been so sudden and wide-ranging.

'How could a transformation of such a profound and far-reaching nature come so suddenly upon us?' asked Henry Kissinger in his memoirs nine years later.[1] It was a break in the continuum which showed up all the limitations of conventional history. Political scientists or economists had taken little interest in oil supplies until it was forced on them and they did not expect that the OPEC producers could assert themselves against their Western masters. But Kissinger and the other Western leaders were too locked in their conventional wisdom to recognise the implications.

Kissinger remained the chief architect of US policy in Washington through 1974. He was determined to break OPEC, to divide it and to force the price down with auctions of oil; he described the cartel as a moral challenge to the Western democracies to face down extortionate foreigners. But the West was now more divided than the Arabs. Washington blamed the 'craven' European governments for competing to make separate deals with the Arabs. But the Europeans blamed the Americans for first squandering their oil and making them all vulnerable to the oil powers.

By 1975 Kissinger and the secretary of the Treasury, William Simon, were becoming more convinced that they could break OPEC as the economic recession reduced oil consumption: storage tanks overflowed, tankers were laid up, and docks were half empty. Leading economists including Milton Friedman, the high priest of the free market, were confident that OPEC would collapse, as was the *Economist*. But OPEC still held together and held up the oil price, for the richest producers were discreetly cutting back their production to prevent a glut. The Seven Sisters were conveniently providing the means to ration the producers. 'Why abolish the oil companies', the Iranian oil minister, Dr Jamshid Amouzegar, asked me, 'when they can find markets for us, and regulate them?' 'With the Sisters controlling everything,' the Shah of Iran explained to me later, 'once they accepted, everything went smoothly.'

And soon the Americans were themselves divided about what the oil price should be: as they wanted to encourage exploration and alternative sources of energy, they were worried that it might come down too low. Meanwhile Britain, which had successfully found its own oil in the North Sea, at great expense, was becoming an honorary member of OPEC, needing to maintain a high price. Within two years of the first outraged response, the proponents for the free market were having to accept that oil would always be a special commodity, likely to swing between acute shortage and dangerous gluts, which required some basic controls.

Who was now running this oil world? The Seven Sisters looked still more like paper tigers, helpless to influence the price or to confront the producers. Aramco, the consortium set up by the four giant American companies which had first exploited the Saudi oilfields and imposed its own price, had been turned into the Arabs' instrument and dared not defy the Saudis for fear of being nationalised. When I visited the chairman of Aramco, in its Saudi compound, he spoke like a Saudi spokesman. The oil executives who had sounded like their countries' commercial diplomats now looked more like mercenaries who could quickly change sides when the money was right. Western governments were exasperated by their obsession with immediate profits. After Kissinger met with senior oil executives he said that they were 'a living disproof of Marx's maxim that the captains of industry always know in the end where their true interest lies'.[2] But the oil companies, dependent on global networks of producers and consumers, refused to identify themselves with their own home governments. The British prime minister Edward Heath faced a moment of truth with the two London-based oil companies when the energy shortage threatened his political future. In October 1974 he summoned the companies' chairmen, Sir Frank McFadzean of Shell and Sir Eric Drake of BP, to Chequers to demand that they maintain full oil supplies to Britain, despite the Arabs' cutbacks. The chairmen explained that, as international businesses, their companies could not discriminate against other consuming countries, and that the British must share the pain. Heath reminded Drake that the British government still owned half of BP, but Drake refused to budge. 'I was deeply shamed', Heath wrote afterwards with asperity, 'by the obstinate and unyielding reluctance of these magnates to take any action whatever to help our own country in its time of danger'.[3] It was BP's first showdown (Drake told me afterwards) with the government which had created it, and it won.

Governments all over Europe were weakened by the oil crisis, much more than companies. Heath was confronted by a strike of coal-miners taking advantage of the energy shortage and called a general election which rashly concentrated on the question 'Who governs Britain?'. The answer could have been 'energy', and the voters preferred the Labour Party. All Western leaders, whether left or right, saw their plans and policies knocked sideways by external forces which they could not influence, and were battered by the high oil price and subsequent inflation: by the end of 1974 Willy Brandt in Germany was to resign, followed two years later by Olof Palme of Sweden. But their successors still grappled with runaway inflation, strikes and declining living-standards. Every country saw its own problems as unique: it was only later that they realised that the oil crisis had changed the tide throughout the West, swinging every boat round; the massive shift of wealth had weakened all the industrial democracies.

*

The Seven Sisters, published in 1975, became my best-selling book, translated into numerous languages and reprinted with each subsequent oil crisis. The big companies, led by Shell, tried to rubbish it, but oil was now attracting a wide readership beyond just oilmen. I spoke at international conferences and testified to the US Senate. I felt I was floating on oil, surrounded by all the arguments, seeing the world differently from the perspective of this murky fluid on which every industrial country depended, and which could undermine the most confident governments and turn dangerous enemies into friends.

How far did the oil crisis of 1973 really shift the world balance of power? Certainly it weakened the ability of the giant companies, and the governments which supported them, to control their resources in foreign countries and to profit at the expense of other people. Certainly it brought a surge of wealth to the rulers of a few developing countries. But oil could always be a curse as much as a blessing. 'God gave us the land', said the Mexicans; 'the Devil gave us the oil.' The oil wealth, without disciplines and democracy to control it, brought inequality, corruption and inflation, which could undermine regimes more than it supported them. Within six years the Shah of Iran, who had sought to reinforce his military power through oil money, had been toppled by an Islamic revolution; by the 1980s two of the biggest oil powers, Iran and Iraq, were at war with each other, and all the Middle Eastern producers were looking less secure.

*

Looking back from thirty-five years on, after the victory over OPEC in 1973, what did the power of the oil-producers really amount to? Certainly the cities of Arabia have been transformed beyond recognition. When in 2000 I visited Dubai, the most spectacular showplace, it had few relics of the pearl-fishing and dhow trades with which it had begun. The Maktoum family, who controlled it, were determined to show how quickly money could defy the desert: Dubai was like an architect's fantasy, with rectangles, domes and cupolas scattered along the horizon. The city centre was a pastiche of Manhattan complete with a mock Chrysler building and – ironically – twin towers with points like hypodermic needles. The straight beach was lined with grand tourist hotels and Sheiks' palaces, culminating in the Burj Al Arab hotel, the tallest in the world, shaped like the sail of a ghostly ship. The coastal desert had been almost obliterated by artificial harbours, islands and bright green lawns and golf courses stretching out to the brown dunes. Everywhere there were high cranes and teams of Indian contract workers mass-producing grandiose villas for rich Arabs, designed in all kinds of styles

– Egyptian, Roman, Byzantine, Moorish – everything except Christian Gothic. The whole place projected global commercial ambition, supported by expatriates from all over the world. Dubai had just unfolded new plans to become a world financial centre; the newspapers were full of news from Pakistan, the Philippines or Malaysia; and every new building was topped with clusters of satellite dishes pointing eastwards. Yet it all looked oddly insubstantial: the brown palaces looked like giant sandcastles which could be submerged by the tide, and in the haze the skyscrapers looked like a mirage. In fact many of them were empty, still waiting for office workers, and the only major industry was construction. All the financial activity on which Dubai based its future depended on external factors, above all the price of oil. Behind all the daring enterprise it was still a feudal state controlled by a billionaire monarchy through a web of agents, contractors and commission-men. And much of the wealth had been squandered on extravagant and useless projects. The inrush of money had not shifted the balance of power or been transmuted into serious political influence in the world; instead it was beginning to undermine the security of the state. As in a fairytale, the wish for riches had been granted and turned into a curse.

For all the Western influences and styles, Dubai was determined to show itself emphatically Muslim. It was the same through the other Gulf states, and particularly in Saudi Arabia. Everywhere brand-new mosques, closed to non-Muslims, were competing for glory, with still-broader domes and taller minarets. The Arab rulers felt obliged to show their credentials as devout Muslims by financing mosques and mullahs and Islamic charities, some of which had dubious purposes, and to express support to fellow-Muslims abroad, particularly the Palestinians in their confrontation with Israel. But they were not prepared to sacrifice their own extravagant lifestyles or their links with America and Europe. Their hypocrisy was increasingly obvious to the more devout and less prosperous Arabs, and the contradiction was literally explosive.

When the twin towers in New York collapsed in September 2001, they brought down with them America's confidence in its oil supplies in the Middle East. Most of the oil-producers were now seen as accomplices of terrorists. Two major oil powers, Iran and Iraq, were depicted by George W. Bush as part of the 'axis of evil'. And all the Gulf sheikhdoms, despite their close links with the West, had underground links with terrorist movements. But the most worrying oil power was Saudi Arabia. Many clues to the bombing pointed to the kingdom. Most of the bombers themselves were Saudis; the country's huge inequalities and corruption had bred fundamentalist rebels, while Saudi funds had financed them: their prophet, Osama bin Laden, was pledged to remove American forces from Saudi Arabia and to restore the original, austere, Muslim faith. The instability of the Saudi monarchy was now much more obvious: there was no convincing civil society to provide an alternative, and the middle-class leaders were caught between autocratic princes and fundamentalist revolutionaries. Sheikh Yamani, who had been seen thirty years ago as the scourge of the West, was now an elder statesman of the international oil industry, running his own global energy institute and representing the Westernised Saudi professional class, but when I met him again soon after September 11 he was openly worried about his country's stability, and his position inside Saudi Arabia was increasingly vulnerable.

The Iraq War was thought by many really to be about oil. Oil had worked its curse across the Middle East, bringing more instability, inequality and potential revolution. The riches it had brought had never provided the rulers with the security and political influence they hoped for; instead they had financed a destructive power which no-one had dreamt of thirty years earlier, threatening not only the local rulers but the security of the West itself.

11

New merchants of death

While I was still promoting *The Seven Sisters* in Washington and looking forward to a long respite, I was given a new tip-off which I found impossible to resist. Jerry Levinson, my mentor in Senator Frank Church's multi-nationals sub-committee, passed me a pile of papers, with his customary sigh and head-shake suggesting dirty work, and said: 'See what you make of *these*.' They were a series of subpoenaed documents revealing a network of bribes and fat commissions paid by the big American aerospace companies to arms dealers and middlemen, mainly in the Middle East, to ensure the sales of fleets of military planes and arms. This wave of bribes followed all too clearly from the oil boom. Western governments were desperately trying to bring back the vast surplus of the oil producers, the 'VSOP' as the British Treasury called it, and were encouraging their arms companies to make deals in the Middle East. The Arab rulers, rapidly enriched by oil money which they could not spend and feeling increasingly insecure, were an easy prey for arms salesmen offering glittering new weaponry. The companies, desperate for orders in the midst of a recession, were competing with massive bribes, negotiated by the middlemen, who pocketed their own share. They soon attracted the interest of the multinationals sub-committee, which now turned its attention from oil to arms, providing an unprecedented, and unrepeated, insight into the most impenetrable business of all. After I pored over the documents I was soon following a new paperchase which led me from Washington and California through Europe to the Middle East and Japan, and gave me sudden glimpses into this seedy underworld where power took its most basic form, as the power to kill.

The story seemed to belong more to mythology than to ordinary politics or business. The arms trade had always carried Wagnerian echoes, evoking the subterranean Nibelungen or Siegfried's sword; and the founders of the great arms companies, such as Alfred Krupp or Alfred Nobel, had seen themselves as supermen who alone understood the real powers and secrets of the world. I had long been intrigued by the character of Andrew Undershaft in George Bernard Shaw's play *Major Barbara*, the benefactor of a model town which depended on making weapons for its prosperity. Marxists and pacifists had warned that capitalism required wars to stimulate production and use up its surpluses, and advised against the 'merchants of death'. Their demonology seemed to belong to a past age, before two world wars had revealed the full horrors of the trade. Now whole regions of California or Tyneside were being revived by selling weapons, and capitalism again seemed to depend on the prospect of war. But the new merchants of death were much smoother and more respectable than the Wagnerian or Shavian villains: they were chief executives of high-tech corporations, genial Arab middlemen, cynical diplomats and unseen intelligence chiefs. I knew I could never fully penetrate the secret lairs of the arms dealers, but the quest would throw more light on them, and I resolved to write a book, which I called *The Arms Bazaar*.

It was California, to my surprise, that depended most dangerously on the new arms trade. Los Angeles, which was so proud of its dependence on movies and Hollywood, was actually much more reliant on the aerospace industry which surrounded it; and the movie and arms industries would often cross-fertilise each other, as we shall see. Through the years of the Cold War the Lockheed Corporation had stretched out through the San Fernando valley north of Hollywood, turning out fighter-bombers or military transports, which reached a peak during the Vietnam War. But it also needed foreign sales to maintain production, and when it began to sell its Starfighter warplane in Europe, competing against Dassault, it had already established a network of agents in every country to forge close links with key decision-makers. In Italy Lockheed had bribed ministers of defence; in the Netherlands it had bribed Prince Bernhard, the consort of Queen Juliana; in Germany it was suspected of bribing the buccaneering Bavarian leader Franz Josef Strauss. In retrospect, these bribes would be seen as part of a broader pattern of American corruption of European politicians in the cause of the Cold War; but it was the arms bribes which set the pace. When Lockheed faced the end of the Vietnam War, and its civilian airliners encountered setbacks, it was looking desperately for foreign buyers to fill the

171

factories, and its president, Carl Kotchian, flew round the world to drum up orders. After the oil shock of 1973 the rulers of the newly enriched states of the Middle East were the most tempting clients for Lockheed's warplanes: they faced no obvious military threat but they were fascinated by weapons as symbols of their new power; and they could be encouraged by well-placed commissions. Bribery in the Middle East had always been part of the way of life. But Lockheed was in a hurry and offered unprecedented funds; and in a few years it raised corruption to a quite different level, where the bribes became more important than the product.

I was determined to paint a convincing picture of the arms dealers as comprehensible individuals rather than lurid villains. In Los Angeles, having digested all the evidence, I gave Kotchian dinner. He was a friendly, likeable man: a thick-set farmer's son from North Dakota, with the rugged build and slow speech of the Midwest, he had risen up through the company as an accountant. But he was a passionate salesman, convinced that he was helping to save not only Lockheed from bankruptcy but the world from communism. He described his predicament with candour and openness: how he felt all the full weight of responsibility for the thousands of jobs of Lockheedians in California with their 'fierce loyalty'. He felt no compunction in bribing officials if he thought he could clinch an order: 'I did it because I thought it was right,' he told me, 'and I still do.' He vividly described his most gruelling ordeal, when he was trying to get an order for airliners in Japan: he waited for days in his lonely hotel room in Tokyo, hoping for news of the crucial order, not knowing who could achieve it. Eventually he had to penetrate behind the 'black curtain' to make huge payments to Yoshio Kodama, the sinister Japanese boss who wielded mysterious influence over the companies. I was engrossed by Kotchian's account, and when I eventually described his network of bribery in my book, and the political damage it had left behind in its wake, I felt a few pangs of guilt that I had betrayed his trust over that dinner. But a few months later, to my amazement, I received a letter of thanks from him saying that it was the fairest account that he had read. I realised the full divide between the critics of the arms trade and the proud self-contained world of the arms salesman, to whom the moral concerns were nothing compared to their heroic mission of protecting their workforce and profits and saving the world from communism. Kotchian seemed the reincarnation of Andrew Undershaft, who proclaimed 'The Faith of the Armourer': 'to give arms to all men who offer a fair price for them, without respect of persons or principles'.

Of course the corruption was always two sided. It took two to make the deal; and the most extraordinary character in the web of corruption in the Middle East was the Saudi arms dealer Adnan Khashoggi, later to become a global celebrity, who was the chief middleman for Western arms companies: in a few years Khashoggi had collected over $100 million in commissions from Lockheed alone. In February 1975, while researching *The Arms Bazaar*, I tracked Khashoggi down to his offices in London overlooking Big Ben, guarded by two tall Korean bodyguards and full of petitioners seeking business. Khashoggi received me with a genial welcome, a portly figure waddling in like a penguin, but immediately generating electricity among his minions. He was very forthcoming to an Englishman: explaining the naïvety of American executives when they moved into Saudi Arabia, not knowing the 'custom of the country', he insisted that 'you cannot transplant American morality'. He saw himself not just as a crucial go-between but as a valuable donor to the Saudi nation and people. He had already explained to the Pentagon how he was really an unrecognised benefactor, for in a monarchy like Saudi Arabia commissions were really the chief means by which the wealth at the top could be distributed among others; and he persuaded the Pentagon that he was really conducting 'an inexpensive aid programme'. It was as if the twentieth century was suddenly receding to sixteenth-century Europe, when quartermasters and courtiers made fortunes from their rake-offs from supplying food and weapons for their monarch's wars.

But behind all this high-minded rhetoric Khashoggi had been shrewdly seducing Lockheed executives with elaborate blandishments and traps – about which I heard details from a former aide who had herself closely witnessed his entrapments. In Paris he would lay on huge glamorous parties in his own mansion for Lockheed executives, who would be goggle eyed, surrounded by flattering guests and beautiful girls. These girls seemed thrilled by the executives' slow jokes and dull conversation, and ready to be seduced. In fact they were call girls hired from Madame Claude's high-price escort service, under instruction to give the men everything they wanted. Sometimes Khashoggi would invite a Lockheed executive to fly down to the

Mediterranean and take a cruise on his yacht, which just happened to be waiting with a crew who needed employment: 'It would be doing me a favour.' In fact the yacht would be specially redirected to pick him up, with a programme of partying and seduction designed to put him under heavy obligation to return the favour, so that the Lockheed–Khashoggi alliance would be established still more closely.

Khashoggi was a postmodern kind of arms dealer, an international playboy and celebrity who thrived on headlines: to him there was no such thing as bad publicity. The earlier arms dealers, such as Basil Zaharoff, the salesman for Vickers guns, had enjoyed some fame as men of mystery; but Khashoggi seemed to belong more to showbiz than to the arms underworld: he was a friend of Joan Collins, Cary Grant and Brooke Shields, and he featured as the hero-villain of a thriller, *The Pirate* by his then friend Harold Robbins. He flew round the world apparently oblivious to frontiers and customs. It was impossible to shame or embarrass him: after I had denounced his arms deals in *The Arms Bazaar* he seemed still more than glad to see me, to talk about the world and show off his wealth: when he gave me a long lunch in London and I asked for a glass of wine he ordered a bottle of Mouton Rothschild '64. When I wanted to interview him at the Paris air show he flew me there in his private DC9 airliner, with a double bedroom, bathroom and luxurious sitting-room. He saw the Western attacks on him as merely a harmless diversion which would not interfere with the real deals with governments behind the scenes; he loved to talk about his meetings with kings and presidents, and saw himself as a master-statesman with a unique understanding of what really made the world turn.

Khashoggi was never as vulnerable as he appeared to the West. His actual wealth remained uncertain: in 1986 a book was written about him called *The Richest Man in the World*,[1] while a few years later he was reported bankrupt and out of favour with the Saudi royals. But he retained his extravagant lifestyle; behind all the revelations and scandals he remained the agent and close friend of Prince Sultan, the Saudi minister of defence, and no-one knew to what extent his dealings were on behalf of his master.

When the Americans had to move into Saudi Arabia in 1990 to defend it against Saddam Hussein, the Saudis' massive buying of weapons appeared to be discredited, since they still could not defend themselves. 'The Saudis

22. 'The Listener': with Sally (*right*) and Louisa Lasdun. (Sandra Lousada)

23. In the study in Ladbroke Grove, 1991. (Christina Burton)

24. Lecturing on the British press at Vincennes. (Barbara Hill)

25. With Sheikh Yamani after publication of *The Seven Sisters*, 1975.
(Commercial Illustrators Ltd)

26. With his Brandt commission colleague Kay Graham.

27. Willy Brandt.

28. AS and Sally at the Oriental Hotel, Bangkok.

29. *Front row, left to right* David Owen, Shirley Williams and Bill Rodgers at the 1984 SDP annual conference in Buxton. AS makes himself inconspicuous between Owen and Williams. (PA Photos/Wirephoto)

30. With David Owen and Oliver Tambo, 1985. (P. W. Temple)

31. Nelson Mandela and Oliver Tambo meet for the first time in more than 28 years, Stockholm, March 1990.

ANC COMMEMORATIVE CARD NO.5
RELEASED LEADERS WELCOMED

32. Oliver Tambo's handwritten note that accompanied the photograph above.

33. AS and Mandela meet at the Dorchester Hotel, July 1996.

34. AS and Trevor Huddleston.
They remained friends for life.

35. Celebrating Jim Bailey's CBE,
May 1996. (James Barnor).

36. With Katie, Ladbroke Grove, *c.*1991. (Emily Anderson)

37. With his grand-daughter, Anna, on his 75th birthday, 2001.

38. Aboard his grandfather's caravan, *Esmeralda*, which he had restored, 1991.

have learnt that it's no good buying arms if you can't use them,' Khashoggi told me in 1991. 'They could see on TV that American technology worked and that their own soldiers were too fat.' But he now accused the Americans of having encouraged Saddam to invade Kuwait, so that they could bring their own forces in: 'Now the US will dominate the region, and American arms companies have been saved by the war.' And he presented himself as a peace-maker to solve the Middle East's problems: there was a real opportunity now for peace, he assured me, provided the Americans could escape from their 'domestic foreign policy'.

*

Cynical Western politicians could claim that arming Saudi Arabia was a harmless way to return some of the oil wealth to the West. The massive bribes seemed a small price to pay for helping to revive the Western economies. But the arms-selling and corruption in Iran were more obviously dangerous. In the 1970s the Shah was obsessed with weaponry, convinced that he could use his oil wealth to turn Iran into a major military power: when I argued with him in St Moritz in February 1975 he assured me: 'There is absolutely no difference between Iran and France, Britain and Germany.'[2] In Iran American and British companies saw a glittering opportunity to provide warplanes, tanks and missile systems to feed the Shah's insatiable appetite. The orders bore no relationship to the actual military threat to Iran, or even to the Shah's exaggerated fears of communist incursions from the Soviet Union: in London, the Ministry of Defence's chief arms salesman assured me that most of the tanks would get stuck in the desert, and the companies and governments knew quite well that much of the money was creamed off in commissions to the Shah's family and middlemen. But the arsenals of the Shah promised prosperity to the arms-producing regions of America and Britain, and their governments put all their diplomatic weight behind it. When I visited the British embassy in Tehran in 1976, it looked more like an arms showroom than a diplomatic mission, plastered with photographs of British weaponry. I argued with the ambassador, Sir Anthony Parsons, a scholarly and much-respected diplomat (who later became ambassador to the United Nations), about British support for a corrupt and oppressive regime; I had heard something of the revolutionary movements from dissident groups in London. Parsons was politely sceptical and stressed the necessity of supporting a loyal ally. As he wrote later, 'there was not, as I saw it, a revolutionary situation in the country'.[3]

But behind all the apparent power of the Shah there was far more revolutionary activity in the mosques and bazaars and back streets than Western intelligence had dreamt of, and the mullahs and young radicals were outraged by the Shah's corruption. In 1979 Ayatollah Ruhollah Khomeini returned to be swept into power; the Shah went into exile and all the weapons supplied by the West fell into the hands of a fiercely anti-Western religious dictatorship. The Foreign Office in London, shocked by its lack of information, wrote to all the British ambassadors in the Middle East to ask them to analyse the likelihood of similar coups elsewhere. Parsons himself, an honest and principled man, later wrote a book in which he acknowledged his mistakes. And in his retirement, when he kept clear of the lucrative boardrooms which most ex-ambassadors sought, he became an outspoken critic of the international arms trade.

The damage to Iran had already been done. How far the Western nations could have restrained the Shah, how far he would have brought about his own downfall, has since been much debated. But what is clear is that both arms companies and governments encouraged his military ambitions and extravagance, which outraged the Islamic militants and hastened the collapse of his regime – at an incalculable cost to Western interests and to peace in the Middle East. In the 1980s Khomeini, who depicted America as 'the Great Satan', was seen as the most intransigent enemy of the West, more dangerous than Saddam Hussein in next-door Iraq, who was secretly encouraged by the CIA to invade Iran, thus precipitating the eight-year Iran–Iraq War – which then provided a new bonanza for arms salesmen furnishing both sides.

*

The world after 1990 seemed at first to offer an opportunity for the major powers to exercise more control over the arms trade, with the collapse of the Soviet empire. Between 1988 and 1993 the total trade quite rapidly diminished. Facing less Russian competition, the Americans were the dominant arms-sellers, with Britain and France lagging behind. The Gulf War of 1990, which had been won by superior American technology, increased the demand for American weaponry, which had now been 'combat proven'; and the American companies had less obvious need to bribe their way into new markets. After the first Lockheed scandals, the US Congress had in 1977 passed the Foreign Corrupt Practices Act, strengthened in 1988 and 1998, which forbade bribery and led to a few prosecutions; and Lockheed, now merged into Lockheed-Martin, took pride in rigorously warning recruits to avoid transgressing the new rules. But the European arms companies were much less constrained and more anxious to sell their systems in the face of American superiority. The Middle East remained the biggest market, but British Aerospace took over from Lockheed the role of chief supplier to the largest single customer, Saudi Arabia – where the huge commissions and bribes remained shrouded in secrecy.

The Gulf War had provoked more concern at the UN about arms-selling, particularly since the five permanent members of the Security Council, which had voted to go to war with Saddam, were the five who had done most to arm him.[4] The Japanese, who were largely outside the arena, took the initiative in trying to reach an agreement, and the UN instituted an arms register in which all nations were required to report their exports of weapons.

But the economic pressures to sell weapons to dangerous regions became more powerful as the Western world went into recession; and new markets were opening up, particularly in east Asia. China was rapidly expanding both its military machine and the exports which helped to finance it, while the Americans saw promising new opportunities in selling to China's fearful enemies, notably Taiwan.

*

It was cheap small arms, not high-price warplanes or missiles, which had caused most of the deaths in battle round the world since the Second World War. And the most disturbing of the arms dealers I encountered was Sam Cummings, who appeared like a modern Mephistopheles. An American small-arms dealer, he was a boyish, jolly man in his forties who relished the role of cynical commentator of the world's follies and massacres: with his wide smile and ghoulish laugh he rolled out creepy jokes and epigrams: 'Arms for the love of Allah! . . . The plainest print cannot be read through a gold sovereign.' He had been a gun freak since he was a child, he told me, and he got his first break in the Korean War, when he identified captured weapons for the CIA. After that he set up his own business called Interarms, which bought and sold rifles, machine-guns and mortars across the world. I first met him at one of his arsenals, a bleak warehouse on the Manchester Ship Canal that few Mancunians knew existed, which comprised six storeys containing 300,000 guns. He took me on a tour, lovingly describing the circuitous routes through which the weapons had reached him, crossing the frontiers from one troublespot to the next, providing a miniature history of regional wars.

Cummings had the style of an educated gentleman: he had been brought up in a private school in Philadelphia; he wore sober dark suits, did not drink or smoke. He had adopted his school's motto for his company, *Esse quam videri* (to be rather than to seem), which sounded appropriate for his secret trade. He was based in Monte Carlo with a Swiss wife and two daughters, and spent holidays in a house in Villars, a Swiss mountain resort. He saw himself as a philosopher of weaponry: he liked to quote the classics and loved to use these lines from Coleridge to describe the arms trade:

> A wild and dreamlike trade of blood and guile,
> Too foolish for a tear, too wicked for a smile![5]

He knew quite well that his arsenals had provided the means for tens of thousands of deaths across the world; but he always liked to invoke the slogan of the arms lobby in America: 'Guns don't kill people, people do'. And he could always blame governments for the carnage: he could not export weapons without licences from his host governments, or without the connivance of intelligence agencies. He insisted that he kept aloof from the CIA or MI6 since his early days in Korea: 'I was never a wild fanatic for the spook business,' he told me. 'I am glad to be out of it, and I prefer more humdrum deals. They'll throw you on the chopping-block well before they throw themselves, and in the end they're just as dumb as you or I.' But he was always a good source for revealing subterranean arms deals across the globe, for his order book depended on knowing where the next demand would come from, or where the next cache of guns would be released. His insights into that underworld were valuable: while defence correspondents and military historians depicted third world wars in terms of rival leaders and their armies, he saw history in terms of the secret journeys of the weapons as they travelled from the Balkans or the Middle East to Africa or Latin America, to lie ready for the next rebellion or civil war. He was less interested in wars than in their aftermaths, when the guns would move on in readiness for the next conflagration.

Cummings's business, like Adnan Khashoggi's, depended on a shrewd combination of publicity and secrecy; and after *The Arms Bazaar* was published in 1977 he was all the keener to keep in touch with me in Manchester or London, providing titbits about new arms deals which usually proved accurate. After the collapse of the Soviet empire in 1990 Cummings was worried by the sudden lack of enemies, and the surplus of cheap guns in Russia and eastern Europe was bad for business. 'The world's awash with small arms,' he told me in June 1991. He went to Russia three times in two years and found that dealers would sell at almost any price: he was offered 60,000 Kalashnikovs for $3 each. There were enough rifles and machine-guns left over around the world to kill millions in any future war: the South Africans were busily shipping weapons to the Balkans to supply the Croats, who would soon make full use of them, and Lebanese businessmen in Beirut noticed that shiploads of arms were leaving for the Balkans. There was less demand for weapons from Cummings's arsenals, but the downturn seemed to make him more philosophical: he joined me at a high-minded conference at Oxford to discuss arms control, where he gave his usual pessimistic analysis and once again blamed governments, but he seemed genuinely keen to help the cause. When John le Carré was preparing his thriller *The Night Manager*, featuring an arms dealer, I introduced him to Cummings, who instructed him as a 'trainee' in his arsenal; some of Cummings's outlook was reflected in Chapter 24 of the book.[6] I lost touch with him until I read that he had died, still only seventy-one, in 1998. But with each new outbreak of fighting I still felt I could hear his ghoulish laugh: 'Arms for the love of Allah!'

But Cummings was only the prophet and personification of the ruthlessness of the gun trade, which was causing growing massacres and miseries and turning much of the developing world into an international Dodge City. In 2000 a White Paper from the British Department for International Development reported the fearful cost of regional warfare: 'Of the forty poorest countries in the world, twenty-four are either in the midst of armed conflict or have only recently emerged from it. This problem is particularly acute in Africa . . . An estimated five million people have died.'[7]

*

The trails of evidence from arms dealers like Cummings or Khashoggi always ended in the dark – in the secret areas where the deals were directed and protected by governments and their intelligence agents. The full truth would not emerge for decades, if ever.[8] Governments were always the main players in the arms trade: the biggest deals by the companies for warplanes or missiles were openly supported by their governments, which saw them as crucial for the economy and jobs at home. British ambassadors in the Middle East liked to boast that they were really arms salesmen, and during the 1980s Margaret Thatcher presented herself as the most aggressive hustler of them all. But in the small-arms trade, which was much more lethal, governments preferred to hide behind the private dealers, surreptitiously giving them licences to supply weapons – which could easily find their way to unsavoury regimes and rebel armies, while ministers or ambassadors appeared blameless. In theory British diplomats, as they kept on telling me, rigorously controlled all exports of weapons through 'end-use certificates', which determined where they would end up, in practice they frequently turned a blind eye to the ultimate destination and in the 'grey areas' of the business, such as Beirut or Amman or Miami airport, the guns could mysteriously be diverted somewhere else, to help to start another war.

Occasionally a government's subterranean dealings would emerge and cause a public scandal, or a new war or massacre would revive public indignation about the trade. The Iranian Revolution of 1979, the 'Iran–Contra' scandal, the Angolan civil war and the Iran–Iraq War all showed the deadly consequences of irresponsible arms-selling. And sometimes a friendly country would suddenly turn into an enemy, revealing all the dangers of selling it weapons. By the end of the 1980s Saddam Hussein in Iraq emerged as a much more dangerous enemy than the ayatollahs in Iran, after the West had helped to support him. And by the 1990s the Western arming of Saddam provided the clearest example of the follies of government connivance. The British had been relatively small suppliers to Saddam's huge arsenal, but a succession of evidence and documents gave a sudden insight into the dishonesty of British policy, and the lack of controls.

British governments continued to insist that arms sales were crucial to the economy, and for providing jobs. The junior defence minister Alan Clark was the most blustering champion of British arms sales to Iran, claiming they were vital to Britain's interests, but in fact many of the deals had been financed by government loans through the Export Credit Guarantee Department, which was soon left by Saddam with unpaid bills. And the economic arguments for arms sales were exploded by the most respected economic journalist Sir Samuel Brittan in 2001:

> Behind the arms promotion lobby is the primitive belief that if one source of overseas sales dries up, the workers and other resources involved would simply waste away. This is rubbish in view of the millions of people who change jobs every year . . . We will never really stop dubious arms sales until the myth of the export drive is nailed once and for all.[9]

Clark's zeal seemed more influenced by his macho need to equate the gun with the penis than by economic policies: when I attacked him in print for his irresponsible policies he retorted by mocking 'the archdeacon of the wanking classes'. But his interest in weapons was part of the wider psychology of male aggression behind arms-selling: in my travels I only met one woman arms dealer, Youtta Simon, an elegant agent in Paris, while much of the campaigning against arms sales was led by very competent women.

The arming of Saddam was to have disastrous consequences after 9/11, where the United States, with Britain by its side, led 'a coalition of the willing' in the Iraq War, believing there to be weapons of mass destruction in Iraq.

12

Saving the world?

It was the poorest countries in the world which suffered most from the oil crisis of 1973, as they had to pay higher prices for the fuel on which many of their hopes of development depended; and the price continued to rise. Six years later, in 1979, I found myself, by another lucky accident, immersed in the problems of this vast inequality: this time not as an outsider looking in, but as an insider looking out.

The 'non-oil developing countries', as the World Bank bleakly described the poorest countries, were now facing a bitter frustration. For ten years before 1973 they had been trying to obtain better terms for exporting their own commodities, such as sugar, copper or cocoa, and had tried to organise a common bargaining-front through the United Nations Conference on Trade and Development (UNCTAD); but they had remained divided and indecisive (some people complained that UNCTAD really stood for 'Under No Circumstances Take Any Decisions'). Some compared themselves to workers in the nineteenth-century industrial countries, who could achieve power only by combining into labour unions: why could they not organise their own unions between countries across the world? But poor countries were much harder to unify than workers, and multinational companies could still beat down the prices of cocoa or sugar by playing one hungry country against another. Without bargaining-power they were condemned to the bottom of the heap, sometimes now called 'the fourth world'.

After the 1973 OPEC victory many countries exporting raw materials hoped to create cartels like the oil-producers: they saw oil as the forerunner of other commodities which must achieve better terms. In 1974 President Houari Boumédienne of Algeria launched a 'new international economic order' at a special session of the UN and argued for fairer prices for all commodities, whether copper, bauxite or sugar: Zambians, Jamaicans and

Filipinos began talking expectantly about a COPEC, BOPEC and SOPEC. Boumédienne, like Henry Kissinger, saw his cause as a moral crusade which could attract a unity deeper than oil. In March 1975 he invited the OPEC heads of state to Algiers, at the high tide of their power: I watched an extraordinary procession into the conference hall, including the Shah and the sheikhs, a black dictator and a Latin American president, who made stirring speeches. Boumédienne reiterated his favourite theme, that oil was the source of life itself; the Shah embraced his old enemy Saddam Hussein of Iraq and together they promised a new age of peace. Was this really the beginning of a new world order?

All the developing countries, with or without oil, were now calling themselves 'the South' as opposed to the industrialised 'North', and the North was becoming more apprehensive of the South, which provided most of its raw materials. In 1975 the Americans and Europeans began a North–South dialogue in Paris at the Conference on International Economic Co-operation (CIEC); the Americans practised their tactic of 'talk 'em to death' and it died out after eighteen months of fruitless discussion.[1] But internationalists in the West were still concerned about the growing rift. Robert McNamara, the former US secretary of defence who had become president of the World Bank, was impatient with the rhetoric of the new order, but he dreaded a confrontation between the two sides of the world which would undermine his plans for development: already the rich countries, grappling with their own economic crises and inflation, were reducing their contributions to aid.[2] McNamara decided to try to break the deadlock by creating a new independent international commission that would find new solutions. For chairman he made a rash and un-American choice: Willy Brandt, the former chancellor of West Germany, a socialist best known for his search for a dialogue with the communist countries of the East.

I was approached to become involved with the Brandt commission, as it soon became known, through a surprisingly old-fashioned Oxford network: a garden party at All Souls College – the traditional meeting-place of the pre-war conservative British establishment. My friend Michael Faber told me that Brandt was looking for an editorial adviser to help put together the commission's final report; was I interested? It was an irresistible opportunity

183

to see world problems from inside and to try to explain them. I did not know I was entering an ideological maelstrom.

In February 1979 I went to my first meeting of the commission, which had already met in Mali, Malaysia and Switzerland. Beforehand I had a long talk with Brandt, who looked more haggard and blotchy than I remembered him, but was still humorous and welcoming, pretending he had read my books: 'I want the report to be Sampsonised.' He complained that there were not enough jokes about development, which suggested there was something wrong; he discussed one joke – 'if there's one thing worse than being exploited by multinationals, it's not being exploited' – and rejected it. He was determined to be impartial between North and South: do we all want to be like the Americans? He quoted the words of Pope John Paul II: 'Development is another word for peace.' He hoped the report could concentrate on three themes: peace, self-interest and justice.

He sounded more like a spiritual leader than a politician, and he warned the commissioners that they must concern themselves with people, not things; there were other powers beyond military forces or capital accumulation – as the Pope had shown in Latin America or Ayatollah Khomeini would later show in the revolution in Iran. The Indian aide next to me scribbled 'Ayatollah Brandt'. Brandt was reflective and illuminating, but he was clearly running the commission on a very light rein, with little sense of direction. He seemed more interested in openings to the East, where, he explained, the communist parties were visibly crumbling; and his closest colleague was his fellow-socialist Olof Palme, the former prime minister of Sweden (who was assassinated seven years later).

The eighteen commissioners round the table represented North and South, left and right; they included bankers and trades unionists, men and women. They made up a kind of microcosm of the world's viewpoints though they included no communists from the East, to Brandt's disappointment. The ten from the South included Layachi Yaker from Algeria and Amir Jamal from Tanzania, as well as smooth bankers like Rodrigo Botero from Colombia and Abdlatif al-Hamad from Kuwait. It was hard to imagine them all agreeing to a consensus.

The secretariat of development economists was even more disparate, with twin heads who were at odds: the senior director was a cosmopolitan Swede,

Göran Ohlin, but he was frustrated by an abrasive Yugoslav, Dragoslav Avramović – later central banker in Belgrade under Slobodan Milošević – who was committed to the dogmas and language of the new order, where words had different meanings and some arguments were taboo. The most difficult taboo was about oil, for it was a divisive subject in the South, and part of the faith of the new order was that oil was not different from other commodities in the South. It was a difficult constraint in trying to write a report, but the North was equally reluctant to discuss its own agricultural protection and rigged markets.

The most heavyweight member from the North was Edward Heath, still sulking four years after being deposed as Conservative leader by Margaret Thatcher. He was not glad to see me: as a journalist I had made fun of his repetitive speeches and his blancmange look, and my interviews were frosty; but I noticed with relief that he was brusque with everyone. He was exasperated by the refusal of OPEC members to discuss oil and by their hypocrisy in lecturing the North about not helping the poorer countries. He was specially irritated by 'Sonny' Ramphal, the Guyanese lawyer in charge of the Commonwealth Secretariat in London, who enjoyed rhetorical sallies against the North. Brandt would not cut short the most verbose delegates from the South, who could speak for more than an hour: how could he, Heath wondered, ever have reached a decision with his Cabinet as chancellor in Bonn?[3]

Heath's irritation was shared by Katharine Graham, the owner of the *Washington Post*, who sat next to him in alphabetical order. Graham had been asked to join by her friend McNamara: she knew little about the third world, she warned him, but he thought it would help educate her and her paper; and she joked about her 'six million dollar education'. The delegates from the South held her, as a media magnate, in some awe, assuming that she could tell her papers what to say; but like most owners she had barbed relations with her journalists. She took her responsibility seriously, championing the cause of women and establishing good relations with commissioners from the third world. She was amused when one Arab member propositioned her in her room. She said: '*Jamais où on travaille,*' and he replied: '*Jamais ne dire jamais.*'[4] But inwardly, like Heath, she was furious with the demands from countries in the South which could not sort out their own problems, particularly their escalating birth rate: 'Why should we help them if they don't help themselves?' She was fed up with Brandt, whom she saw as a moralising lefty; and she and Heath forged a close bond of resistance. In the middle of one marathon session Heath whisked her off to Paris to attend the gala opening of Alan Berg's opera *Lulu* with its third act completed. Graham disliked the opera and was largely ignored at the grand reception afterwards because Heath did not bother to introduce her; she was assumed to be a reporter for the *Post*, until it finally clicked that she was one of the most powerful women in the world.[5]

The Brandt commission continued its endless discussions through 1979 in Austria, Belgium and West Germany. The delegates from the South wanted a new world institution which would be responsible for a 'massive transfer of resources' from the North using the abstruse form of currency called the special drawing right, which was described as 'the money of moneys'. The secretariat produced millions of words which I attempted to boil down to plain language, trying to avoid apparently harmless words like 'restructuring', 'remunerative' or 'basic needs' which turned out to have coded meanings in the battlefield of international conferences. My closest ally was the distinguished British economist Robert Cassen, but even he resented some of my simplifications. 'I suppose you realise', he said one day, 'that most people think *journalistic* means "superficial".' 'And do you realise', I replied, 'that *academic* means "irrelevant"?'

While the arguments rolled on, the world outside was becoming darker. The Iranian revolution and its Islamic fanatics were a reminder that economic growth and military power were not everything, while the interruption of Iran's oil supplies had caused a new energy crisis and another redoubling of the price, which had further impoverished the poorest countries, while the rich countries went back into recession and looked for more protection. The cross-purposes between North and South were worsening. In the midst of the energy crisis UNCTAD held a meeting in Manila attended by 3,000 delegates, which ended with a communiqué that never mentioned the word 'oil'.

Brandt himself was unhurried, goaded neither by the urgent need to produce a report nor by the economic disasters sweeping through the world. He quoted Luther: 'If I heard that the world was coming to an end tomorrow, I would still plant an apple tree.' I found him refreshing company, particularly when he was happily drinking in the evenings, speculating about the world with women friends, and telling risqué stories about Eastern communists or the Pope, with his naughty-boy look. He loved telling anti-German jokes. Once the whole commission was stuck on a German train between Bonn and Brussels which kept stopping, and he was delighted by the evidence of German incompetence. But he seemed reluctant to concentrate on the commission, particularly when his new girlfriend (known as Sugarbush) arrived on the scene, and his indecisiveness made my own job difficult. At one point he hoped I could bypass the secretariat and produce my own report directly for him, but that was soon frustrated.

In October 1979 the commission met in the gloomy Palais Egmont in Brussels for its last scheduled meeting, supposedly to approve a report. A few commissioners tried to force the pace by working out their own compromise, led by Pete Peterson, the American banker who had been secretary of commerce under Nixon. He was an impatient tycoon who kept complaining 'Mego' – 'my eyes glaze over' – and left meetings before the end, but he had an eye for a big deal. In Brussels he beckoned me into a private room where he and three other commissioners, Ramphal, Palme and al-Hamad, had worked out a deal which would give the North security of oil supplies and orderly price rises in return for a large transfer of funds and sharing power with the South. Peterson handed me a bundle of rough notes and asked me to put them into shape. I worked on a draft until dawn, which Peterson cut down ('leave out all the idealistic crap') and passed onto Palme, who presented it to the full commission the next day. But it was followed by the usual marathon speeches, which Brandt did nothing to interrupt as the final deadline approached. 'At no time', as Heath wrote afterwards, 'did Willy Brandt bring the commission to the point of reaching a decision on any topic.'[6]

The next day Brandt invited the Brussels journalists to a lavish lunch, beginning with salmon pâté, turbot mousse and mussels, which turned out to be only the hors d'oeuvres – seemingly out of keeping with the grave warnings about global hunger; Brandt talked indiscreetly to the *Time* correspondent and his pretty wife. Afterwards the commissioners reconvened to hear still more speeches, but Brandt was clearly the worse for wear, red faced and breathing heavily. Suddenly he exploded with an angry outburst: 'We're making no progress . . . I am deeply depressed . . . Resolutions do not make revolutions.' He welcomed Palme's draft, and proposed leaving it to a small editing group, but warned: 'You can leave the chairman out.' Heath replied, saying 'with great respect' six times, insisting that the commissioners could not delegate the report to a small group. But Brandt replied, looking still more haggard, that he was not feeling well, and departed to spend the evening with his girlfriend, who had arrived from Bonn. Aides explained that he had a heavy cold, but some commissioners were less sympathetic: I tried to persuade Kay Graham that he had been under heavy pressure but she cut me short: 'Tony, he's a fucking lush. I know what they're like, I've had to live with them.'

The commissioners reassembled for dinner in gloom, bewildered and leaderless, with no hope of a consensus. But the two men who had at first been at loggerheads, symbolising irreconcilable differences between North and South, Heath and Ramphal, now agreed to work together in London to achieve a report – to the amazement and relief of the others. 'If *they* can agree,' al-Hamad said, 'we all can. And they can, because they're both politicians.'

The scene shifted to London, where for two months the two politicians with their aides thrashed out an agreement. Ramphal knew that the South must make concessions about oil if it wanted to share more power and receive more aid; Heath believed that the North must reform its institutions, to avert a crisis of international debt and mass starvation in the third world. At the end of the year the commissioners met again, behind the moated defences of Leeds Castle in Kent, where Heath, with Ramphal's agreement, presented a draft report. Brandt could not arrive until after dinner, to Heath's visible relief. They all approved it with only minor changes, and agreed that the question of oil should be at the centre.

The Brandt report was published in March 1980, with the title *North–South: A Programme for Survival,* and was launched by Brandt: North–South relations, he said, were 'the biggest challenge to mankind for the remainder of the century'. With all its negotiated language it was much less direct and readable than I had hoped, but it did spell out the predicament of 800

million destitute people in the third world and the nature of the crises of
energy, trade and the world economy. 'Taken together they threaten the
whole structure of our political, industrial and financial institutions, unless
we move urgently and adequately to deal with the basic causes.' And it put
forward proposals to avert disaster, including an emergency aid programme
of $4 billion a year, and international taxation.[7]

In Britain Heath now became the champion of the programme, launching
it with vigour and supporting it in the House of Commons with a combativeness sharpened by his contempt for the prime minister, Margaret
Thatcher, who consistently opposed it. He soon became an ardent
propagandist for a fairer deal, which brought him new friends in the third
world, including Fidel Castro, who welcomed him in Cuba and saw him as
his 'esteemed friend'.[8] Working alongside him I was impressed by his total
commitment and consistency, and to my surprise found him a real friend –
still more after we later became neighbours in Wiltshire. I was reassured by
his 'grumpy integrity' as Roy Jenkins called it, and for me he seemed to make
an exception to his deep distrust of British journalists.

The report achieved a success in Britain which surprised almost everyone,
including the publishers, Pan, who sold more than 100,000 copies in paperback. It inspired a mass demonstration outside Parliament and a revival of
interest in development problems. But in Europe it had a more mixed
reception. It was greeted enthusiastically in the Netherlands, where Queen
Juliana became an ardent supporter. But the French were lukewarm, and in
Germany the chancellor, Helmut Schmidt, was worried by the dangers of
inflation. He received the commission at a reception at Schloss
Charlottenburg in Berlin, but he had private reservations about the goodwill
of OPEC countries. I had an inside view of Schmidt's attitude through a
comical accident. I had arrived with German friends who reproved me for
wearing a light grey suit, but when I was introduced to Schmidt he took me
aside and explained why he resented OPEC's intransigence, which had done
so much harm to the German economy. I wondered why he was confiding
in me until he looked round the hall and said: 'Do you know, we're the only
two people wearing light grey suits.'

In the United States the report was received with either boredom or
hostility: when Brandt came to Washington to promote it the president,

Jimmy Carter, was only reluctantly persuaded to receive him. Kay Graham was very disappointed by the report: 'It turned out to be exactly what it was designed not to be,' she wrote afterwards, 'with the various commissioners basically representing their own states or constituencies.' She still tried to publicise it, and asked Ben Bradlee to give it prominence in the *Washington Post*; but it was relegated to page 25, while the *New York Times* put it on page 3. Graham was so angry that she did not speak to Bradlee – for a day. She did persuade the editors of her other paper, *Newsweek*, to produce a cover story about it, but they were glad to tell her afterwards that it was the worst-selling issue of the year.[9]

With the arrival of President Ronald Reagan in 1981 the tide turned more completely against any dialogue with the South. The West faced a more serious recession, and both Reagan and Thatcher refused to recognise the South as a single entity. They both reluctantly agreed to attend the global summit advocated by Brandt, which was held at Cancun in Mexico later that year; but there was no meeting of minds, and the Western conservatives insisted that the poorer countries must help themselves. The cross-purposes were summed up in an exchange between Reagan and Julius Nyerere, the president of Tanzania. 'I will help you buy the fishing-rod,' said Reagan, 'but after that the rest lies with you. You must fish in your own pond to support yourselves.' 'But what happens', asked Nyerere, 'if you haven't got a pond with any fish?'[10]

The North's worries about energy supplies faded as the oil price fell and OPEC became increasingly disunited: the war between Iran and Iraq made both countries determined to pump out more oil, and put them both in conflict with the Saudis. Americans sank back into complacency about oil, while their economy began to recover at the cost of higher interest rates, draining capital from elsewhere.[11] Increasingly the commercial banks took over the role of the International Monetary Fund as huge lenders to the more dynamic countries of the developing world, on their own tough terms, and any idea of 'massive transfers of resources' was forgotten.

In terms of economic and military power, the North had won the confrontation with the South, where the falling oil price had brought bankruptcies and political upheavals; and the fear of Arab states using oil as a political weapon against Israel or America rapidly receded. The grave warnings of the Brandt commission about impending economic disasters in the North proved alarmist or at least very premature.

But there had always been a deeper dimension to the North–South problem, as Brandt had emphasised from the start; and while the North had won the economic war, it was losing on the moral and religious battlefields. Oil financed Islam, which advanced as Christianity receded, while many young people in the most impoverished countries turned to fundamentalism and took consolation in the rewards of the afterlife. The Saudis financed mosques, whose domes and minarets sprung up everywhere, in contrast to the rectangular skyscrapers and temples of commerce; but many of the mullahs who controlled them – often unnoticed by their original benefactors – were preaching religious revolution and confrontation with the evil forces of materialism and capitalism. Many of the rebellions and wars at the end of the twentieth century, from Sudan to Afghanistan and Indonesia, were based on religion, and fanatics who were prepared for suicidal bombing were able to wreak vengeance on the most highly organised military machines. The war in Iraq, and the terrorist attacks in Madrid and London, following on from 9/11, meant that the threat to the North was never greater.

*

In the two decades after the Brandt report the South faded further from the consciousness of the North. The poorer countries were increasingly ineffective in their negotiations for better terms of trade, and after the end of the Cold War they were no longer wooed or supported as important allies against the enemy, while many of their once-precious minerals and raw materials lost their value as new sources opened up. The global capitalism which spread through the ex-communist countries had little use for nations which were still struggling to lift themselves from a subsistence economy: Africa, which included most of the poorest countries, felt increasingly marginalised, off the economic map. The new conservatives in the West were sceptical of the whole usefulness of aid, and America and Europe spent proportionately less on their aid budgets; the poor countries only hit the headlines and TV screens when they were devastated by famines, natural disasters or civil wars. The prospects of a new order or a unified front of developing countries disappeared, as they were humiliated by their powerlessness.

Was there any way in which the South could attract the North's attention or assert some leverage? The Brandt commission had in passing discussed the danger that it might in desperation turn to terrorism as its ultimate weapon. And soon after the publication of the report William Clark, who had been a vice-president of the World Bank under Robert McNamara and a keen supporter of the commission, became more seriously concerned about the danger. With some help from McNamara and senior diplomats and bankers, he published in 1984 a fictional book called *Cataclysm*, which purported to describe 'the North–South conflict of 1987'. It described how, as major developing countries defaulted on their debts, bankers and governments in the North withdrew their support. In the ensuing protests Chicago was racked by black rioters and its buildings set on fire, and a terrorist group called 'the Black Hand' launched a global campaign including 'inconvenience terror', which immobilised electronic accounting, and bioterrorism, which poisoned water supplies and spread deadly diseases. Chaos spread through the West, Wall Street crashed, and South Africa and Israel became flashpoints. With the threat of nuclear war, China and Japan initiated a conference to save the West and to create a new World Central Bank, which would ensure fair terms for poorer countries.

The warning was not taken very seriously, but the North was to renegotiate the vast sums lent to the South, which were often seized by those in power and which left many countries facing famine and disaster. The North–South divide was to continue as a growing concern to the world.

13

Breaking the mould

I took some time to realise how deeply Margaret Thatcher was transforming the mood of the country, and dividing it after her victory in 1979. When I wrote my earlier Anatomies I had found it relatively easy to find some kind of middle ground. Both main parties roughly adhered to the post-war settlement, which included maintaining full employment, allowing a mixed economy of private and public industries, accepting trade unions and maintaining high taxes to finance public services. They took similar attitudes to most British institutions, from nationalised industries to the army and the monarchy. When Edward Heath came to power in 1970 the middle ground was shrinking, and when I mentioned consensus to him he snorted: 'There never *was* a consensus in the sense of a deliberate effort of will and thought to create a particular situation . . . Even the idea of "Butskellism" was sloppy and inaccurate.'[1] But Heath soon moved towards the centre, as he intervened to rescue industries, conciliated the trade unions and maintained high taxation. And when a Labour government returned in 1974 under Harold Wilson and then James Callaghan, they resisted further socialist policies including more nationalisation.

But Thatcher soon insisted that she was not a consensus politician but a conviction politician: and she had fixed convictions, most of them inherited from her father. When I interviewed her in the drawing-room in Downing Street and mentioned the dread word 'consensus' she reacted ferociously, striding up and down the room, protesting that it really meant surrender, both in Britain and in Europe. 'Consensus? Consensus? Poof! What sort of consensus was there between the early Christians and the Romans? Look at Peter Carrington. He's just come back from Brussels with what he thought was consensus: it just meant giving in to the French.' And in the next few years the consensus did indeed disappear out of sight, as the Conservatives lowered taxes, privatised industries and confronted the unions, while Labour reacted with more drastic socialist policies. Both sides turned against the middle ground.

Thatcher's attitude to the jobless showed how decisively she had broken with the post-war settlement. She allowed unemployment to rise to levels unheard of since before the Second World War. Denis Healey warned that if the number of jobless reached a million there would be rioting in the streets: but it went up to a million, two million, three million, and they still did not riot: indeed many of them turned out to be voting for Thatcher, attracted by her militant patriotism and unleashing of individualism, while Labour's collectivism was now deterring many working-class voters.

Thatcher could easily depict her liberal critics as guilt-ridden idealists who dodged the real problems. 'I'm a plain straightforward provincial,' she had told me back in 1977. 'I've got no hang-ups about my background like you intellectual commentators in the south-east. When you're actually *doing* things you have no time for hang-ups.'[2] She was misrepresenting herself, of course: she was much more of an intellectual ideologue than most liberals or journalists, and she was living comfortably in the south-east, married to a millionaire. She was ruled by ideologues, particularly by Friedrich Hayek: when I had to admit I had not read one of his early works she commanded: 'Go away and read it.' But she certainly had little guilt about putting people out of work or increasing inequality between rich and poor.

Thatcher was soon making Britain's anatomy look very different. She was upsetting the whole system of checks and balances which many people had seen as crucial to Britain's democratic system. In 1962 I had depicted the power structure as a necklace of interlocking rings, with a gap in the middle. Now Thatcher herself was filling much of the gap and saw herself as the central structure. 'I think I have become a bit of an institution,' as she had then explained, 'and the place wouldn't be quite the same without this old institution.'[3] She talked much about cutting back the power of the state, but she was exercising her own power to the limit, with relish,[4] and more crudely and thoroughly than any prime minister since Churchill. 'If you look back at ministers' memoirs of the sixties,' her private secretary, Charles Powell, told me in 1992, 'my seven years with her belonged to a different world. There was never any risk of rebellion in Cabinet, no sitting on the edges of chairs.

Often you never heard of the Cabinet.' She did not worry about maintaining balance or fair play between the parties: she only wanted to promote people who were 'one of us'. (Tony Blair was to assume a similar approach when he was elected in 1997.) Nearly all the institutions I had anatomised began to look different. She elevated the military and the police, demoted diplomats and civil servants, eclipsed the monarchy and consigned trade unions into the shadows. She mocked the bishops, whom she associated with wet collectivism, and projected her own version of Christianity as the faith of individualists against the forces of socialism: 'I've always regarded individualism as a Christian mission,' she told me.

She even seemed to be undermining the class system, which had seemed so much part of Britain's anatomy. She was amazed, she explained before she became prime minister, to hear the Tories depicted as the party of privilege and the establishment: 'If that's so, what am I doing in it?'[5] She had certainly broken the political influence of the landed aristocracy and the 'knights from the shires', as she sacked the Tory patricians from her government. Old families lost their hold on both politics and business, while the old 'deference vote' was rapidly disappearing. But she was really reverting to more Victorian class distinctions based on money, promoting a new plutocracy with many more tycoons and financiers in the House of Lords. She gave businessmen a confidence and status they had not enjoyed since the nineteenth century, and removed any stigma from being 'in trade'. She praised the traders and shopkeepers like her father, and promoted entrepreneurs into national heroes, bringing them into the heart of Whitehall. In fact only a handful of true risk-taking financiers really emerged, and the British never really accepted the entrepreneurial society. But the tax cuts and incentives for businessmen unleashed commercial ambitions among the Thatcher generation which took older Britons by surprise. Industrial managers made the most of the new freedom to hire and fire. A few years earlier chairmen would boast of how many people they employed: now they would be judged and rewarded according to how many they had sacked. High salaries became the yardsticks of status on the American pattern. When shareholders forced directors to disclose their emoluments the publicity only increased their competition to achieve the maximum 'score'.

Thatcher's bark was often worse than her bite. After all her diatribes against the welfare state she did not cut it back, and increased spending on the National Health Service; she worked closely with the civil service, which she purported to despise. But in politics a bark could be as sharp as a bite, and she was loud enough to project a quite different Britain, both at home and abroad. The image of a country in decline, which had haunted every post-war government, was superseded by one of a combative and commercial Britain ruled by an Iron Lady. 'I have changed everything,' she would boast, and she persuaded many people it was true.

*

For myself I felt disoriented and displaced in Thatcher's Britain: sitting on the middle ground I felt as if an earth tremor had opened up a wide crack beneath me. I was split between the two sides of the crack with an inevitable ambivalence. I welcomed the reinvigoration of business, the release of young energies and the assault on class barriers; but I was deeply disturbed by their replacement with the cruder divisions based on money and gross inequalities. Was this the only choice, between harsh money values on the right and defensive state socialism on the left? And I was more repelled by Margaret Thatcher's vision of Britain in the world as she reverted to the insular spirit, whether in regard to Europe or developing countries. She seemed determined to reverse the sense of involvement and responsibility which so many Britons had felt over the post-war decades, and to return to a purely commercial ambition and competitiveness, like the mid-Victorians or the more provincial Americans. Was this really Britain's destiny as a post-imperial power, to reject the responsibilities and experience of its long history in the world and to accept a dependent role in an American empire?

I could not see much more hope from the Labour opposition. I had voted Labour in each election since 1950, but I was appalled by the resurgence of insularity there too after Labour returned to power in 1974, when the anti-Europeans reasserted their influence. In the 1979 election our Labour candidate in Kensington was a shrill young woman committed to getting Britain out of Europe. Our Labour canvasser turned out to be an old *Observer* friend, Bob Taylor, who shared my European views. He said: 'If I were you

I would vote for the Liberal.' So I did, and so did Sally, who had previously been a Labour voter.

I was still more exasperated by Labour after Thatcher came to power, when the leftwingers in the trade unions and constituencies strengthened their hold. When they chose as leader Michael Foot, the fiery anti-European and favourite of the unions, they seemed set on a course of further nationalisation and withdrawal from the EEC which I could never vote for.

My Labour friends were almost all European minded and alienated from the leadership. Shirley Williams, whom I knew well through Europe and Africa, was in despair at the triumph of insular militants; she was joined by Bill Rodgers, her old ally from Liverpool, and more surprisingly by David Owen, who was disgusted by the leftward shift. In June 1980 they formed the 'Gang of Three' (as the left called them contemptuously). Roy Jenkins was in Brussels as president of the European Commission, but he had made speeches advocating a new alignment in British politics, and in January 1981 he returned to Britain, where he soon made the gang up from three to four. The Labour Party's adoption of a new constitution was the last straw: the four broke with the party and proclaimed the 'Limehouse declaration' in 1981, committing them to break away and set up a 'Council for Social Democracy'. They aimed, as Jenkins put it, to 'break the mould' of the British political system.

After my global travels I felt detached from the British political scene, so I was surprised when Shirley rang to ask me if I would join a hundred people to sign a declaration supporting the Limehouse declaration. I hesitated. Could any group of individuals change the pattern of British political parties that was so entrenched? In my Anatomies, the two main parties had seemed an essential part of the power structure, while the Liberals seemed destined to remain the powerless third party ever since they had split in 1916. Could a fourth party really achieve power, starting from scratch? Shirley had warned that a centre party would have 'no roots, no principles, no philosophy and no values'.[6]

The Labour rebels were themselves soul-searching. The party was like a church which had provided their home and nurtured their faith. And the Labour Party had learnt the hard way that it could only beat the Tories if it held together. European and American history was full of warnings about the dangers of splitting the opposition. The divisions on the left had helped to put Hitler into power in the 1930s and enabled the right to dominate post-war western Europe.[7] Yet honest politicians must have their limits to supporting policies they totally disagree with. The Gang of Four had fought as hard as they could from inside the party, and had been defeated by activists who did not represent the majority of Labour voters. They knew that Labour's policies were running it into a dead end which would make it unelectable. And the Labour Party was already looking much less like a church, as everyone became more rootless.

For myself, I thought that a new party had an outside chance of replacing Labour as the main opposition party; but even if it did not replace Labour, it would compel them to adopt its policies in order to regain power. In any case, I could not honestly vote for Labour's insular policies. I wrote in the *New Statesman*:

> The ordinary voter must come to a point when he can no longer regard his party as a church or a nation, which he feels compelled to defend whatever its shortcomings. In the end he must look for individuals who agree with his principles and attitudes; and if they have a real chance of coming to power he has a duty to support them.[8]

As a journalist I felt awkward about being committed to a new party. I felt free to criticise anyone. I had mocked colleagues like Robin Day or Ludovic Kennedy, who had been parliamentary candidates in 1959; and I discounted journalists like John Cole or William Rees-Mogg who liked to sound independent while remaining loyal to their party. But I wanted to share in an adventure with which I totally sympathised and I felt uneasy with the artificial relationship which binds a journalist to a politician, the outsider to the insider, so close yet so distant, like a shopper looking through a plate glass window. A politician, however friendly, is always preoccupied with the overriding need for publicity, the desire for a favourable mention in a newspaper – or a book. What were those politicians really thinking and talking about, behind those guarded indiscretions with journalists? I longed to smash that plate glass window and break into the shop to inspect the real goods on the shelves.

So I hurled my small brick and found my name among a hundred others in an advertisement in the *Guardian*, including thirteen ex-Labour ministers, an array of academics, the actress Janet Suzman, the businessman David Sainsbury, a solitary trade union leader, Frank Chapple, and three other assorted journalists: Marjorie Proops, the agony aunt of the *Daily Mirror*; Polly Toynbee of the *Guardian*; and the broadcaster John Morgan.

I was then a director of the *New Statesman*, whose young journalists were fiercely left wing, and I was writing a column for the *Observer*, which remained staunchly loyal to Labour: Cole, its deputy editor, had written a leader in 1979 firmly supporting his friend James Callaghan, and he tried to deflect me from writing columns criticising Labour. At the Gay Hussar, my favourite restaurant, much frequented by Labour leaders such as Michael Foot and Roy Hattersley, the atmosphere was frosty.

But I was quickly swept up in the preparations for a brand-new 'Social Democratic Party', which included the thirteen ex-Labour ministers and a solitary Tory, Christopher Brocklebank-Fowler, a genial backbencher irreverently nicknamed Dogger-Bank Trawler. It was launched in the Connaught Rooms on 26 March 1981 as a spectacular media event with 500 journalists, banks of TV cameras and global commentators. The event was triumphant: the new party had responded to the profound discontent of voters on both sides of the party lines. Behind the shop window it was exhilarating to be suddenly involved in busy committees, discussing policy, or media or communications, sitting alongside psephologists, economists or businessmen while the four leaders rushed in and out. The new party seemed to be releasing all the energy which had been constrained by the rigidities of the two old ones. But I soon realised how little organisation lay behind the confident slogans and speech-making and how uncertain were the policies. Six weeks after the launch Roy Jenkins summoned a meeting at the Charing Cross Hotel to discuss economic and social policies. There were some formidable economists present, including the Nobel laureate James Meade, and many ex-ministers and officials, who put forward well-argued and deeply felt theories. But after all their experience of government the policies remained surprisingly uncertain: the authority on industrial policy, Sir Leslie Murphy, the former chairman of the National Enterprise Board, explained his attitude as 'suck it and see' – hardly a reassuring slogan for a party of experienced leaders. They had all rejected socialism without finding any alternative ideology. The policies were (as the later historians of the party called them) 'beads without a string. They lacked an underlying theme or big idea.'

There was an obvious problem, as Shirley had foreseen, for a new party growing up without roots; and it was more difficult because the leaders were all convinced internationalists and Europeans. I had seen enough of European politicians and bureaucrats to realise how much they could become disconnected from the lives of their own people, as they rushed between airports and international conferences gabbling away in the dehumanised language of Eurospeak. The language and lifestyle of the Euro-politicians had little appeal to ordinary local voters.

Jenkins seemed to personify the European grandee: he made no secret of his delight in foreign travel, luxury hotels and grand European *confrères*. Brussels, he admitted, might have 'left too much of a patina of high living'.[9] His speeches (and later his memoirs) were full of references to good food, airports, hotels and wine. He compared the new party to an experimental plane, its image to whisky without a label;[10] he compared Shirley Williams to Sarah Bernhardt playing Phèdre.[11] He presented himself as an aristocrat of Labour, the polished product of Balliol, Oxford and wartime intelligence, rather than as the son of a Welsh miner; when he addressed trade unionists I noticed his evident tension. He enjoyed his alternative role of distinguished political biographer and of man of letters, which could exasperate his colleagues: when my literary agent, Michael Sissons, gave us both lunch to finalise an urgent book about the new party, Jenkins was quickly distracted into reminiscing about authors. He sometimes seemed to be caricaturing himself with his donnish mannerisms. Denis Healey, his Balliol contemporary who maintained a down-to-earth image, made fun of Jenkins's casual Edwardian style[12] and thought he was more interested in preferment than policies. Jenkins in turn was irritated by Healey's know-all arrogance and his need to lecture him on 'every subject under the sun'. But the contrasted styles were anyway misleading: Jenkins had more consistent principles than Healey, and extraordinary raw political courage: he was now taking the biggest gamble of his life.

And Jenkins's patrician manner was countered by David Owen, who cultivated a much more combative style, loving to ruffle feathers, particularly of diplomats (when I visited him as foreign secretary he was shouting to his secretaries: 'Take away all that bumf!'). His medical background meant that he was a passionate anti-smoker, so he was cross when a small plane he and Jenkins were travelling in filled up with smoke from Jenkins's Havana cigar. Owen had his own intellectual arrogance, but he gave a sense of toughness and realism to the party which contradicted any image of diplomatic grandees.

The most popular of the four was Shirley Williams, whom I knew much better. She came from a more academic and literary background than Jenkins and had strong American links, but she was a child of the Labour movement and she could relate instantly to ordinary voters with her chummy style, untidy hair and casual clothes. She had become even more immersed in politics after the break-up of her marriage to the philosopher Bernard Williams, and living alone made her empathise with ordinary people all the more: she appeared as a warm antidote to the punishments of the governess Margaret Thatcher. She had a valuable supporter in Bill Rodgers, the junior member of the gang, who had his roots in Liverpool and was never afraid of angry crowds.

The new party maintained a breathtaking momentum and it soon had a chance to test its appeal when Jenkins boldly contested a by-election in Warrington, a working-class area on the Mersey with a safe Labour majority. When I canvassed for him in the bleak terraces, I appreciated his full rashness in trying to woo workers to a new middle-class party. But his enthusiasm, energy and brilliant doorstep skills seemed to cross class barriers, and the SDP won 42 per cent of the vote. Even Healey was having doubts about Labour's future. 'For a moment it looked as if Roy Jenkins was right,' he wrote later, 'and that the new centre grouping had broken the mould of British politics.'[13] And the prospects seemed still better when the Liberal Party voted by a huge majority to join an electoral pact to create the Alliance.

Soon afterwards the SDP held its own first 'rolling conference', with delegates travelling by train to Perth, Bradford and London, making for a much jollier atmosphere than the more formal big-party rallies in Blackpool or Brighton, where the faithful followers were lined up in rows. The rolling conference attracted much publicity, and in the halls the media sometimes outnumbered the delegates, though they drew attention to the lack of roots: was the new party the result of an upsurge of popular feeling, or a travelling circus which depended on television cameras to create its illusions? But in November Shirley Williams displayed all the attractions of the SDP to mass voters, when she contested a by-election in Crosby, the normally safe Tory seat in Liverpool.

As a fellow-campaigner, I found it a heady experience, like a throwback to an earlier era of mass meetings and street crowds: Shirley rushed from one packed hall to the next in a whirl of high-octane enthusiasm and won the seat with a 5,000 majority.

The mould of politics seemed really to be breaking: a sensational Gallup poll in December showed that 51 per cent would vote for the Alliance at a general election. The two big parties were both becoming more extreme and more unpopular: Michael Foot was leading the Labour Party towards the wilderness while Thatcher sacked the moderates in her Cabinet and was still losing support as the economy languished. The polls suggested that the SDP was taking more Tory voters than Labour. In March 1982, a year after its inception, the SDP scored a new triumph when Jenkins won the by-election at Hillhead, the last Tory stronghold in Glasgow, and re-entered Parliament.

It was the last triumph. A week later the political furniture was overturned when Argentina invaded the Falklands, Thatcher went to war and patriotism, as so often in history, cut across the party alignments. Thatcher emerged as a national heroine and gained support from Labour voters as well as returning Tories. The Tories' poll ratings went up from 30 per cent to 45 per cent.[14] More important, the economy was improving with lower inflation, which reassured the Tory doubters. Liberal intellectuals watched with dismay as the old-fashioned war upset their rational expectations and aroused old chauvinist instincts in the British public.

And the war helped to foster divisions within the SDP, particularly between Jenkins and Owen. When parliament debated the Falklands, Owen provided macho gusto and military expertise while Jenkins felt ill at ease among the bellicose speeches. Parliament was already showing up Jenkins's old-fashioned style: he was finding its debating much tougher, as militant MPs like Dennis Skinner mocked his elaborate Oxford rhetoric, while Owen (as Jenkins lamented) was 'master of the quick in-and-out intervention, delivered with a darting tongue'. When the SDP elected its leader in June 1982, Jenkins won, but Owen stood against him and achieved 44 per cent of the votes to Jenkins's 56; and he was (as Jenkins recalled afterwards) 'an unforgiving loser'.[15]

I still felt closely committed to the new party and intrigued to watch it from inside; to my surprise I was elected to the national committee, as one of the eight so-called *prominenti* chosen by members. We were an odd mix, including a fiery young mother with a baby which kept interrupting with screams. The debates were not very decisive and I realised once again how the big decisions are always taken somewhere else – in the policy committee. I began to understand the problems of holding a party together. Egos were constantly competing, yet they were much more seriously dedicated to politics than most journalists as they argued over fine points of policy and listened patiently to the committee bores. I was embarrassed to find my eyelids drooping until I noticed our leader Jenkins dozing off (he was having undiagnosed trouble with his thyroid, which later worsened). At party conferences the politicians vied more openly for publicity: I found myself sitting up on the platform alongside MPs who kept jockeying for the best position for the TV cameras, and I felt uneasy on the other side of the great media divide. After I delivered a careful short speech I was upset to be mocked in the *Telegraph* by the acid columnist Frank Johnson – until I remembered how I had mocked media politicians twenty years before.

The brave new party continued in the doldrums. In March 1983, it expected a victory in the crucial by-election in Darlington; but its candidate was an inexperienced TV sports commentator, whom Jenkins failed to replace – a mistake he would always regret – and the SDP lost. When Thatcher declared a general election for June 1983 she had regained her popularity, boosted by the Falklands victory and by an upturn in the economy, while the two leaders of the Alliance were at odds. Jenkins appeared too lethargic and aloof, while the Liberal leader, David Steel, was visibly impatient.

The election results showed a hollow triumph for the Alliance: they began with a poll rating of 14 per cent and ended with 25.5 per cent of the votes, only just behind Labour's 27.6 per cent; but the two-party system was entrenched. The Liberals had thirty MPs in the new parliament, but the SDP was almost wiped out: only five of the twenty-nine sitting members kept their seats, including Jenkins and Owen but not Williams or Rodgers, while only one new SDP candidate won a seat, the 23-year-old Charles Kennedy, who was later to lead the combined Liberal Democrat Party. The tiny band of Alliance MPs revealed all the unfairness of Britain's electoral system of 'first past the post' but the British public remained apathetic about constitutional reform.

Most of the former SDP MPs saw their careers destroyed. Some would never really recover but many were remarkably resilient. I would admire politicians all the more after watching their courage. As a journalist I had an alternative day job; I could charge up the two-year adventure to a unique education and retreat behind the plate glass.

I suffered a relatively minor setback to my own career. I had rashly embarked on a new Anatomy, but I could not maintain my earlier political detachment and I knew that I would now be under fire from both right and left, as I warned my publishers. When *The Changing Anatomy of Britain* was published in September 1982, nine months before the election, I soon paid the price: I had written the political chapters too hastily, and Labour and Conservative critics seized on my mistakes with glee. Most of the attacks were fair game in the cut and thrust of politics; but I was more seriously hurt by being rubbished in my old paper, the *Observer*, by its new deputy editor, Anthony Howard. It effectively ended my connection with the paper, and I would never again attempt a full Anatomy. But whatever my own misjudgements, the mixed reactions to my book were also signs of the more fundamental sea change in the country: the broad consensus at the centre which was the basis of my first Anatomies was now breaking up.

I remained loyal to the SDP, but after the 1983 election it never recaptured its early enthusiasm and unity, while the Gang of Four began to quarrel like the conspirators in *Julius Caesar*. Jenkins stood down as leader, replaced by Owen, who gave the party a more combative character with his abrasiveness. But Owen lacked the ultimate confidence to work with his co-equals: Shirley Williams, who remained president, felt excluded by 'fierce David', while Jenkins compared him to the Javanese upas tree, which poisoned everything around it. And Owen was soon at odds with Steel and the Liberals, disliking their compassionate rhetoric and weak attitude on defence; he was becoming a 'nuclear fetishist', Jenkins complained,[16] obsessed with the details of weaponry.

At the 1987 general election the Alliance still received 23 per cent of the popular vote, and the Liberals kept seventeen MPs; but the SDP now had just five MPs and only Owen among the Gang of Four remained in Parliament. When Sally and I went to a post-election party at Bill Rodgers's house it seemed more like a wake, and the few Labour guests were determined to see off their SDP rivals. Most members of the SDP now wanted to merge with the Liberals, which they painfully achieved the next year, to form the Liberal Democrat Party. But Owen was implacably hostile and maintained his own independent SDP, with a few loyal supporters including Polly Toynbee. They continued unsuccessfully fighting by-elections until May 1990, when they contested Bootle and received only 155 votes, compared with 418 cast for Screaming Lord Sutch's Monster Raving Loony Party – after which the independent SDP collapsed.

A year later I went to a party in Holland Park to commemorate the tenth anniversary of the SDP, which was already fading into history. 'It couldn't have been wrong', said Jenkins in his speech, 'to have tried to change the whole system, and to have nearly succeeded.' But had it achieved anything at all? Could any newcomer break the two-party system? Most Labour Party leaders maintained that the SDP had succeeded only in splitting the opposition to the Tories. Its chief result, wrote Denis Healey, 'was to delay Labour recovery for nearly ten years and to guarantee Thatcher two more terms in office'. The historians of the SDP, Ivor Crewe and Anthony King (who had advised the party at the beginning), wrote that 'the existence of the SDP did not materially affect the outcome of either election' and its contribution to political ideas was 'almost negligible'.[17] But I still believed that the SDP leaders had to break away from the Labour Party to preserve their integrity and to proclaim sensible policies; that it was a time to stand up and be counted; and that the new party compelled Labour to come to its senses. 'Without the harsh reality of our nearly overhauling them in 1983,' wrote Jenkins, 'they would not have begun to reform themselves on the whole range of issues on which they were willing to lead the country into a dogmatic and sullen isolationism.'[18] And Rodgers claimed with some reason that 'the threat from the Alliance was the main reason for the modernisation of the Labour Party'. Certainly the policies and attitudes of Tony Blair's New Labour government were closer to the SDP than to Old Labour.

It was the accidents of history, rather than the movements of public opinion, which had brought down the SDP. The Falklands War had revived the Conservatives; and a year later the SDP's failure to win Darlington stopped its momentum. If the Alliance had won Darlington it could have overtaken Labour in the 1983 election and changed the face of politics.[19] The new party had not succeeded, as Jenkins had hoped, in 'breaking the mould'. And ironically it was their right-wing enemy Thatcher who did much more to change the whole alignment of British politics.

14

Money kings

The most obvious legacy of Thatcherism was the explosion of interest in money-making which swept through the 1980s, as taxes went down, salaries went up and stock markets boomed. It was a psychological as much as a political phenomenon: the money mania burst out all the more fiercely for having been suppressed, like sex in the 1960s. Having been a taboo subject, it was now talked about everywhere. Doctors and professors compared earnings, home-owners compared property prices, managers boasted about their 'golden hellos', chairmen saw their salaries as their 'score', multi-millionaires competed to be at the top of the 'rich lists'. Academics who had dreaded mentioning money talked about it endlessly at high tables, ancient foundations competed to raise funds, while their halls were rented out to businesspeople for conferences or corporate dinners. Fastidious scholars who became masters of colleges were shocked to find themselves judged by how much money they could extract from brash tycoons.

For many of my generation, who had been brought up not to discuss money and had lived through wartime austerity and post-war controls, it seemed like a throwback to the past as much as a vision of the future. As a schoolboy I had read about Victorian greed and extravagance in *The Forsyte Saga* or *The Way We Live Now* with amused surprise at the materialist values that had been rejected and deemed outdated. Now the High Victorians had returned in modern dress, with still more ambition and preoccupation with money. But they were much less romantic without period costume or horse carriages, and much harder to pin down or observe, for they were more mobile and detached from their country. The Victorian plutocrats were based in their city mansions or country estates surrounded by personal servants; but the new rich preferred to fly between luxury flats and hotels, looked after by anonymous servants, without any real contact with their own compatriots. And the new poor were further out of sight, imported from the developing countries.

After the years of commercial restrictions there were initially only a very few genuine entrepreneurs in Britain, most of them foreign born. The British, under the spell of money, were apt to regard them with uncritical awe, as if they were set apart from normal legal constraints; and the more unscrupulous had huge scope for crookery. The most flamboyant and ruthless of them was Robert Maxwell, who had already been disgraced but bounced back in the 1980s to build up a new empire including the *Daily Mirror*, acquired in 1984, which he used as his base for corrupting the media. I was curious to discover how he fitted in with Britain's anatomy. He was glad to explain: when I lunched with him at the *Mirror* he showed me round his grandiose offices, full of presents from foreign dictators, with a heliport on the roof. With his overbearing presence he was a physical caricature of the power of money. But he seemed to operate outside any British framework: to describe him, Lord Goodman advised me, 'you need someone from the Meteorological Office'. He used the trappings of wealth – the yacht, the helicopter or the Oxford mansion – to seduce or bully any opponents, and recruited supposedly dignified public figures to become his lackeys. Once he was safely dead, mysteriously drowned off his yacht, he soon became a favourite scapegoat; few people cared to recall how deeply he had corrupted Britain's political system.

*

Revisiting the City of London in the mid-1980s I found it barely recognisable as the complacent Square Mile I had first explored in the 1960s, when a few English families and networks controlled much of the country's finance. It had been transformed at a stroke in October 1979, soon after Margaret Thatcher came to power, when her chancellor, Geoffrey Howe, announced that all exchange controls would be lifted. This would permanently change the whole context of British finance – and of British politics. 'International capitalism has defeated democracy,' Tony Benn told his diary; and twenty years later David Kynaston, the leading historian of the City, commented: 'It is not yet clear that he was wrong.'[1] The City was soon booming as never before, with rising share prices, huge bonuses and neoimperial palaces. It was the centre of the new money mania, as it became liberated from high taxation and controls. Young dealers, men and women, could make fortunes in a few years: the gloomy old beer joints were transformed into champagne bars, and high-price restaurants appeared all over the West End to satisfy the appetites of the conspicuous new rich from the City. This was of course to be repeated under New Labour and Tony Blair, twenty years on.

But international capitalism was also routing the old British financial establishment, which paid a price for its new wealth. The inrush of foreign money was overwhelming its protective traditions: its networks of family and school, its reliance on personal trust and informal agreements: 'my word is my bond'. The old City institutions were soon unable to rival foreign giants, with their resources across the world. The old-boy networks showed all their shortcomings as protective closed circles.

The most dramatic debacle was at Lloyd's of London, the group of insurers which dated back to Edward Lloyd's coffee house in the seventeenth century, which was most proud of its reputation for trust and personal responsibility. When I wrote my first Anatomy I was fascinated by the spectacle of the Lloyd's Room, where individual underwriters sat in their narrow boxes collecting signatures from the brokers, to insure ships, aircraft or factories across the world; they seemed to personify the principle of individual responsibility compared to the anonymous bureaucracies of companies. I was impressed by the continuous history of Lloyd's: I identified the underwriters with Antonio, the Merchant of Venice, who insured argosies on the Rialto. I was curious to know how the business felt from the inside, as a participant, not just a spectator.

I was given lunch once a year by a charming old Oxford friend in the insurance business who kept suggesting I should become a member of Lloyd's. Each time I explained I didn't understand it, but I was curious to know more. My friend introduced me to his underwriter friends, who were not altogether convincing: bluff sportsmen, ex-army officers, 'splendid fellows' in red braces. They had no obvious analytical skills, but at least they were identifiable individuals who seemed responsible for their own decisions, and they described persuasively how they balanced their risks between sea, air and earth. I was tempted to join; like Antonio, I could reassure myself:

'My ventures are not in one bottom trusted.' Compared with the perils of book-writing, which depended on one uncertain talent, Lloyd's under-writing seemed far more secure; and it offered the prospect of some income when my own production dried up. So after eight lunches I said yes and became a 'name'. I received a modest cheque, followed by two more.

Then the catastrophes began. Gales and hurricanes raged across Britain, capsizing oil rigs and blowing down forests, causing huge losses for insurers. But I was much more worried that the industrial insurers, the 'non-marine' underwriters, were revealing the full rashness of their earlier risks: they turned out to have insured thousands of companies against asbestos poisoning, and these companies were now making huge claims which would stretch for decades ahead. As the losses piled up, the faults of the whole system began to show themselves, like garbage on the beach at an ebb tide. Underwriters turned out to be insuring each other, so that when they went bad their losses multiplied in an endless spiral. I began to realise the full meaning of 'unlimited liability' as the splendid fellows sent their demands for cash.

The flaw in their individualism was now all too clear: through the fat years, many underwriters had been free to feather their individual nests, without serious regulation or political interference. 'The trouble with Lloyd's is that the Labour Party never attacked them,' explained my friend Ian Hay Davison, who was briefly chief executive of Lloyd's and tried to clean it up. 'Labour weren't interested, because it was just the rich stealing from the rich. So Lloyd's never needed to reform.' As the losses and lawsuits continued, the old confidence and trust were blown away: my charming lunch friend retired out of sight to the country while his agency merged with others three times, into a big, anonymous company where I knew no-one.

It was a painful but instructive lesson in the shortcomings of British capitalism. Many of my journalist colleagues enjoyed some schadenfreude: Bernard Levin in the *Times* relished the spectacle of rich British land-owners and layabouts brought down by their own folly and greed, now desperately trying to dodge their liabilities. In fact Lloyd's had opened its doors to all kinds of middle-class professional people: doctors, lawyers, actors and other suckers; and most of them were scrupulous in paying up. I took some consolation from sharing the ordeal with others who were much worse hit.

In the worst year of losses I went to Lloyd's AGM in its great futuristic cathedral with two friends who had lost heavily: a retired diplomat who had had to sell his house, and a widow who was working out what she called her 'DFG' – distance from the gutter. As we listened from the gallery to the fat-cat chairman rolling out smooth clichés, I was full of admiration for the courage of the members, many of them almost ruined. Some whom I met had become more interesting people, as their lives were turned upside down, tipped out of complacency into real challenges and dangers. But many faced retirement with much less security.

At last, after three years of mounting losses, a new chairman faced up to the need for Lloyd's to restructure itself and found people clever and persistent enough to reduce the infinite to the finite. They came from right outside the old-boy net, led by an ex-monk from Hull and a female mathematician from Switzerland. The new Lloyd's team cajoled and bullied the agents, underwriters and accountants to shore up the tottering institution, producing a settlement which allowed names to leave Lloyd's at manageable expense and which brought in corporate members, who could handle potential new losses. I thankfully withdrew, at a cost which was less than I had dared to expect, while I realised that I could still earn money from writing.

*

Lloyd's was only one of the old British financial institutions which was losing its influence and status as the City became exposed to world competition. The proud merchant banks that had been at the heart of the old estab-lishment were no match for the foreign giants, mostly American, which gradually bought them up, one by one. Barings, the most English of them all, was brought down in 1995 by a single crooked trader in Singapore, and was bought by a Dutch bank. Even S. G. Warburg, the dynamic newcomer which had overtaken its traditional rivals and pioneered new international loans, was taken over by a Swiss bank the same year. 'There was never any sense that old English bankers were competing with us in any way,' said the American banker-writer Michael Lewis in 1996. 'It was much more, how much did we have to pay them to clear out of town and do something else with their lives.'[2] The last humiliation came when in 1997 Barclays Bank sold its investment subsidiary BZW to the Swiss bank Credit Suisse First

Boston. 'I am sorry to announce the demise of the City of London,' wrote the commentator Christopher Fildes.[3]

I could not weep many tears for the old City, which had been the bastion of hereditary privilege and which had excluded so many talented outsiders. But the new City was much harder to understand – and to write about. It had no real autonomy and few dominating personalities. It was part of an international system with a much smaller role for personal trust, controlled not by a governor but by lawyers and regulatory authorities. And much of the dynamic as well as the money came from outside Britain, from bankers and investors in Hong Kong, Tokyo or New York.

*

Money was making the world go round in the 1980s and 1990s, much more obviously than ever before; and entrepreneurs and investors were achieving a greater scope to transform whole communities and even countries, even greater than the nineteenth-century financiers like the Rothschilds or Cecil Rhodes, much less trammelled and limited by governments. Many of them were confident that they could impose their own benign and rational solutions, breaking down national barriers and opening up a new era of prosperity and peace. But how much real power did they have to change the world? I was curious to know more about the new money kings, and I had a chance to investigate further when I embarked on a television series, with my producer friend Mick Csaky, called *The Midas Touch*, which enabled me to interview some of the chief actors at length.

It was New York, rather than London, which was the obvious centre. I found the atmosphere of Manhattan transformed much more dramatically than London by the new money mania, with baroque financial palaces, stretch limos blocking the sidewalks, and a wave of conspicuous consumption as the new rich were determined to flaunt their wealth. Whole magazines and television programmes were dedicated to praising the rich and famous, and the new rich lists revealed the world's wealthiest people. 'There have never been so many rich made so quickly with so much,' said Malcolm Forbes, the exuberant owner of *Forbes* magazine, which published the most prominent list. The new greed took even neo-conservatives by surprise. 'Do you realise the greed that came to the forefront?' Ronald

Reagan's budget director David Stockman, asked his friend William Greider in 1981. 'The hogs were really feeding. The greed level, the level of opportunism, just got out of control.'[4]

And New York bankers and financiers saw their power extending across the world. 'There is no hiding-place,' said the most articulate of them, Walter Wriston, the chairman of Citibank, who proclaimed his mission with sardonic aggression. 'There is no power on earth like the power of the free marketplace,' he said, 'and governments hate it, because they cannot control it.'[5]

It was Forbes who was the most enthusiastic promoter of the global marketplace, and who sailed round the world on his yacht *The Highlander*, with its helicopter proclaiming 'Forbes: The Capitalist's Tool'. I had happened to meet him when I was visiting Shanghai in 1988 and gatecrashed a party on the yacht. Forbes was a genial host, wearing a baseball cap and grinning like the Big Bad Wolf. He had been cruising through east Asia with rather bored-looking guests who included Harry Oppenheimer's daughter, Margaret Thatcher's son and the would-be king of Bulgaria, spreading the faith of American capitalism. Forbes explained how he had first enlightened the Chinese by leading a motorbike tour through China five years before and by introducing them to ballooning. In Shanghai he was using *The Highlander* to show off to his Chinese guests, who included the deputy minister of culture.

A year later I interviewed Forbes back in his office building in Manhattan, which housed his museum filled with toy soldiers, Fabergé eggs and rows of gowns from his honorary degrees. I asked him his view of the power of money, and he compared himself to the Medicis, who likewise flaunted their wealth and converted it into power: 'Wealth simply represents power, and power is consequential to anybody that's around it.' He saw nothing wrong in displaying his wealth to the poorest people in the world: 'If you aren't guilty for having your money, and are grateful, why should you not enjoy it?' He explained that a rich man is compelled by his own bodily limitations to seek a wider purpose than mere money-making: 'His stomach doesn't contain more than somebody with less money.' Yet he sounded frustrated by his lack of recognition and real political power; and the frustration continued in the family: after he died, his son Steve tried to become president of the

United States: he spent $40 million on his campaign, then a record, and failed ignominiously.

Many of the new global billionaires craved political power, but the most dramatic contender was the financier Sir James Goldsmith, who became a semi-mythical figure on both sides of the Atlantic. I had first met him in a plush London casino, an appropriate setting for a compulsive gambler. He looked so filmic, with his powerful eyes and his mellifluous voice, that I half-expected him to say: 'In a few minutes I will have to blow up the world, Mr Bond.' His father had once said that he would either rule the world or go to jail, and by the late 1980s he seemed on his way to the first. Like other global operators he seemed thoroughly placeless, with no settled home: I was reminded of Citizen Kane, who had been taken away as a child from his beloved Rosebud. Goldsmith had been brought up in both Britain and France, often staying in hotels which his father owned. 'Dynamism is usually the result of disequilibrium,' he told me. 'I'm a Jew to Catholics, a Catholic to Jews, an Englishman to the French and a Frenchman to the English.' But his detachment gave him a shrewd understanding of the mobility of money, and by the mid-1980s he had become a billionaire through a succession of spectacular raids on established corporations, selling off parts of them and then moving on to discover new prey. He loved to depict himself as a predator, a shark in the ocean of money, preying on the bigger fish to protect the small minnows: 'If you eliminate predators you will have a dead industry.' He was the enemy of all bureaucracies, whether General Motors, the Vatican or the Kremlin; and he saw himself as liberating industry from the dead hand of 'corpocracy'.

When I interviewed him at length for the series in his baroque mansion in Paris, he looked like a pasha, surrounded by ornate furniture and libidinous paintings. He eloquently explained the benefits that entrepreneurs brought to the world, by moving their billions to where they were most productive and compelling ideological governments to come to terms with reality. He was modest about his own scope: 'An individual fortune today will never be as powerful as it was in the nineteenth century, nor should it be. It will always be a marginal person thing compared to the major power of the state.' But he agreed that the unregulated power of money could cause revolutions more serious than those in the nineteenth century. 'There are a lot of destructive forces around. We will have to learn to live with them . . . How do you regulate the world? I don't know.'

Goldsmith longed to achieve serious political influence, but never succeeded. He had hoped to become a press baron, first through the French magazine *L'Express* and his own news magazine *Now!* and then making an unsuccessful bid for the *Observer*. Then he campaigned to protect the environment, influenced by his brother Teddy; he established a huge game reserve in Mexico, where he built his own Xanadu palace and planned a university dedicated to ecology, which never materialised. Eventually he went directly into British politics in the 1997 election by setting up his own Referendum Party, which wanted to take Britain out of the European Union and promised a referendum on this issue. It gained no MPs and only succeeded in damaging the Conservative vote. In the meantime he was secretly suffering from cancer and he died soon after the election – leaving behind a huge fortune for his eight children but no serious political legacy. One of his sons, Zac, was to become a leading ecologist, following his uncle.

I found a much more interesting guide to the money world in George Soros, the Hungarian master-speculator, who shared my interest in Africa and the developing world. I had first met him before he became famous, when he was interested in my book *The Money Lenders*, published back in 1981, which dealt with the problems of debts in developing countries. He sounded like a sparkling academic, with his bright eyes, his love for ideas and a quiet Austro-Hungarian courtesy. He seemed quietly detached from the marketplace: one afternoon in London, when Wall Street had just taken a dive, he took me on a long walk through Hyde Park discussing Latin American politics without any apparent concern for the falling share prices. Later I had kitchen suppers with him in his Park Avenue flat, with his young wife Susan, who was an expert on William Morris; when he began talking about world finance she soon stopped it: 'Are you going to talk shop all night?' In London he appeared bored by social climbing or grand occasions: he gave parties to which he would invite important people without introducing them, and he would move from one group to another, listening more than talking (Europeans had an advantage over Americans, he told me, because they knew how to listen). I did not realise he was seriously rich until I was dining out with him and a mutual friend, Ronald Dworkin. When the bill came Soros said: 'I see the *New York Times* says I have the second-biggest income in America. I think I should pay.'

He had built up his fortune by speculating across the global markets, based on careful analysis but also on gambles: like Goldsmith he needed danger, and he enjoyed dangerous sports like helicopter skiing. But he was also a moralist, unlike Goldsmith, whom he saw as a kind of Mephistopheles; and he had a kind of Messiah complex, as he admitted. He soon became more interested in spending money than making it, and set up foundations across the world dedicated to the 'Open Society' – a concept he took from his first mentor, Karl Popper. He was scathing about conventional aid: 'The last remnant of the command economy,' he complained, 'because it is designed to satisfy the needs of the donors, not the needs of the recipients.'[6] He thought that philanthropy went against the grain 'because our civilisation is built on the pursuit of self-interest' and wanted to be clear about his own self-interest: he had been motivated by the dangers and challenges of his childhood, when he hid from the Nazi occupation in Hungary, and then escaped from the communists to England at the age of seventeen. He wanted to promote the Open Society, as he put it, to 'make the world safe for Jews'. He had no difficulty in equating the world's problems with his own: 'My whole life has been one long effort to integrate the various facets of my existence.'[7]

Soros had made his first disbursements to black students in South Africa, which he had visited in 1980, but he was frustrated by the constraints of apartheid and retreated – to his later regret.[8] Later he turned to eastern Europe, and his philanthropy increased massively after 1989 when the communist governments collapsed. He was convinced that Russia needed help to establish democratic institutions that would stabilise it: he poured money into his foundations and urged Western governments to follow his example with much larger resources: in spring 1989 he proposed a new 'Marshall plan' to be financed by the Europeans.[9] He was disappointed by the Western leaders who did nothing, particularly by Margaret Thatcher, whose influence could have been decisive but who was hostile to all foreign aid. And his forebodings were justified: Russia was overwhelmed by ruthless capitalists and its fragile democracy began to disintegrate under corrupt leaders. (When I asked Soros about Boris Yeltsin he replied: 'I can think of several nouns for him in Hungarian but only one in English: "bounder".')

But Soros was also caught up in his own contradictions: the global marketplace which had enabled him to make his billions was also making it harder for any government to commit itself to any such long-term intervention. And within Russia he could not resist the temptation of investing in the new financial markets which were serving to destabilise the democracy that his foundations were trying to stabilise. They were, as he said, like the robber-barons of nineteenth-century America.

Soros soon became more interested in fame. He wanted publicity to give him access to top politicians; but he became a celebrity because of his money, not his philanthropy.[10] He became much more famous in Britain when he made a billion dollars by gambling on the devaluation of the pound in 1992 following Black Wednesday, when sterling left the ERM and which sounded the death knell for John Major's government. His profit cost every Briton £12 but he was unrepentant: 'Every citizen of Great Britain should have contributed £12 to the transformation of Eastern Europe. I'm happy to have delivered that aid.' I saw him less as he spent more time in New York, embraced by rich society and charity galas, and I felt his speculations were cutting across his philanthropy. Once he connived with Goldsmith and Jacob Rothschild to buy gold shares, and quickly pushed up the price. Wasn't it dangerous, I asked him, to play up to the suspicions of eastern Europeans about capitalist plots? 'It may be,' he replied with typical candour, 'but I couldn't resist it.' He was well aware that he was a prime target for anti-Semitic conspiracy theories. 'If there was ever a man who would fit the stereotype of the Judo-plutocratic Bolshevik Zionist world conspirator, it is me.'[11]

I remained fascinated by Soros, both as an electric individual and as the personification of global money power, with all its opportunities and dangers. But he never really resolved the contradictions. He saw clearly that global capitalism was making countries less stable, but his own shrewd speculations served to destabilise them further. He was always questioning his role and power. 'What does that power consist of?' he asked himself in 1995. 'Can I move markets? Perhaps, but only if I guess correctly the direction in which markets want to move. Can I influence governments? I am beginning to be able to, but only because of the reputation I have built up.'[12] But his reputation with governments was limited by his public image as a speculator who could make blunders as well as quick killings, and he never persuaded them to back democratic institutions as he had hoped. He remained a brilliant exponent of the dangers of uncontrolled global money.

*

After my talks with the money men I was much more sceptical about the theory that the globalisation of finance would in itself bring peace and prosperity to the developing world by drawing it into a benign capitalist system based on America, as optimistic prophets like Francis Fukuyama assumed.[13] I had seen in Latin America and Africa how short-term profit-making could be devastating for developing nations which were trying to build up their own fragile financial systems, only to be undermined by sudden outflows of capital. When I revisited Moscow after the collapse of the communist regime I saw how rapidly the new Russian robber-barons had established their power base and exploited the international banks. Back in England I asked a partner at Salomons how they could make such big profits from Russia. He replied: 'Oh, the usual way – plunder and pillage.' Soros was proved right in his warnings that the global system was inherently unstable. And by the end of the millennium the unleashing of private greed was causing chaos in the wilder parts of Africa or Asia, and closer to home in the Balkans, as arms dealers and mercenary armies began translating money into guns and massacres, and the humiliations of poverty began provoking massive reactions from nationalist and religious extremists, who saw American capitalism as threatening their dignity and the bankers' skyscrapers in Manhattan as the headquarters of evil.

Some Britons liked to compare the new world system based on America to the *Pax Britannica* of the nineteenth century; but, as the Oxford historian Niall Ferguson reminded them, the British capitalists were not able to prevent the eventual catastrophe of the First World War, which destroyed the whole system.[14] A century later, the power of money still needed countervailing political powers to control its corruption and exploitation, supported by armies when necessary. The future peace of the world depended on courageous and visionary political leaders rather than shrewd investors and speculators.

The more I saw of the global entrepreneurs and bankers, discussing developing countries in terms of financial statistics, growth rates and bottom lines, the more I wanted to see the problems through the eyes of the people at the receiving end who were supposed to benefit from them, particularly Africans, who were the most vulnerable to uncontrolled greed on the edge of the economic system. And I was all the more drawn to the problems of the people I knew best, the black South Africans, who were at last seeing a prospect of freedom.

15

Revolutionaries and capitalists

I had been out of touch with South Africa during most of the 1970s, distracted by my travels round the world pursuing oil companies and arms deals. I depended on Nadine Gordimer and other friends in Johannesburg for news of developments, and they reported few signs of effective black opposition to apartheid. But in June 1976, there was a sudden explosion: the Black Consciousness movement, which had been growing up out of sight of the whites, suddenly erupted into a lethal showdown in a setting where few people expected it: in the schools of Soweto. Schoolchildren demonstrated against being taught in Afrikaans and were met with murderous reprisals from the police. The local revolt spread into a national uprising. 'You knew twenty years ago that it would happen and would go on happening,' wrote Nadine, 'getting more terrible and being ignored more callously and insanely every time.' But this time, she explained, 'for the first time, I have been afraid'.

The next year brought a further horror when in September 1977 Steve Biko, the leader of Black Consciousness, which had encouraged the revolt, died under brutal interrogation. 'From the point of view of our downhill race to a fascist state,' wrote Nadine, 'this was the biggest single week of progress ever.' The atrocity appeared for a time to galvanise Western governments into more serious confrontation against apartheid from several countries, including the United States, but this increased interest proved short lived. When I visited Washington a month later I doubted the good faith of President Carter's administration: 'Are they really being serious?' I asked in a column.[1] In London David Owen, then foreign secretary, told me that sanctions should be kept as a loaded gun but should not be used, while he complained about his deeply conservative diplomats and the impossibility of controlling arms sales to Pretoria. I saw Harry Oppenheimer, the chairman of Anglo American, in his London office; he had by now come round to approving of Western pressure, but he was pessimistic about influencing the Afrikaner government, whose members were feeling still less secure: 'You mustn't expect them to commit political suicide.'

I was determined to revisit South Africa after eight years' absence, but it was now harder for a journalist to get in. In November 1978 I got a commission from a glossy German magazine to write a travel article on Namibia, which sounded innocuous and which enabled me to stop in Johannesburg on the way, remaining incognito, without needing a visa. The immigration official glanced at my passport, which said 'Writer'. 'What do you write?' 'Books, mainly.' He looked bored and let me through.

I could only stop over for three days, staying with Nadine, who was now much more isolated as one of the few white supporters of the banned African National Congress. The cultural life of Johannesburg was shrinking still further: the big Colosseum cinema had been converted into a rifle range. Nadine still kept in touch with black writers, but they were more suspicious of white contacts, as both sides became more polarised. I found it still harder to make any real contact with serious black leaders or journalists. *Drum* was now politically muzzled by censorship and had retreated to entertainment and sport. I talked to brave reporters at a small black Christian newspaper, the *Voice*, where the noisy presses prevented eavesdropping, but they could not publish anything about politics or the police. I drove to Soweto to visit Nthato Motlana, the fast-talking doctor whom I had known twenty years earlier as Harrison Motlana, an ANC activist and friend of Nelson Mandela. In his small surgery he described how the police had penetrated all the schools and churches with their informers. Motlana was still an unashamed capitalist, criticised by left-wing militants, but he despaired of those Western governments who refused to impose sanctions. 'Why are you worrying about losing your own jobs and trade? Why do you hide your stick behind your back when you deal with South Africa?'

Back in London, I felt that there were new hopes when the prime minister, John Vorster, resigned in the wake of corruption scandals. But the hopes did not last. 'Jericho just never falls; it's a myth,' Nadine wrote soon afterwards. And it was soon clear that his successor, P. W. Botha, would be much tougher: he easily co-opted big-business leaders to support his increasingly militarised state. And by 1980 the political mood in London and Washington was much less promising, as both Margaret Thatcher and Ronald Reagan showed themselves more sympathetic to apartheid governments and refused to have contacts with the communist-influenced ANC.

It was South Africa which showed up, for me, the true crudity of Thatcherism: the lack of compassion, the simplifications of the Cold War, the belief that free enterprise in itself would bring freedom and democracy. Thatcher had always had an instinctive sympathy with white South Africans, encouraged by her husband Dennis, who had business friends in Durban. She was impatient and had been bored by the protests of Africans across the continent. But during the 1980s she could not evade the mounting confrontation in South Africa, which showed up all her combativeness and stubbornness in caricature.

*

In the early 1980s black South Africans were showing a new wave of resistance from the grass roots, with one of those spontaneous surges of rebelliousness which journalists or historians find it hard to trace. They were showing a determination and fearlessness which few whites had predicted, demanding Mandela's release and beginning a campaign of sustained violence which the police could not suppress.

Representatives of all the non-white peoples came together in the United Democratic Front (UDF), comprising church leaders and trades unionists as well as politicians, which provided a cover for the banned ANC. By 1985 many townships had become no-go areas for the police. In March, the twenty-fifth anniversary of Sharpeville, the police killed nineteen protesters at Uitenhage, which set off demonstrations and sabotage. The country seemed to be moving ineluctably towards civil war. And at the beginning of the year Oliver Tambo, the president of the ANC, had re-emerged into the headlines from his exile in Zambia, by making a bold New Year message: 'Make South Africa ungovernable.'

I had been fascinated by Tambo, whose name was always associated with Mandela, ever since I had first met the two of them in the 1950s in their law office in Johannesburg. He was a gentle, self-effacing man, a protégé of Father Trevor Huddleston who sounded more like a priest – which he had wanted to be – than a revolutionary politician. Before Mandela went to jail Tambo had escaped, ending up in London, instructed by the ANC to build up the resistance abroad. He had pleaded for support from the British and US governments, but in vain, and reluctantly had to accept weapons and money from Moscow. I had last seen him in 1970, when I had stopped in the Zambian capital, Lusaka, the headquarters of the ANC in exile, where he was the commander of guerrilla fighters making sporadic and dangerous forays into South Africa. He was surrounded by militants and Marxists, but he still retained his detachment from communism and his Christian commitment. He took eucharist whenever he could, and saw his troops not as guerrillas but as Christian soldiers. His ordeals in exile were in many ways more testing than Mandela's in prison. But he retained his faith in the victory of right against wrong; and he remained puzzled that the British, who had so heroically stood up to Hitler, were so ambiguous towards the apartheid governments.

Tambo was in a lonely predicament during the 1970s, trying to confront the massive forces of apartheid from this outpost, with few Western friends and with the ANC effectively suppressed inside South Africa. The revolt of Steve Biko and Black Consciousness was in many ways embarrassing to the ANC, since it had little to do with the ANC and went against its principles of multiracialism. Tambo shrewdly realised that he must come to terms with the revolutionary mood, remembering how he had shared their views when he was a young militant; he had welcomed the thousands of refugees that had come up to Zambia and converted many of them to the ANC's policies. But the ANC had remained ineffective in South Africa until the new surge of rebellion in the early 1980s. Now in 1985 Tambo was once more in the forefront, as the champion of a new defiant campaign against apartheid.

I was writing a fortnightly newsletter at the time, feeling sadly out of touch with black South Africa. In July 1985 I was surprised to read newspaper reports that Tambo was calling for much more violent tactics, including assassinating white leaders in South Africa, so I tried to ring him at ANC headquarters. It was a frustrating task since they had only two erratic telephones: 'How can they expect to run a country', complained my assistant, 'if they can't even organise their telephones?' But suddenly Tambo himself rang back and began talking candidly and openly in his precise and

223

measured style, as if the fifteen years since we had last talked were obliterated. He assured me that the reports about assassinations were a total fabrication, and he sounded full of optimism about the ANC's prospects: apartheid was breaking down in many townships. More surprisingly, he had been encouraged by talking to businessmen in America who were sympathetic to the ANC and were bringing pressure on Pretoria.

I interpreted this as heralding a new prospect: that the ANC could break out of its isolation and its dependence on Moscow to make bridges with Western capitalists. David Astor, my old editor, now in retirement, quickly took up the idea: why should Tambo not begin talks with British companies, who were much bigger investors in South Africa than the Americans? With his usual discreet methods David set up a small committee, including Mary Benson and me, to arrange for Tambo to visit London to meet British businessmen and Conservative leaders, in an attempt to break through Thatcher's veto.

In the meantime, on 20 July 1985 President Botha declared an emergency, giving the police much more drastic powers. I was determined to witness the new crisis for myself, and precipitately flew out to Johannesburg in August, staying at the Carlton Hotel in the middle of town. Police and soldiers were everywhere. 'It's not a police state – it's a military state,' said the writer Mothobi Mutloatse. 'I watched the army arresting 800 children in Soweto.' But my old *Drum* friends soon convinced me that the young black generation had a militancy which could not be suppressed. 'Sharpeville was a revolt by the parents,' said Peter Magubane, the veteran photographer. 'Soweto was the children. Now it's both.' 'My nine-year-old daughter attacks me for being too polite to the white man,' said the columnist Obed Musi. 'The parents can't control the children as they could in '76', said the editor of *Drum*, Stanley Motjuwadi. The emergency was uniting the black communities more effectively against the police. 'There's no room for informers in Soweto today,' said one old *Drum* colleague; 'there are safe houses for freedom fighters even in small Afrikaner towns.' The new militancy among blacks was based not on despair but on the expectation of winning, which I had not found before: most of them now expected to be holding, or sharing, political power within ten years. Middle-class blacks were worried about being seen as Uncle Toms, identified with the losing side. Even whites shared the expectation of change: a poll had just shown that 63 per cent thought that apartheid would not exist in ten years' time.

And international capitalists were at last beginning to change sides. In August Chase Manhattan Bank in New York, which had long been a loyal lender to apartheid regimes, abruptly decided to stop rolling over its loans. This was not due to any sudden fit of morality, I ascertained later in New York, but to a hard-headed calculation: the anti-apartheid campaigners were depriving Chase of valuable business in Manhattan, which was much more important than profits from South Africa. But it was all the more deadly coming from the marketplace, inducing a rapid run on the South African rand and a drop in its credit rating.

It was fascinating to watch the sudden confusion of businessmen as they hedged their bets and tried to distance themselves from apartheid. They hoped that Botha would promise Mandela's release; but he made a speech which offered no serious concessions. On the next day, 27 August 1985, Black Tuesday, I went to the Johannesburg stock exchange and watched the hysterical dealing and yelling as the rand collapsed and investors bought gold shares to protect themselves. At the end of the day the government announced the suspension of all dealing for four days and a freeze on repayments of debt for four months; while the head of the South African Reserve Bank, Gerhard de Kock, toured America and Europe trying desperately to negotiate an emergency loan. Politics was now in full collision with business, and most stockbrokers reckoned that the first step to renewing confidence would have to be Mandela's release. Two days after Black Tuesday the Association of Chambers of Commerce called on the government to negotiate with black leaders 'even if some of them are currently in detention'.

I made a quick tour of the South African tycoons who were now rapidly trying to build bridges with the black leaders they had for so long ignored. Mike Rosholt, the chairman of the mining group Barlow Rand, insisted to me that businessmen must now play a bolder role: 'When you think about it, compromises are part of our daily activity, every time we make a deal. We're more used to them than politicians.' When I lunched with Harry Oppenheimer, now retired as chairman of Anglo American but still influential; he was at last exasperated by Botha's intransigence. He asked me what I knew about ANC leaders and suddenly said: 'Do you know, I would rather like to meet Oliver Tambo.' I suggested that since they were both often in London, it would not be hard to arrange.

Two weeks later Tambo did have a major breakthrough, when a group of influential businessmen flew up from Johannesburg on 13 September to see him in Lusaka, including Gavin Relly, successor to Oppenheimer (who felt 'twitchy', he told me, about the expedition). 'It was one of the nicest days I've ever spent,' Relly said after six hours of talks. 'It was a marvellous meeting', said Tambo. Both sides returned with some euphoria, but it was short lived: just before Christmas a bomb in a shopping-centre near Durban killed five white shoppers, and the businessmen quickly backtracked from their enthusiasm for the ANC. Tambo denied that the bomb was linked to the ANC, and was puzzled by the turnabout. 'It was because of the violence', he told me, 'that they came to see me.'[2]

Back in London, David Astor's little group planned for Tambo to meet businessmen and politicians in October 1985. We arranged a tea party at the House of Lords, a speech at Chatham House, a lunch at the *Economist*; and I invited a group of chairmen to our house in Ladbroke Grove, making the most of my contacts as an Anatomist, for private talks with Tambo. It was a tense gathering, including conservative chairmen such as Sir Alistair Frame of Rio Tinto Zinc as well as more flexible directors from BP and ICI, and it was joined by Michael Young, an adviser to the most die-hard company of all, Gold Fields, who surprisingly invited himself. They were clearly apprehensive of meeting the leader of a terrorist, part-Marxist, movement. But I had invited two friends whom I knew to be more sympathetic to black aspirations, David Sainsbury and Sir James Spooner, chairman of Morgan Crucible, to try to break the ice. Tambo, looking like the would-be priest that he was, brought with him his aide Thabo Mbeki, who did most of the talking. I had last seen him as a student in South Africa in 1962; eventually he would succeed Mandela. The businessmen were understandably worried by the ANC's policies of nationalisation, but Mbeki skilfully defused some of the suspicions in his best Anglophile style. They departed without being convinced while wanting further contacts. But the rest of Tambo's encounters in London were more productive and by the end of the week even the *Times* had its main story: 'Talk to Tambo'.

In South Africa the whites were once again in a volatile state of mind, longing for peaceful settlement but terrified of chaos. By 1986 their mood had changed back to intransigence, and in June Botha declared a much more stringent emergency, enabling police offers to arrest anyone they suspected of endangering public safety. I flew back to Johannesburg soon after. The white suburbs had an eerie normality, even boredom. The city was celebrating its centenary, proclaiming its spectacular growth from a gold-mining camp with hardly any reference to the blacks who had dug out the gold. The lack of news in the heavily censored papers encouraged euphoria rather than fear and the government had created a siege economy with strict financial controls, which had produced a local mini-boom. I found it impossible to get into Soweto, which was encircled by roadblocks: when I turned my car round I was pursued by police who questioned me thoroughly about why I was driving in the area. The only public gathering that the police dared not ban was the Sunday service in the Cathedral, addressed by Archbishop Desmond Tutu, who delivered a passionate and fearless sermon: 'No state of emergency', he said, 'has ever produced lasting peace.' I spotted only two businessmen – both of them Jewish – who dared to appear alongside the mainly black congregation. When I had dinner with Tutu the next evening, together with the Archbishop of Canterbury's envoy Terry Waite, he seemed almost totally isolated.

The police had detained more than 4,000 blacks, including most of the key activists, which revealed the effectiveness of their intelligence. But from the Carlton Hotel I was still able to make some contacts with the resistance: indeed a few leaders were actually holed up in the same hotel, rightly reckoning that the police would not search in the most obvious and respectable place. I could still slink into the *Drum* office where Stanley Motjuwadi was contemptuous of Botha's clampdown: 'The more people he detains, the greater the armies of his enemies . . . We're still scared of shooting, but the children don't care a hoot.' 'The emergency was a deadly mistake,' said Percy Qoboza, the editor of *City Press*; 'the leadership is already regrouping and the jungle telegrams are still working.'

The remaining black leaders were increasingly anti-capitalist. 'The alliance between big business and the apartheid regime has gone on too long', said Cyril Ramaphosa, the miners' leader, who had escaped from the

227

country, 'and is soaked with the blood of workers who have reaped nothing from the free-enterprise system.' 'Botha retains his power because of big business,' said Popo Molefe, the former secretary of the United Democratic Front, who was now on trial for treason. But the local businessmen were now once again taking fright, and rallying behind Botha's state of emergency: 'Anglo-Saxon businessmen are coming closer to Afrikaners,' said the Afrikaner editor Harald Pakendorf.

I was depressed by my visit, which seemed to show how easily an authoritarian regime could corral anxious tycoons. But in London big businessmen were now more sympathetic to Tambo, despite Margaret Thatcher's boycott. Following on from the earlier tea party, I had invited leading corporate chairmen to a lunch at the Connaught Rooms – generously funded by David Astor – to meet him and members of the ANC executive. To my surprise they nearly all came: they included the chairmen of the two biggest banks in South Africa, Sir Timothy Bevan of Barclays and Lord Barber of Standard Bank; Evelyn de Rothschild, the chairman of Rothschild's; representatives from Shell, Courtaulds, BP and Gold Fields; and George Soros. They were joined by two courageous business leaders from South Africa, Tony Bloom of the Premier Group and Chris Ball of Barclays, though the biggest company, Anglo American, was noticeably absent. Tambo welcomed the businessmen warmly and explained how important they were to his country's future, and they agreed to the joint statement which I had drafted, saying that they should all 'contribute what they can to help ensure that South Africa becomes a democratic and peaceful country'.[3]

For the next three years I could not get back to South Africa: during my visit I had written a long article for the *Observer* and soon afterwards I received a bleak letter from the government, informing me that my exemption from a visa had been withdrawn – in other words, I was banned. But the more South Africa was deadlocked, the more important London and Washington became.

I was drawn more closely into the South African vortex by my growing friendship with Tambo. Sally and I saw him frequently in his house in Muswell Hill – which the South African philanthropist Clara Urquhart had bought for him – filled with African curios and visiting revolutionaries, where his formidable wife Adelaide, known as 'the Duchess', brought up her three children. Oliver was constantly flying between London, Lusaka and other capitals, in failing health and often exhausted, searching for new openings and support. He was in a lonely situation, with little help from the small ANC office in Pentonville, which was strikingly inefficient – perhaps deliberately, for its chief representative, Solly Smith, was later revealed as an agent of the Pretoria regime. Tambo was still shunned by Thatcher's government as the leader of a dangerous communist terrorist organisation, while he had his own problems with his communist allies. He needed help from Moscow, but found that they did not try to intervene with ANC policy: in fact they thought the ANC should give less emphasis to nationalisation. And he was not worried about the South African communists taking over: 'Our people will decide,' he told me in New York in January 1987, 'and they're not very interested in a socialist state.' And the South African Communist Party was beginning to modify its revolutionary policies. I had watched its members celebrate the party's sixty-fifth anniversary with a rally at the Conway Hall in London, addressed by their chairman, Joe Slovo, alongside old British party members: the style and rhetoric was like an old-fashioned Stalinist rally, but Slovo was strikingly realistic, insisting that there would still be a mixed economy under majority rule and warning that the ANC could not 'pole-vault into socialism and communism the day after the overthrow of white rule'. When he rang me the next day I asked him if his speech represented new thinking by the Communists. 'Well, it represents thinking. We've been catapulted into a new situation. We've been used to being an agitational opposition, not an alternative power.'[4]

In London there were also some hopeful signs of new openings to the Afrikaners. I had several visits from Frederik van Zyl Slabbert, who had resigned in February 1986 as leader of the opposition party, the Progressive Federal Party, in order to campaign for negotiating with the ANC. The next year he achieved an important breakthrough, when fifty leading Afrikaner intellectuals met with ANC leaders in Dakar.[5] Thabo Mbeki described to me afterwards the emotional scenes when the Afrikaners sang the ANC anthem with tears in their eyes, and he was all the more exasperated by Thatcher's continued intransigence.

Many big companies were now beginning to reinsure themselves against the possibility that the ANC might come into power before long. The mysterious Michael Young was soon brokering a succession of secret talks in a country house owned by Gold Fields, where Thabo and other ANC exiles discussed possible future negotiations with Afrikaner academics and businessmen who had their own back channel with South African intelligence. It was a fascinating insight into how a big company could play it both ways. In public Gold Fields maintained an unwavering hostility to the ANC: it published a centenary history written by the right-wing polemicist Paul Johnson, fulminating against the black terrorists. But in private it was reinsuring itself by making links with a likely black government.

Most British multinationals were now hedging their bets on South Africa, and Frene Ginwala, an ANC representative in London who later became speaker in the South African parliament, often held secret talks with them. Shell felt a special need for contact for it had been singled out for boycott by the ANC, which had lost it some custom from motorists – particularly in the Netherlands, where young campaigners had set fire to some filling-stations. I was not very popular with Shell since writing *The Seven Sisters*, but I had got to know Sir Peter Holmes, the chairman, who was an unusual tycoon: an intrepid mountaineer and amateur historian with a special interest in Africa, he had run Shell in Nigeria when it had been nationalised and he was determined to avoid a repeat in South Africa. He asked me to arrange a discreet meeting with the ANC, and in January 1987, over two long dinners at Shell-Mex House, Ginwala presented the details of Shell's connivance with the apartheid government, including allowing military installations at its refineries. Holmes promised to investigate the facts, and the dialogue continued.

There was one area in which British business could most obviously be helpful: providing education and training for future African managers and leaders. While many people talked about the ANC coming to power within ten years, few Africans in South Africa had had any experience of government or administration under apartheid, and most of the exiles had seen more of communist than capitalist countries. 'Supposing President Botha suddenly told Mandela and Tambo: "I've had enough, you take over,"' said my friend Nat Masemola. 'We wouldn't know what to do with it: we've got no-one who knows how to run government departments, banks or factories.' David Astor was struck by the problem when he received a message from Winnie Mandela early in 1986 asking for help in training fifty young ANC recruits in administration in Britain, a need which Tambo soon confirmed. David took up the idea and provided some funds to attract others – while the Thatcher government would not consider it. Just at that time I had been invited to New York to advise the Rockefeller Brothers Fund, which was much more adventurous than most foundations (much influenced by Peggy Dulany, David Rockefeller's daughter): when I told them about the project they seized on it and agreed to help fund it. A few weeks later, back in London, I mentioned it to Peter Holmes, who believed strongly in the need for education and training everywhere, and he also offered funds. The ANC recruits were now ironically receiving key support from legendary capitalist strongholds without realising it – the Rockefellers, the Astors and Shell.

David Astor, who was always quick to convert ideas into execution, set up a discreet outfit with a deliberately unmemorable name, the South African Advanced Education Project, and found an ideal director, Anne Yates, an ex-South African educationalist (who had arranged twenty years earlier for Mbeki to study at Sussex University). Tambo put his weight behind the project, and Yates was rapidly flooded with applicants, sponsored by the ANC, for short training courses in everything from banking to viticulture. Many of them were exiles who had been trained in eastern Europe or Cuba, and with patient ingenuity Yates found British companies and institutions who could show them how capitalist businesses and Western governments worked from the inside. In 1987, as the South African scene worsened again, it was still difficult to imagine them being able to make proper use of their new experience in government, and plans were made to 'park' them in jobs while they waited; few of them thought they would be back in South Africa, legalised, in three years.

From my odd vantage point, I felt a still greater need to build bridges with the ANC, for the transition that was bound to come. It was the law which offered the first alternative to war and the safeguard for a future peaceful shift of power, and I realised how deeply Tambo was imbued with the law since I had first known him as Nelson Mandela's partner in the 1950s. When in 1987 the British foreign secretary, Geoffrey Howe, at last agreed to see

Tambo he told him that whatever their disagreements they could still under-stand each other as two lawyers. When Tambo told me this, it occurred to me that it might be possible to persuade South African judges – who were all white – to meet ANC lawyers in Britain to find common ground; and in May 1987 I invited Tambo and two of his colleagues, Mac Maharaj and Jacob Zuma (who would later become the ANC's deputy president), to a lunch party at our house. It included Ronald Dworkin, the American lawyer-philosopher, David Astor and Franklin Thomas, the president of the Ford Foundation, which was then deeply involved in South Africa. I put forward the idea, which the ANC members promptly supported. Franklin promised to finance it and Ronald undertook to organise it – with a total commitment which left me breathless with admiration.

Over the following months Ronald and his wife Betsy patiently persuaded cautious South African judges to take the risk of meeting lawyers from a banned organisation. Eventually, after much intimidation and many setbacks, the judges arrived at Nuneham Park outside Oxford in June 1989 to meet the ANC lawyers, led by Tambo. The lawyers included Ismail Mohammed, Albie Sachs and the remarkable Dikgang Moseneke, who had taught himself law on Robben Island and become the first black barrister in Pretoria. Ronald skilfully mediated and established principles of rule under the law which they could all accept; and afterwards an extraordinary mix of participants assembled for supper at David Astor's house nearby. The news of the meeting had already leaked out in South Africa. 'One of the most important meetings between South Africans opposed to apartheid and exiles of the banned ANC is being held in Britain this weekend,' wrote the *Sunday Tribune*.[6] President Botha tried to prevent it, and the chief justice, M. M. Corbett, explained that it was 'a small private symposium . . . to discuss on a scholarly and academic basis legal problems and issues'.[7] But the judges were impressed by the moderation and dedication of the ANC lawyers, and more reassured that the future continuity of the law could be maintained.

Amid all the shifting sands Margaret Thatcher remained adamant that she would not recognise Tambo and his terrorists, but in July 1987 she did send out a new ambassador, Robin Renwick, who was much shrewder and more agile than his predecessors. I already knew Renwick from when he was helping to negotiate Zimbabwe's independence in 1980, together with his colleague Charles Powell; and before he left to become ambassador he explained to me over lunch that he did not see communism as a serious menace to South Africa, and he was convinced that the ANC would be crucial to future peace. He could not, however, risk appearing pro-Tambo in Pretoria, or having any direct contacts with him. Could I pass on any messages or concerns from him? The assignment gave me a ringside seat to the coming punch-up: when a few months later in Vancouver Thatcher denounced the ANC as 'a typical terrorist organisation', Renwick and Powell both assured me that she had lost her temper and that it would make no difference to their ANC contacts, which were developing through intelligence sources. But Tambo was exasperated by Thatcher's intransigence as the violence worsened and he felt that time was running out, as his health deteriorated. 'I don't know what is going to change diplomatic attitudes in London, they're so insensitive,' he told me in January 1989 when he was recuperating from exhaustion. 'Perhaps only a massacre. It's very difficult to excuse Mrs Thatcher for saying that the ANC are terrorists while we are the victims. She is totally blind.' Three months later Tambo's lieutenant Mbeki came to see me for a whole morning. 'What is she really up to? In South Africa the Afrikaner establishment are pressing to start talks, so why is she moving in the opposite direction?' Mbeki showed his mastery of the complex diplomacy, and I passed on his concerns to Renwick, who replied with some reassurances. In fact most of the key advisers to the UK government were in favour of open talks with Tambo and the ANC, including the prime minister's foreign policy expert, Sir Anthony Parsons, whom I had previously met when he was ambassador to Iran. 'It's only she who stops them,' explained Powell. 'She really *is* conservative.'

By mid-1989 Tambo's prospects at last seemed more hopeful. Botha, diminished by a stroke, received Mandela from prison in his office in Cape Town, clearly looking for a way to release him; and soon afterwards he was superseded as president by the leader of the National Party, F. W. de Klerk, a more flexible politician whom Tambo thought 'capable of being persuaded by reality'. Tambo was now straining himself to achieve agreement between the ANC and the neighbouring African states to prepare for a settlement, and at last on 21 August 1990 they all signed the 'Harare declaration', which promised to end the armed struggle if the ANC were unbanned and the prisoners released. But the week before, on 12 August, Tambo had been struck down in Sweden by a serious stroke and flown back for emergency treatment at the London Clinic, arriving incognito as 'Mr Reginald'. Mbeki mistakenly tried to suppress the news for three days, but the truth could not be concealed: Tambo could speak only haltingly and was effectively out of action. When I visited him at the clinic in November he was talking slowly but confidently with a twinkle about his contacts with Mandela in prison, and how he must tour Africa after his release; but he was clearly unable to lead the ANC through the crucial months to come, and it was left in the hands of an uneasy triumvirate of exiles.

Those last months of 1989 were an extraordinary time of uncertainty across the world: for while South Africa was in the balance, eastern Europe and the Soviet Union were also facing upheavals after forty years of unchanging oppression, as the communist regimes collapsed. There was a power vacuum everywhere, and no-one knew who would fill it. In October I had lunch with George Soros, who had just returned from Poland, which he compared with South Africa: he quoted the Polish saying 'only the impossible is possible: only the powerless have power'. But in South Africa the uncertainty was more alarming, for the future stability of the country rested on one man, Nelson Mandela, who had been in jail for twenty-seven years.

16

Mandela

By the end of the 1980s Nelson Mandela the prisoner had become an icon with little connection with reality. I could not relate the icon to the revolutionary I had known in the 1950s. For almost thirty years no photograph of him had appeared. 'We all talk about him', said my daughter Katie, who was inspired by his story, 'but let's face it: we know nothing about him!' In 1985 I had watched Oliver Tambo unveiling the huge bust of Mandela outside the Royal Festival Hall, but I could barely recognise the head, with thick lips and bull-neck like a Soviet workers' hero, quite unlike the expressive face I had known in the early 1960s. Newspapers and TV programmes kept preparing for his release and looked desperately around for anyone who knew anything about Mandela. 'You mean you actually *knew* him?' a CBS interviewer asked me with astonishment. I was tempted to romanticise a friendship with a legend and to suppress my first impressions of him as a touchy and arrogant man; and in truth I knew little about how he had developed in jail, though his lawyer, George Bizos, assured me he was a formidable presence. I still dreaded that his release would prove an anticlimax, revealing a tired old man of seventy-one emerging like Rip Van Winkle, hopelessly out of touch with the modern world. How could he confront a powerful military state and shrewd Afrikaner politicians determined to divide the black opposition? Mandela was worried while in prison, as he himself told me later, that his overblown fame had made people believe he was a superman. How much power could be wielded by a myth?

And after forty years watching the emergence of independent Africa I could not feel very optimistic about the black leadership. The British as well as Africans had hailed a succession of new presidents as charismatic heroes who would be their country's saviour – Nkrumah, the Redeemer of Ghana; Kenyatta, the Father of Kenya; Amin, the Field-Marshal of Uganda – only to see them follow the same path towards autocracy, paranoia and dictatorship. By the 1980s the pattern was looking unavoidable, with only a few smaller countries such as Botswana and Cameroon as exceptions. For Western conservatives the message was clear: the Africans were simply unfit to govern themselves. For myself I was inclined to blame the colonisers more than the colonised: the imperial powers had done little to prepare them for democracy, and American and Soviet cold warriors had done more than anyone to corrupt the new leaders and encourage their illusions of grandeur. But I could not help being disappointed by the ruthlessness of the new African dictators, who seemed determined to replay the civil wars and vendettas of medieval Europe, from the Wars of the Roses to the Thirty Years' War. Yet it was not correct to suggest that Africa was more 'backward' than Europe; for European history could also move backwards, as was shown by Hitler and would soon be shown by leaders in the Balkans.

Would Mandela and his colleagues be the same when they gained independence? After this African history I had to be sceptical. But since I had known them as young men I had always found the black South African politicians quite different from others in the continent, with their long history of patient resistance, their sense of discipline and their exposure to Western ideas. And I had seen and heard enough of Mandela to know that he had developed into a much more serious leader than the demagogues in the north.

I was still banned from South Africa, to my growing frustration; I longed to show Sally the country she had never seen. So in late 1989 I called on the friendly new South African ambassador in London – crossing the cordon of protesters who were picketing the hated fortress in Trafalgar Square – to plead with him personally for a visa. He reminded me courteously that I was still banned, but then explained that his government wanted the world to know how rapidly the situation was improving and eventually gave me a visa overwritten with the strange stipulation 'TO ASSESS THE CHANGING SITUATION IN SOUTH AFRICA IN EIGHTEEN DAYS'.

The country was changing much faster than I had ever imagined. In February 1990, two days before Sally and I flew to Johannesburg, President F. W. de Klerk made his historic speech to Parliament, announcing that the African National Congress was unbanned and that Mandela would shortly be released. At Johannesburg airport the global media were already converging to report on the world's most famous prisoner. We stayed with Nadine Gordimer and watched with her the liberation of old friends who had been banned for thirty years, returning like ghosts from the past. The Johannesburg *Star* published long lists of people who were suddenly unbanned, including many old *Drum* writers, most of them dead, like Todd Matshikiza, Bloke Modisane or Can Themba, listed with aliases from the police files as if they were big-time criminals: 'Daniel Canadoce Temba, alias Temba Dan Can, alias Themba-Dorsay Can, alias Mvalise'. Nadine gave a party where our old friends speculated about the extent of the change. Zeke Mphahlele was still sceptical: 'It's easy for those in power to unban people: it doesn't mean they lose control.' Bram Fischer's daughter Ilse explained that her dead father's ashes were still banned, kept in prison. But we were thrilled to watch the crumbling of apartheid and the end of the 'collective madness' as Nadine called it, and I was delighted to see again politicians I had known thirty years before, with their values and ideals unchanged by prison, apparently oblivious of the hiatus. When I arranged to meet Ahmed Kathrada, Mandela's jail colleague, he suggested we meet 'near the flat' – meaning the place where we had last met when we were both in our twenties. I found Walter Sisulu, Mandela's mentor and jail colleague, in the Soweto box house where I used to see him in the 1950s. As he came out to welcome me, white haired but sprightly, he warned me to lock my car: 'Remember how Pat Duncan had his coat stolen.'

Mandela was still in jail, but six days after we arrived we heard that he would be released the next day. The following morning we caught a plane to Cape Town, to watch him make his first speech at the City Hall; but the streets were solid with crowds, so we drove to the British embassy, where we were now staying. We watched the historic event on television with the ambassador, Robin Renwick, and his colleagues, who gave us the diplomats' view. As Mandela spoke from the balcony in the fading twilight their faces fell and Renwick quickly left the room to telephone London. Mandela was reading a speech which had clearly been drafted by an ANC committee, reaffirming the militant policy and the armed struggle, while the diplomats had expected that he would present himself as an independent statesman and peace-maker. But it seemed to me that Mandela could only be useful if he remained loyal to the ANC: he could only make peace if he carried his people behind him.

What was the British government's real attitude to Mandela and de Klerk? Over the next days I argued with Renwick, perhaps the most brilliant diplomat of his generation, and I still was not clear where he stood. He had certainly consistently urged de Klerk to release Mandela, but he was also very supportive of Mandela's main rival, Chief Mangosuthu Buthelezi: he explained that Buthelezi's power was a fact of life which the British could not ignore. Renwick was very close to his prime minister, Margaret Thatcher; and I suspected that she, as well as de Klerk, was deliberately building Buthelezi up as a counterweight to Mandela, in the classical British tradition of divide-and-rule, to maintain white supremacy.

Mandela soon flew up to Johannesburg to address a mass rally and then returned to his small house in Soweto. When I telephoned the house Winnie answered. 'I keep pinching myself to believe that it's true,' she said, putting me straight through to Nelson, who talked as if nothing much had happened in thirty years. 'Hello, Tony, when are you coming here? How's the family?' Two days later I drove out with Sally to the box house in Vilikazi Street where I had visited him in the 1960s. An ANC flag was flying from the concrete garage – the flag which had been illegal two weeks before – and the house was surrounded by photographers and TV vans, which made it look like a stage set: schoolgirls were peeping through the garden wall into the small patch, where a tall black man with grey hair was talking to a TV team. At the door was Peter Magubane, the veteran *Drum* cameraman who was now Mandela's personal photographer, the most privileged of all. Over the past years he had frequently been detained for supporting the ANC, and had seen many false dawns: 'Is this really It?' I asked him.

'Yes, it's It. They can't put it back.'

In the house we were greeted by Winnie, who was playing the model housewife, preparing a meal in the kitchen. Mandela strode in, looking far too big for the room, perfectly groomed in a double-breasted suit: his white hair looked premature and his shaky walk betrayed his seventy-one years while his hug revealed the bony body beneath his tailoring. But he seemed much more serene than the man I remembered: his smile was no longer a wide showbiz grin, but the relaxed, amused smile of someone at peace with himself. He sat down with his big boxer's hands resting on the dining-table, and asked about his London friends, Mary Benson and David Astor, who had sent him law books in jail. He was interested in Oliver Tambo's meeting with the judges and wanted to take it further. He looked Sally up and down and said: 'I remember Tony as a bright young man. He didn't tell me about you; he's kept things from me.'

A few days later I went back again with three liberal journalists; there was still a queue of dignitaries waiting to see him – which was soon jumped by his tailor, Yusuf Surtee, carrying a new pair of trousers. This time Mandela was the pure politician: he eloquently thanked the media for keeping the cause of liberation alive, and stressed that South Africa must have a free press. He talked about books, praising Nadine Gordimer and saying that my *Anatomy of Britain* had been the first book he had received in prison. He played down his own role and emphasised that he remained the loyal servant of the ANC. 'They may say: "Well, you are a man of seventy-one, you may require a pension." Or "Look, we don't like your face, please go." I will obey them.'

Could this old man in the small house really take power? When I drove back into the white suburbs they seemed totally disconnected. The whites were relieved that Mandela had been released calmly and that South Africa was being praised by the world. But they did not expect him to affect their very comfortable lives, their mansions or servants; they were still in a quite different country. At the end of eighteen days I could not yet 'assess the changing situation' as my visa demanded.

Back in London I still kept some contact with Mandela, for he practised diplomacy in a very personal way, relying on individual friends rather than bureaucrats. When I was able to see him later in Johannesburg he discussed how the ANC could rectify false reports in the British media: he gave me his home phone number and said: 'Why don't you just ring me when you see something that needs correcting?' – as his aide looked on in despair. Later he sent an urgent message through the ANC's London representative: 'What can you do about R. W. Johnson?'[1] I saw him again in April, when he paid a short triumphant visit to London with Winnie, who appeared the ideal consort, gracious and attentive to his needs. He attended a pop concert at Wembley Stadium, addressing a crowd of 75,000 young people, to thank them for their past support: 'You elected not to forget.' It was televised live by the BBC, which was attacked by right-wing conservatives who complained of political bias, and I was asked to give a commentary which excluded any hint of fund-raising. In the interval Mandela moved through a crowded reception room, welcoming admirers. Katie was introduced to him as my daughter, and he replied firmly: 'Remember you're a person in your own right.'

There was much speculation about a meeting with Thatcher; Mandela's ANC colleagues insisted he must postpone it, but he persisted with his personal diplomacy. One Saturday night in June 1990 I was just going to sleep when Adelaide Tambo woke me with an odd request: 'My brother is in England and wants to see his girlfriend tomorrow morning.' I was cross until I realised the code: it meant Mandela wanted to see Thatcher. I rang her private secretary, Charles Powell, who was quite unsurprised: 'I know that Mandela is staying the weekend in Kent. The prime minister is at Chequers and it *is* rather short notice to send a helicopter, but I'll see what I can do.' Early the next day Thatcher made a long phone call to Mandela, as I heard from both sides. Mandela urged her to maintain sanctions against Pretoria, without success; but she disarmed him by showing a maternal worry about his forthcoming trip to America: 'If you go on like this you won't come out alive.'

After touring America Mandela came back to London, where Thatcher and her ministers were anxious to show their respect. Douglas Hurd gave a private lunch for his friends, including Trevor Huddleston, Helen Suzman and myself: Mandela was courteous and appreciative but restated the need to maintain sanctions, despite 'my sister Helen'. He went on to see Thatcher for the first time, a person whose power came from the opposite end of the political spectrum. Robin Renwick had urged her to let Mandela talk uninterrupted, since he had been waiting for twenty-seven years incommunicado; he spoke for fifty-two minutes, before she replied for half an hour. She was warm and charming, Mandela told me, and he resented critics who complained he should not have talked to any enemy who had denounced him as a terrorist. He had to work with people who had done far worse things in South Africa, he explained: 'I didn't even mention slaughters.'

In London the crowds gazed upon Mandela with reverent awe, which exasperated his critics, especially those who pointed to his conviction for terrorism. In fact he was never a terrorist in either the Palestinian or the Israeli sense: he had taken up arms as the last resort to confront a terrorist state, and he had avoided any attack on civilians. But he was certainly never a spiritual leader: he was a master-politician who understood the nature of power, and at his engagements in London – the foreign secretary's lunch, the House of Commons, a gathering of editors – he never lost sight of his objectives.

In any case the image of the Mandelas as a saintly couple was crumbling behind the scenes, as the truth emerged about Winnie's murderous gang in Soweto in the late 1980s and her corrupt financial dealings. Most of her closest friends, like Adelaide Tambo, were reluctantly disillusioned, but Mandela had idealised Winnie in jail and was for a long time too dazzled by her presence to face up to her infidelities and betrayals. At last he had to accept the necessity of separating from her. It was the loneliest time of his life, compounded by the death of his closest colleague, Oliver Tambo: an unhappier time than any in prison.

His private misery coincided with growing violence between blacks and political frustrations, and President de Klerk soon appeared as the peace-maker contrasted to the ineffective Mandela. 'What the blacks need', wrote Hugo Young in the *Guardian* in April 1991, 'is a leader as competent as de Klerk.'[2] De Klerk could show that Mandela could not control his own people, as the ANC faced a growing rebellion from the Zulus led by Chief Buthelezi.

But the Zulu revolt, I was convinced, was much less spontaneous than it looked. I had watched Buthelezi's career with alarm. I had first met him when he visited the *Drum* office in 1952, when he had just been expelled from Fort Hare University for supporting the ANC; but since then, while Mandela was in jail, he had become a Zulu nationalist and ferociously attacked the ANC for communist policies. He gained many right-wing supporters in Britain as well as South Africa. Thatcher often received him at No. 10, encouraged by her Afrikaner guru Laurens van der Post. And he was encouraged in his violent opposition by a group of multimillionaires including the casino-owner John Aspinall (who called himself 'The White Zulu'), Sir James Goldsmith and Conrad Black, the owner of the *Daily*

Telegraph. In July 1990 I was invited to a big meeting of the conservative Centre for Policy Studies, where Buthelezi was the star speaker: he explained that the ANC wanted 'to shoot themselves into power', while Aspinall proposed splitting South Africa into thirty tribal components and the journalist Bruce Anderson complained that the Zulus were not being violent enough. I tried to suggest that the ANC could resolve the conflict with peaceful negotiations, but I was far outnumbered by the Zulu lobby, which had no solution except violence.

At least apartheid was now totally discredited; I wryly watched its old supporters and appeasers, whether diplomats, businessmen or bureaucrats, rewriting their stories as the tide changed. No-one, it now seemed, had ever believed in apartheid, as no-one in post-war Germany had been pro-Nazi. Many Afrikaners had genuinely been converted. One day in London I was visited by Professor Johan Heyns, the moderator of the Dutch Reformed Church, which had long provided theological and social support for apartheid, but who was now bravely building bridges to the ANC: he told me how he had visited them in Lusaka just before Mandela's release and afterwards urged his college friend de Klerk to make contacts. Heyns explained that he was still mainly interested in theology and ethics, and that his only weapons were words, but they could be effective, and he was determined to change people's hearts. He was a charming and avuncular man who seemed too good to be true. And he was: a few years later he was murdered by right-wing Afrikaners.

One day I was visited in London by Patrick 'Terror' Lekota, the ANC leader who would later become its chairman, whom I had last seen in a police cell when he was on trial near Johannesburg. He brought with him another ambiguous turncoat, an unlikely Afrikaner colleague called John Horak. Horak, a journalist, showed me his CV of previous employers, beginning with the *Diamond Fields Advertiser* in Kimberley and ending with assignments for the *Sunday Times*, and explained he was now looking for a job in Britain. Then Lekota interrupted: 'It's not quite simple: you see, he's also a colonel in the South African police.' Horak, he explained, had simultaneously pursued a parallel career as a police spy providing information about the ANC, but while spying on Winnie Mandela he had been turned to become a double agent. Now his cover had been blown, his old police colleagues were out to get him, and the ANC had flown him to London to protect him and find him a job. I could not offer much hope for a job in British journalism, but suggested that he write his memoirs. He told me fascinating stories about the methods and codes of apartheid's secret agents: how for instance they used gamekeepers in the game reserves, employed by the World Wildlife Fund to catch poachers, who doubled up as police agents pursuing ANC freedom fighters on the run. The memoirs did not materialise but he ended up working for ANC intelligence in Pretoria.

I went back to South Africa frequently, which was still suspended between two disconnected worlds. When I called on Mandela and his colleagues in their brand-new office in Johannesburg they sounded confident that they would soon achieve power, yet in the interim they lacked any formal authority; while the whites in the suburbs appeared quite unaware of impending change and were doing little to adapt to it. Mandela, the old man who had been out of the world for a quarter-century, was now, as Nadine Gordimer said, 'the personification of the future'; while many young whites were stuck in the past. The future at last began to take some shape when the government agreed to begin negotiations in the Convention for a Democratic South Africa (CODESA), which were conducted in an appropriately futuristic building called the World Trade Centre, near Johannesburg airport: when I talked with the ANC delegation there they sounded confident that Mandela would soon become president and de Klerk his deputy; but there were all kinds of spoilers among other delegations, including Buthelezi and the right-wing Afrikaners, waiting to disrupt any agreement. The negotiations continued on and off over two years with recurring breakdowns, culminating in June 1993 when the thugs of the neo-Nazi Afrikaner Resistance Movement invaded the building, smashing through windows, to try to bring the talks to a halt – a terrifying image of the potential future anarchy. But at last at the end of 1993 Mandela and de Klerk agreed on a new constitution and elections based on a simple one-person-one-vote system, and the first democratic elections were fixed for April 1994.

Mandela was well aware that elections depended on cash: he had been raising funds round the world for the ANC ever since he left prison. He was never embarrassed by using his prestige to extract large sums of money from questionable people or former opponents. He asked me to introduce him at fund-raising receptions in London, where he preserved a very personal style. At the Dorchester Hotel in May 1993, before the election, he addressed a grand reception attended by the chairmen of most of the big companies, including Lord Weinstock of GEC and Lord King of British Airways, most of whom had opposed the ANC before it was legalised; now they queued up to shake Mandela's hand. In among them were scattered veteran anti-apartheid campaigners, who bristled as Mandela smiled and chatted with their ex-enemies. Trevor Huddleston, the president of the Anti-Apartheid Movement, was still filled with 'holy anger' and complained to me fiercely: how could Mandela forgive these villains? It was odd to hear the Christian father rebuking the political campaigner for being too forgiving. But Mandela had no time for recriminations and he raised huge sums which eventually dwarfed de Klerk's election chest.

The plans for elections went ahead, surrounded by hazards and uncertainties. The Afrikaner right wing refused to participate, and a band of extremists invaded the neighbouring bantustan of Bophuthatswana, until they met an ignominious defeat. 'South Africa braced itself for a race war and civil war yesterday,' wrote the *Sunday Times*, the chief prophet of doom in London. Buthelezi also boycotted the elections and organised a march of Zulus through Johannesburg, which provoked deadly reprisals from the ANC. Buthelezi continued to hold out, and conservatives still predicted a bloodbath. Then a week before election day he finally gave in, after pressure from all sides, and joined the elections.

I flew out to Johannesburg with Sally to watch the elections in April 1994: the last surrender of white power in Africa. The walls and lamps were plastered with Mandela posters: the initials ANC, which had been banned until four years before, were now everywhere. They seemed at odds with the street names like Empire Way or Eton Road, or a new estate called Settlers' Park. In the lily-white northern suburbs the prospect of a black government still seemed unimaginable. But Nadine's house was an island of continuity, the same as forty years ago, and parts of Johannesburg were reverting to the multiracial existence which I had known before apartheid had first separated it: Sally and I went together with Nadine to the musical *Sophiatown*, which featured the now-legendary *Drum* writers.

Mandela was already being hailed as the victor. We went to the final ANC rally in the huge stadium near Soweto, where he arrived by helicopter and strode through the arena, with an entourage of drum majorettes, witch doctors and pop singers. He spoke like a president: when a gun went off he sternly rebuked the crowd. As he left in his car he reached out to shake my hand, but a security guard quickly intervened and closed the window. Two days later, at a press conference at the Carlton Hotel, Mandela radiated authority. The only disturbance came from the British paparazzi. Mandela insisted on the importance of gun control and community policing: when he was asked about his personal feelings he would only say: 'Certain things cannot be expressed in words.'

The mood was still tense with fears of violence: on the eve of the election a bomb exploded at the airport, and on polling-day another went off at the ANC headquarters downtown. But the voting-stations in the townships were suffused with an extraordinary calm, as patient blacks lined up in winding queues for three or four hours waiting to vote, while monitors from the United Nations or the Commonwealth watched for irregularities or intimidation. All the political violence was dissolved by the passionate faith in democracy.

The next day I talked to Mandela at the Carlton Hotel, when he was clearly about to become president. Did he ever imagine forty years earlier that he would be in this position? 'No, we were too busy fighting apartheid; and I was a junior then. I was convinced that there was no better leader than Tambo.' He rejected any praise of his personal leadership: 'No single individual can be elevated above others.' Could he not go too far in practising forgiveness and forgetting about evil? 'No,' he answered firmly. 'Men of peace must not think about recriminations or retribution; courageous people don't fear forgiving, for the sake of peace.'

That evening we had dinner with Nadine, joined by Lakhdar Brahimi, the Algerian diplomat who was supervising the elections for the UN, whom I had known well as ambassador in London and who had a long experience of revolutions. He warned us about the problems which had beset his own country after independence, when its revolutionary leaders were promoted without experience of administration. But he was confident that the election results, though rough and ready, would produce an outcome which most parties could accept, and he was right. When the ANC victory was announced, with just short of two-thirds of the vote, there was no serious dispute. After all the predictions about bloodbaths, the power had been transferred from whites to blacks with little disruption. Most British and American media shared the admiration for the peaceful elections and large turnout, which seemed to revive the idea of democracy in their own countries: 'It was like being alive in the time of Lincoln,' wrote the *New York Times*. Only a few conservative journalists dissented: 'Dawn of freedom my foot,' wrote my old sparring-partner Peregrine Worsthorne in the *Sunday Telegraph*. 'Black majority rule in South Africa should send a shudder round the world.'

Certainly no-one who had followed the history of black Africa could believe that democracy in itself would produce a fair and peaceful society. I could not forget how ten years earlier the world had hailed the victory of Robert Mugabe in Zimbabwe, who was already looking more like an autocrat than a democrat, and who was to bankrupt his country. But South Africa was embarking on a much more thoughtful transfer of power, with a mature leadership and strong constitutional safeguards, and I had far more faith in Mandela as a genuine democrat.

Mandela's insistence on reconciliation was much easier said than achieved, and my old friends argued hard about the conditions for the settlement with the Afrikaner government. The ANC would have to give amnesty to some of its worst persecutors; yet it could not simply forget and obliterate the past: 'You can't heal a wound if the shrapnel is still inside it,' said my friend Raisaka, who had seen his own brother beaten to death by the police. Lawyers like George Bizos, who had investigated some of the worst police atrocities, were haunted by the prospect of letting the police go scot free. Nadine quoted the words of Milan Kundera: 'The struggle of men against power is the struggle of memory against forgetting.' But from these fierce arguments there gradually emerged the idea of a 'Truth and Reconciliation Commission', which would promise amnesty only on condition that the perpetrators would first tell the full truth about their crimes – an idea which would prove to be South Africa's most imaginative contribution to peaceful transitions round the world.

On our last day Sally and I went to a celebration lunch party given by

Adelaide Tambo in her luxurious villa where Walter Sisulu, the eighty-year-old father figure of the struggle, was guest of honour. Adelaide gave a gracious speech thanking the foreign guests including the British MPs Paul Boateng and Bob Hughes, David Dinkins, the mayor of New York, and myself. It was a first glimpse of old revolutionaries as they faced the responsibilities of power. Sisulu hugged me and said: 'We've done it.'

What had they done? A few months later I visited the new ministers enjoying the trappings of power in their government offices. The guerrilla leader Joe Modise was now minister of defence; the ex-head of the Communist Party, Joe Slovo, was minister of housing. Parliament was transformed from an Afrikaner stronghold into a multiracial assembly full of bright tribal costumes. 'I love this dream,' said Archbishop Desmond Tutu. 'You sit in the balcony and look down and count all the terrorists. They are all sitting there passing laws. It is incredible.' The young minister Pahad drove us on a tour of the ministers' houses, enclosed in the beautiful and secluded Groote Schuur estate outside Cape Town. The old freedom fighters looked very unradical in those comfortable surroundings: we found Govan Mbeki, the Marxist firebrand, listening to Alistair Cooke's *Letter from America*. 'Now I know why you were all so keen for power,' I teased Pahad.

'But the funny thing is,' he replied, 'we didn't know all this was here.'

It was like a caricature in black and white of those sudden British transfers of power, like Labour taking over from the Conservatives in 1945. When a minister asked me for advice on how to handle civil servants, I proposed that they watch the TV series *Yes, Minister*, but he replied: 'Oh, we've already seen the videos.' The transition on the surface was smoother than many had expected: the bureaucrats were keen to please, and the Afrikaner secretaries and security guards were soon calling the black ministers 'Sir'; power in the end had no colour bar. But the obstacles were greater than they looked. The terms of the settlement required the ANC government to work alongside Afrikaner ministers and officials who had been their enemies and there was still much unseen resistance to reforms, incompetence and non-communication between races. 'Yes, Minister' could often mean 'No', much more decisively than in Whitehall.

Mandela himself moved into the grand presidential offices as if he had always been groomed to be head of state: confident and courteous, springing out of his chair to greet a visitor, and introducing his Afrikaner PA, who brought the tea. I found him always welcoming and personal, asking about my family, reminiscing about old *Drum* friends, talking about London and the Queen Mother. But he was never off guard. He knew the impact of anything he said: if he said something slightly indiscreet he would instinctively put his hand over the tape recorder and he would always veer away from discussing his personal feelings.

*

I was still fascinated by the story of how this serene president had developed from the headstrong revolutionary I had known in the 1950s; so I was excited when my publishers in 1995 suggested I write his authorised biography. Mandela asked me to breakfast in his house in Johannesburg, and said with customary flattery that he knew no-one more qualified to write it: he wanted a biographer who had known him in his earlier political years, provided I didn't mention we had met in a shebeen. He would let me see his letters and key documents, while letting me make my own judgments: 'I don't want to be seen as *not a person*; I'm no angel.' So I embarked on a three-year assignment which proved both more exacting and more exciting than I had foreseen. It was potentially tricky, I was warned, to write an authorised biography while the subject was still alive; but Mandela largely kept to his promise of not interfering; and I had the unique privilege of being able first to read historic documents, and then to question the central character in the story.

It was moving to retrace Mandela's long career through the underside of white South African history, like re-entering a country house through the servants' entrance and up the back stairs before reaching the grand rooms. Sally and I tracked down the remote kraal where he had been raised, driving down the long dirt track full of ditches and boulders, to find the little group of round huts where he had lived with his guardian, the acting paramount chief. We visited the two mission schools where he had endured his very English education, to find their confident stone buildings now forsaken and decaying, crumbling relics of the liberal heritage which apartheid had destroyed. In Johannesburg I revisited the little gingerbread building where he had worked as a lawyer in the 1950s, and sought out old haunts such as the Oriental Restaurant or Kapitans where he had plotted revolution. I could relive my own youthful experiences when Mandela enjoyed reminiscing about the musicians, sportsmen or writers of that vibrant decade when I had first known him: when he held a reunion for 'veterans of the struggle' he invited two stars of that time, Dolly Rathebe and Thandi Klaasen, to sing the old township songs with poignant nostalgia, while the veterans jived on the grass. What had happened, Mandela wondered, to the vigour and humour of the old *Drum* tradition? The 1990s, with all the new-found freedoms, could never quite replace the creative optimism of the struggle in the 1950s.

It was still hard to link up all the disconnected images of the contemporary President Mandela as I followed him round. I saw him on very different stages: in his grand offices in Pretoria and Cape Town, at banquets, at party rallies, at Robben Island, in parliament, or at his home in Johannesburg. Occasionally I saw him off guard, suddenly despondent with his mouth turned down in a circumflex; but the next challenge would jerk him back into life. Everywhere he seemed at home, relating to all newcomers as if they were uniquely important, remembering faces and names: the perfect politician.

In Britain I watched him entertaining the Queen at a banquet, arguing with academics at Oxford, jiving at the Albert Hall, embracing children in London streets. I found it odd, having first known Mandela among the slums of Soweto, to see him so completely at ease on my home ground. He loved talking about his English education and influences, and he often sounded less like an African president or chief than a Victorian gentleman, maintaining old-fashioned attitudes that the British had lost. He would quote from Tennyson's *In Memoriam*, from Wordsworth or from W. E. Henley: 'I am the master of my fate'. He enjoyed recalling his conversations with the Queen Mother, who had visited South Africa as queen in 1947, or his walks in the garden of Buckingham Palace. Like other colonial subjects, including his own mentor, Jawaharlal Nehru, he seemed to have absorbed English ideals of fairness and morality more thoroughly than the English themselves.

Yet he had been through an experience quite unlike any Englishman's, culminating in twenty-seven years in jail. How can you write an interesting biography, I was asked, when half the life was in prison? It was those years which provided the real drama and significance of his life. They were like an austere play, reduced to a small cast on a bare stage backed by a high wall, compared with the confusing pageant with a cast of thousands which makes up most political lives.

And it was in prison that Mandela developed his inner strength and leadership which enabled him quietly to dominate both his fellow-prisoners and his warders. Through long interviews with them I tried to piece the story together; and eventually I managed to penetrate the prison archives, an Aladdin's cave which gave crucial clues about his relations with the authorities. A hundred big box files contained all the correspondence and reports about the prisoner Mandela, meticulously preserved, including all his intercepted mail and the original manuscript of the autobiography which he wrote in his cell in 1975. The boxes recorded how effectively Mandela had imposed his own personality and confidence on the prison. Already in 1969 the commissioner had to remind him: 'Nelson, you are *a prisoner*'. Eleven years later the minister of justice received a detailed analysis of Mandela's state of mind which emphasised his extraordinary self-confidence: 'His period in prison has caused his psycho-political posture to increase rather than decrease, and with this he has now acquired the characteristic prison-charisma of the contemporary liberation leader.'[3]

It was in prison that Mandela developed his most remarkable asset – his capacity to empathise with his opponents, which would be the key to the negotiations which followed. He was determined to understand and placate the fears of the whites. He astonished the Afrikaner politicians who visited him by showing that he was aware of their past history, as a people who had been themselves oppressed by the British, and who had suffered and fought to gain their independence, as the Africans had fought in their turn. It was this understanding which was most crucial to an eventual settlement, for it enabled Mandela and his colleagues to gain the trust of their ex-enemies, and to set the foundations of a new constitution which both sides could accept. It was the ultimate test of his leadership and it was the rarest of all gifts. Other parts of Africa and the world, including the Middle East and Northern Ireland, had the same desperate need for this kind of peace-making, to bring together two sides who were building up hostility to each other in a vicious circle. But they lacked a courageous and imaginative leader who could reach across the high walls of hatred.

Was he too good to be true, with his infinite patience and forgiveness? I sometimes felt exasperated, like many of his colleagues, by his insistence on seeing the best in everyone: rich businessmen who had made fortunes out of apartheid, Afrikaner politicians who had changed sides at the last moment, right-wing British bankers who had denounced the ANC as terrorists and then curried favour with them. Like many ex-radicals – like Tony Blair or Bill Clinton – he seemed naïvely impressed by rich men. 'How does that man come to be so rich?' Mandela asked one of his colleagues after talking to a flamboyant Afrikaner tycoon. 'But don't you realise, Madiba,' his colleague replied, 'he made his money out of *you*.' After his years of prison isolation, when he welcomed any old movie or TV programme, he was susceptible to showbiz and would give the Spice Girls priority over heads of government. But I still could not penetrate behind the hearty and amiable style of the man who was so near yet so far. He was always the politician, who had merged his public personality with his private feelings everywhere except in his home. Richard Stengel, who ghosted his autobiography, had forewarned me: 'The man and the mask were one,' and Ahmed Kathrada, who had been in prison with him for twenty-five years, had admitted: 'He's impenetrable.'

*

What did Nelson Mandela really achieve in practical terms, with all his charisma? Returning frequently to South Africa, I watched its bright image steadily deteriorating in the West. The first months of Mandela's government were a honeymoon for the whites, who basked in the miracle of the peaceful revolution and the rainbow nation, repeating feelgood stories about reconciliation and forgiveness. They were relieved to be saved from a bloodbath, to be rid of sanctions and boycotts, and to re-enter the world community of sport, culture and the global marketplace. But the rainbow remained more in the sky than on the ground. The whites soon took peace and reconciliation for granted as they pursued 'business as usual'; and they began complaining bitterly about the mistakes and incompetence of the black government, the wave of crime, the incipient corruption and the demands for affirmative action. And most Western media and business people took their own views from the white South Africans.

The whites had been accustomed to being a privileged minority, an outpost of the first world, protected by a ruthless police force and draconian laws. They found it hard to adjust to being part of the developing world, with all the messiness and intractability of countries like Brazil or India. The problems of poverty which had been fenced off and contained in the townships and rural areas were now overflowing onto their doorsteps, as armed robbers, car-hijackers or rapists invaded the white suburbs. The proud city centres, with their Victorian town halls and statues of white generals and pioneers, became symbols of decay, piled with plastic litter and broken glass, degenerating into centres of crime, drugs and violence. The more privileged whites, the ladies of Constantia or the businessmen of Sandton, retreated behind gated fortresses to become expats in their own country; big corporations arranged to transfer their headquarters and capital to London; young doctors and lawyers emigrated to Australia or Canada. Writers such as J. M. Coetzee, Rian Malan or Christopher Hope expressed all their subconscious fears about the barbarian hordes.

And for most Westerners South Africa now looked less important and less interesting. Its gold mines and minerals were no longer crucial to international capitalism and were now much less valuable. Its seaports and bases no longer mattered as strategic outposts in the Cold War. It was no longer a 'white redoubt', a stronghold of Western capitalism against the Marxist republics further north. It now looked more like the rest of Africa, marginalised on the economic map of the world and full of bad news, beset by limitless problems which could not bear much thinking about: the explosion of organised crime, the creeping corruption and the rapid escalation of AIDS, which was sweeping like a medieval plague through the continent. For most Western businessmen and bankers South Africa was descending into the chaos of the continent, 'going down the tubes'.

How far could this be blamed on Mandela's government? It is true that they were unprepared for the extent of the problems. As Mandela admitted, 'we were taken from the bush, or from underground outside the country, or from prisons, to come and take charge. We were suddenly thrown into this immense responsibility of running a highly developed country.'[4] But most of the problems were inherent in the sudden transition from a white oligarchy to a multiracial democracy, and from a police state to a free country. The police had been trained to suppress political agitators rather than track down criminals, and they had been corrupted by bribery. The hospitals had been segregated between efficient treatment for whites and minimal facilities for blacks, before they were opened to all. The black schools had been based on providing basic literacy for a servant class. The problems were limitless: they could never be neatly solved, as problems in the first world were solved.

Each time I returned I was reminded to what extent South Africa was still two countries. The burgeoning black middle class had a very different perspective from the whites. They were equally concerned about crime, and still more about AIDS: both affected them much more than whites. But they saw their lives against a much wider horizon and a longer timescale. The children of my old *Drum* colleagues with whom I kept in touch faced expanding prospects: their parents had come up against a dead end of frustration and closing doors, but the new generation were facing a future which, however hazardous, was full of opportunities and self-expression. They knew they would make mistakes, like any young country; but they were their own mistakes, which they had to learn for themselves. They wanted help from the whites and the West, but on their own terms.

The black millions who lived in the slum townships had much less reason for hope, and their problems were multiplied by more millions immigrating from the rest of Africa to the southern tip of the continent. Cape Town, where they could go no further, was full of homeless people from Congo or Angola speaking French or Portuguese, or fleeing from Zimbabwe, living in cardboard shacks or containers. But most of them still retained their patience and faith in gradually improving conditions, with more water taps, electricity and housing. And the most destitute people still showed the African capacity for improvising and surviving in their own way, like Dickensian cockneys in London slums. Western visitors to Cape Town were appalled by the miles of shacks in Khayelitsha, alongside the motorway to the airport, with their walls of sacking and cardboard roofs; yet that improvised slum was still able to produce black artists, writers and musicians who were more creative and vital than their white spectators.

As I moved again between these disparate societies with such massive inequalities, South Africa looked scarcely more unified than under the years of apartheid. But white and black still desperately needed each other to work out their future, and the country still held together. The real nightmare was the possibility of disintegration into a failed state like many so-called nations to the north, whose private armies and marauding bands competed for minerals and land, while the government was helpless to prevent them.

This sense of nationhood was Mandela's major historical achievement; without it nothing else could be achieved. Like other founders or refounders of nations, like Cavour, Lincoln or Bolívar, he was able to represent the aspirations of quite different people, through his own career and sacrifice. He had risen above the bitterness and factions of the struggle for freedom, and achieved the respect and trust of both sides.

*

And Mandela's influence still stretched round the world. He was convinced that South Africa's experience could be extended to other regions with continuing conflicts and civil wars, such as the Middle East and Northern Ireland, and that they could resolve differences by talking rather than fighting. And he was determined to mediate between the West and pariah countries – particularly those, for example Cuba and Libya, which had given him support when he most needed it. He remained loyal to his past friends, and he reacted angrily to any suggestion that he should drop them: 'The enemies of countries in the West are not ours.' When the US State Department tried to dissuade him from making a state visit to Libya he burst out: 'How can they have the arrogance to dictate to us who our friends should be?' He infuriated Washington, but he retained his moral authority with the West, and his mediation produced important results: in 1997 he helped to persuade Colonel Gaddafi of Libya to hand over the two suspects in the bombing of the Pan Am flight over Lockerbie, who were then tried and sentenced in the Netherlands. This provided a landmark in the enforcement of international law.

Mandela became more outspoken after he retired as president in 1999, aged eighty, when he extended his role as a peace-maker. He always championed the UN, which he saw as the arbiter of international peace, independent of America or Europe. 'I am resentful about the type of thing that America and Britain are doing,' he told me after the Kosovo war. 'They want now to be the policemen of the world.' When I talked to him after September 11 he was quick to condemn the attacks on the twin towers. He had close links with Muslims, both within South Africa and abroad, who had given him much support in the past. In November 2001 he gave a press conference in Washington after meeting President Bush, supporting the war against Afghanistan, and later said that the terrorist strongholds should be destroyed. But after strong protests from South African Muslims, he regretted having given them offence. He was opposed to any attack on Iraq without UN approval, and he warned that 'the United States must avoid any course of action which will be as unpopular as that of the terrorists'. And when Israel invaded the West Bank he made a scarcely veiled reference to 'a terrorist state'. Like many black South Africans, he always saw parallels between the Israeli occupation and the apartheid government's domination of the bantustans.

He remained a single individual, loyal to his party, the ANC, but often critical of it, and increasingly at odds with his president, Thabo Mbeki, who did not invite him to state occasions and did not always return his calls. He could only rely on his personal reputation and his myth.

So what was the real power of that myth? To many cynical commentators the question was irrelevant in the world of realpolitik, like Stalin asking: 'How many divisions has the Pope?' Yet the history of South Africa, I believe, does not bear out that cynicism. For Mandela's leadership depended, in the end, on his moral authority, which had eventually demoralised his opponents. It was his consistent stand on his principles through his years in prison which had mobilised campaigners across the world to boycott supporters of apartheid and undermine the South African economy. And it was when Afrikaner governments lost their belief in the rightness of apartheid, and at the same time their religious support, that they lost the will to impose their system with the ruthlessness which it required. And it was because Mandela had risen above the political fray that he commanded the moral high ground, with an authority granted to no other politician in the contemporary world.

17

The fire and the rose

When I was sixty-two I had a sudden reminder of mortality. In New York in November 1988 I was preparing the television series *The Midas Touch* (see Chapter 14), and was reciting a commentary to the camera about the power of money against a background of the twin towers of the World Trade Center. I felt a sudden chest pain which stopped me continuing, and I went back to my hotel for a rest, where I found I was too weak to walk. I was rushed to hospital, where a doctor explained that I had had a heart attack; soon afterwards I was told that I must have a bypass operation urgently. I had to take a more serious interest in my own anatomy.

My hectic life in Manhattan suddenly contracted to a hospital room. Sally flew out immediately from London to join me, and New York friends whom I associated with fleeting encounters and parties rallied round to my bedside, bringing books, gossip and flowers. New York suddenly ceased to be a fantasy city and became a home from home, full of reassurance and sympathy; it was not until I was wheeled down for a four-hour operation that I felt suddenly alone. When I awoke from the long anaesthetic to see Sally standing beside me I felt only just alive, with aches across my chest and down my legs; but it was surprisingly unalarming. I suddenly remembered what Montaigne had said: 'Why should we fear death, when there is so little difference between being old and death, compared to being young and old?' I knew I would recover when Sally brought me a recording of *Rigoletto*, and I recuperated steadily, in a house lent by a generous New York friend, until I could fly back to London for three months' convalescence.

I eventually felt much fitter than before, but it had been a warning against overexertion and I now had a rather different perspective: family and friends loomed much larger while politicians and power looked more distant and less important. I still felt the *insanabile cacoethes scribendi*, the incurable mania for writing; but I realised it was indeed incurable. One day I met the Canadian economist John Kenneth Galbraith, now nearly ninety, striding through Green Park, and asked him whether he was still writing. He replied: 'Any day I don't write I feel destabilised.' I could hardly imagine him ever being unstable, but I knew what he meant.

I was still restlessly curious to discover the world changing around me. I finished my television series. I wrote another, very brief, Anatomy, entitled *The Essential Anatomy of Britain*, published in 1992, and examined the history of corporations in *Company Man*. I was once again caught up with South Africa: I wrote my biography of Nelson Mandela and took my whole family, including my granddaughter Anna, on holiday to Cape Town, which rounded off my forty-year interest in the country. But it was harder now to take Britain's power nexus so seriously, and as I questioned a new generation about their jobs and power struggles, their answers seemed more glib and predigested. I heard myself replying 'fascinating' or 'how remarkable' while I was thinking 'what rubbish' or 'can you really believe that?', and longed to ask questions which were beyond my remit, like 'has that brought you happiness?' or 'what did your family think?'.

My stage was contracting from a cast of thousands to a more intimate play, while the passage of time speeded up like a tape at the end of a reel. Party conferences, American elections or French governments followed each other with bewildering frequency, faces blurred, and all seemed less significant in fast-forward mode. Each new prime minister and president was hailed as a reformer and innovator before he or she was bogged down in compromises and scandals, while civil servants looked remarkably like their predecessors: as they said in Whitehall, 'only the names have changed'. They all looked less like guided missiles than boats struggling against the wind and the tides of history, and I was less sure of how far they affected human happiness:

> How small, of all that human hearts endure,
> That part which laws or kings can cause or cure![1]

But people became more interesting as individuals in the context of retirement. As a lone writer I had always been semi-detached, aware that

257

most others were enclosed in their corporate castles. Sometimes I felt I was playing the childhood game of sardines, where you have to search through a house for a child, and then join him in a cupboard or wardrobe: I was still alone, wandering outside those cupboards. Whenever I attended a conference, everyone else seemed to have a name tag proclaiming their company or institution, while I had just a name. When I rang up a friend in his office I was constantly asked: 'Who do you represent?' I was tempted to reply: 'The human race,' though I usually said rather apologetically: 'I'm just a friend.' But as friends reached retirement they left their corporate castles and became more rounded people. A few were determined to remain busy-busy, with directorships or committees: 'never been busier in my life . . . must keep myself out of mischief' (what kind of mischief, I wondered, did they have in mind?). But most became more interesting in the context of leisure and reflection.

I found myself, like many others, rediscovering satisfactions that took me back into my childhood, as if my life was beginning to come full circle. 'All true happiness consists in the fulfilment of childhood dreams,' wrote Freud; 'that is why money is so unsatisfying.' I relished travelling in ships and in fast continental trains, which recalled the old Simplon-Orient-Express. I was revived by stormy seas and wide beaches, which brought back childhood holidays by the seaside. I kept remembering lines of Shakespeare that I had learnt as a child. I enveloped myself in our Wiltshire garden, which reminded me of my grandfather's botanical garden in Cambridge. I cultivated ambitious climbing roses like Rambling Rector and Climbing Lady Sylvia, which now seemed more remarkable than climbing people, as they rampaged up pergolas and trees, searching for the sun and the sky. Viewed from the rose garden the world of politics looked very remote, and I kept recalling another image from childhood: the fairground which we visited every year on Hampstead Heath, with its loud organ music, gilded horses, coconut shies, crashing dodgems and mazes of distorting mirrors. As we children were taken home I would look back on the fairground from the hill above: the merry-go-round horses still went up and down and round and round but the music faded and the spell was dissolved.

I became more curious to solve the family mysteries which had hung over my childhood and I wanted to know more about my grandfather, the gypsy scholar whose private life had cast a pall over my parents, and about my aunt Mary, his illegitimate daughter. After she died I tried to piece together the clues to my grandfather's secret escapades with gypsies and his young women assistants, which ended up in a bigamous life in Liverpool. My father had been sadly damaged by the deceptions and humbug, but for me and my family the alternative life was a romantic discovery of a lost world. With Sally I visited the small village in north Wales where my grandfather caroused with gypsies in his bow-topped caravan and compiled his massive Romani dictionary, and we climbed the nearby mountain where the gypsies had scattered his ashes. I wrote *The Scholar Gypsy*, which tried to retrace the hidden Victorian story and to exorcise the family ghosts.

I had tracked down some descendants of my grandfather's gypsy friends and talked with contemporary Romani experts. One of them told me that my grandfather's original caravan was coming up for sale, and I rushed up to Macclesfield to find it decaying in a suburban garden. I quickly bought it, transported it to Wiltshire and had it restored to its glory, installed at the end of our garden as a reminder of childhood dreams, an escape from the modern material world. For my seventy-fifth birthday in 2001, in the garden the most appreciative guest was Anna, then aged six, who delighted in showing guests the caravan and dancing among the roses. I was reminded by my sister Dorothy of a remark by J. B. Priestley which Sally and I had discovered when we compiled *The Oxford Book of Ages*: 'There can be a rewarding relationship between the sevens and the seventy-fives. They are both closer to the world of mythology and magic than all the busier people between those ages.'[2]

It is always impossible to give a real shape to human lives, which are inherently shapeless. Everyone has their own contradictions and discrepancies between aspirations and realities, between Don Quixote and Sancho Panza: they may try to make sense of them, but they seem less sensible to others. It is still harder to give shape to the life of a journalist, who must be driven by curiosities in every direction, at the mercy of unpredictable world events and changes in the marketplace. Why was I driven? What was I looking for that I never found? I could never really join up the intense early experiences in Africa, shared with small groups of friends, with my later investigations into politics, business and power across the world. But

I was fortunate to be able to see the world in terms of friendships with individuals from all kinds of different backgrounds, to have a front seat on many dramas over half a century: to watch the changing relations between North and South, left and right, rich and poor, at first hand, and to see the era of apartheid come and go. I was luckier still to watch it from a secure base, with the same wife and family, which gave a sense of unity to a disparate world.

And I still felt the urge to connect up the fragments, to connect the fire and the rose, which drove me to write this book.

Notes

Chapter 1: Englishness

1. Robert Kaiser, *Cold Winter, Cold War* (New York: Stein & Day, 1974).
2. W. G. Sebald, *On the Natural History of Destruction*, tr. Anthea Bell (London: Penguin, 2004), p. 10. See also Ian Buruma, 'The destruction of Germany', *New York Review of Books*, 21 October 2004.
3. W. B. Yeats, 'An Irish Airman Foresees His Death' (1919).
4. Witter Bynner, 'To a President'.
5. *The Demi-Paradise* (General Film Distributors, 1943).
6. Roy Campbell, 'On Some South African Novelists' (1930).

Chapter 2: Drum

1. Quoted in Pippa Stein and Ruth Jacobson (eds), *Sophiatown Speaks* (Johannesburg: Junction Avenue Press, 1986), p. 56.
2. *Drum*, 23 August 1952.
3. Quoted in Anthony Sampson, *Mandela: The Authorised Biography* (London: HarperCollins, 1999), p.75.

Chapter 3: Observer

1. Michael Astor, *Tribal Feeling* (London: John Murray, 1963), p. 147.
2. Richard Cockett, *David Astor and the* Observer (London: Andre Deutsch, 1991), p. 276.
3. Ibid, p. 275.
4. Office message, *Daily Mail*, 1918. See Reginald Pound and Geoffrey Harmsworth, *Northcliffe* (London: Cassell, 1959).
5. See *The Bedside* Guardian *8: A Selection from the* Manchester Guardian *1958–59* (London: Collins, 1959).
6. 'The appointment of the *Observer*'s editor in 1993, Jonathan Fenby, was sanctioned by the Trust, but did not fully involve it, to the dissatisfaction of some trustees,' explained the official booklet about the Scott Trust. 'The

principal reason given by the Trust's chairman for taking a short-cut on this occasion was that there had to be a swift appointment given the rapidity of the final take-over. However, it is now clearly recognised by the Trust that any future appointment to the *Observer* will conform to established practice.' Philip Schlesinger, *The Scott Trust* (Manchester: Guardian Media Group, 1994).

Chapter 4: Anatomy

1. Peter Hennessy, lecture at Chatham House, 13 March 2002; see also *Secret State: Whitehall and the Cold War* (London: Allen Lane, 2002).
2. W. H. Auden, *Making, Knowing and Judging: An Inaugural Lecture Delivered before the University of Oxford on 11 June 1956* (Oxford: Clarendon Press, 1956), p. 15.

Chapter 5: The other Africa

1. Harold Macmillan, *Pointing the Way 1959–1961* (London: Macmillan, 1972), p. 119.
2. Ibid., p. 122.
3. Ibid., p. 130.
4. Anthony Sampson, *Macmillan: A Study in Ambiguity* (London: Allen Lane, 1967), p. 181.
5. See Alistair Horne, *Macmillan, vol. 2: 1957–1986* (London: Macmillan, 1988) ch. 7.
6. Anthony Sampson, *Mandela: The Authorised Biography* (London: HarperCollins, 1999), p. 132.
7. 3 February 1964.
8. Alastair Niven, 'Reading the World', lecture to the Royal Society of Literature, 2 November 2000.

Chapter 6: 'Only connect'

1. Francis Thompson, 'The Hounds of Heaven'.

Chapter 7: Young Europeans

1. François Duchêne, *Jean Monnet: The First Statesman of Interdependence* (London: W. W. Norton, 1994), p. 393.
2. Jean Monnet, *Memoirs*, tr. Richard Mayne (London: Collins, 1976), p. 496.
3. Ibid., pp. 21–9.
4. Anthony Sampson, *The New Europeans: A Guide to the Workings, Institutions and Character of Contemporary Western Europe* (London: Hodder & Stoughton, 1968), p. 8.
5. Monnet, *Memoirs*, p. 519.

6. Ibid., p. 496.
7. Sampson, *New Europeans*, pp. 11–12.
8. Ibid., p. 49.
9. Ibid., p. 42.
10. Quoted in Larry Siedentop, *Democracy in Europe* (London: Allen Lane, 2000), p. 33.
11. Sampson, *New Europeans*, p. 410.
12. Jean Lacouture, *De Gaulle*, tr. Frances K. Price (London: Hutchinson, 1970), p. 211.
13. Sampson, *New Europeans*, pp. 130, 417.
14. 'The new student battlefield', *Observer*, 3 August 1969.
15. Quoted in Anthony Sampson, *Company Man: The Rise and Fall of Corporate Life* (London: HarperCollins, 1995), p. 129.
16. Monnet, *Memoirs*, p. 490.
17. Sampson, *New Europeans*, p. 180.

Chapter 8: The boss from Hell

1. See Anthony Sampson, *Sovereign State: The Secret History of ITT* (London: Hodder & Stoughton, 1973), p. 244.
2. Quoted in Robert Sobel, *ITT: The Management of Opportunity* (New York: Times, 1982), pp. 335, 334.
3. Sobel, *ITT*, pp. 322, 255.
4. Joel Stein, 'Bosses from Hell', *Time*, 7 December 1998.
5. Henry Kissinger, *Years of Upheaval* (London: Weidenfeld & Nicolson, 1982), pp. 399, 405, 410–11.
6. William Pfaff, 'It's government by and for US corporations and their values', *International Herald Tribune*, 18 January 2001.

Chapter 9: Nixon's America

1. Quoted in *Observer*, 26 May 1974.

Chapter 10: The power of oil

1. Henry Kissinger, *Years of Upheaval* (London: Weidenfeld & Nicolson, 1982), p. 855.
2. Quoted in Anthony Sampson, *The Seven Sisters: The Great Oil Companies and the World They Made* (London: Hodder & Stoughton, 1975), p. 310.
3. Edward Heath, *The Course of My Life: My Autobiography* (London: Hodder & Stoughton, 1998), p. 503. Also private conversation with the author.

Chapter 11: New merchants of death

1. Ronald Kessler, *The Richest Man in the World: The Story of Adnan Khashoggi* (New York: Warner, 1986), published in the UK as *Khashoggi: The Story of the World's Richest Man* (London: Bantam Press, 1986).
2. Quoted in Anthony Sampson, *The Arms Bazaar: The Companies, the Dealers, the Bribes – from Vickers to Lockheed* (London: Hodder & Stoughton, 1977), p. 256.
3. Quoted in Anthony Parsons, *The Pride and the Fall: Iran 1974–1979* (London: Jonathan Cape, 1984), p. 16.
4. Anthony Sampson, *Independent*, 6 April 1991.
5. Samuel Taylor Coleridge, 'Ode to Tranquillity' (1801).
6. Letter from Cummings to le Carré, 28 June 1993.
7. Department for International Development, *Eliminating Global Poverty: Making Globalisation Work for the Poor* (Cm 5006, 2000), paras 78, 83.
8. The military historian Sir Michael Howard has told me that the British Foreign Office is still withholding intelligence secrets concerning the Napoleonic Wars which it fears would offend the French.
9. Sir Samuel Brittan, 'The Ethics and Economics of the Arms Trade', speech at the Royal Society of Arts, 28 March 2001.

Chapter 12: Saving the world?

1. Anthony Sampson, *The Money Lenders* (London: Hodder & Stoughton, 1981), p. 283.
2. Ibid., p. 285.
3. Edward Heath, *The Course of My Life: My Autobiography* (London: Hodder & Stoughton, 1998), p. 608.
4. Katharine Graham, *Personal History* (New York: Alfred A. Knopf, 1997), pp. 587–8.
5. See Heath's account: *The Course of My Life*, p. 608.
6. Ibid.
7. Sampson, *The Money Lenders*, p. 290.
8. Heath, *The Course of My Life*, p. 615.
9. Graham, *Personal History*, p. 588.
10. Quoted in Heath, *The Course of My Life*, p. 611.
11. Ibid., p. 613.

Chapter 13: Breaking the mould

1. Anthony Sampson, *The New Anatomy of Britain* (London: Hodder & Stoughton, 1971), p. 100.
2. Anthony Sampson, *The Changing Anatomy of Britain* (London: Hodder & Stoughton, 1982), p. 41.

3. Hugo Young: *One of Us: A Biography of Margaret Thatcher* (London: Macmillan, 1989), p. 543.
4. Ibid., p. 539.
5. *International Herald Tribune*, 8 February 1978.
6. Quoted in Ivor Crewe and Anthony King, *SDP: The Birth, Life and Death of the Social Democratic Party* (Oxford: Oxford University Press, 1995), p. 68.
7. Ibid., p. 108.
8. Anthony Sampson, 'Why I am a Social Democrat', *New Statesman*, 25 March 1981.
9. Roy Jenkins, *A Life at the Centre* (London: Macmillan, 1991), p. 570.
10. Ibid., p. 545.
11. Ibid., p. 523.
12. Denis Healey, *The Time of My Life* (London: Michael Joseph, 1989), p. 328.
13. Healey, *The Time of My Life*, p. 484.
14. Crewe and King, *SDP*, p. 147.
15. Jenkins, *A Life at the Centre*, p. 567.
16. Ibid., p. 589.
17. Crewe and King, *SDP*, pp. 466–7.
18. Jenkins, *A Life at the Centre*, p. 604.
19. Ibid., 575.

Chapter 14: Money kings

1. David Kynaston, *The City of London, vol. 4: A Club No More 1945–2000* (London: Chatto & Windus, 2000), p. 585.
2. Ibid., p. 740.
3. Ibid., p. 783.
4. Quoted in William Greider, 'The Education of David Stockman', *Atlantic Monthly*, December 1981.
5. Quoted in Anthony Sampson, *The Money Lenders* (London: Hodder & Stoughton, 1981), p. 81.
6. George Soros, *Soros on Soros: Staying Ahead of the Curve* (New York: John Wiley, 1995), p. 174.
7. Ibid., pp. 113, 145.
8. Ibid., p. 114.
9. Ibid., p. 161.
10. Ibid., p. 238.
11. Ibid., p. 239.
12. Ibid., p. 238.
13. See Francis Fukuyama, *The End of History and the Last Man* (New York: Free Press, 1992).
14. See Niall Ferguson, *The Cash Nexus: Money and Power in the Modern World* (New York: Basic, 2001); Robert Skidelsky, 'What Makes the World Go Round?', *New York Review of Books*, 9 August 2001.

Chapter 15: Revolutionaries and capitalists

1. *International Herald Tribune*, 16 November 1977.
2. Anthony Sampson, *Black and Gold: Tycoons, Revolutionaries and Apartheid* (London: Hodder & Stoughton, 1987), pp. 193ff.
3. Letter to Anthony Sampson, 1 July 1986.
4. Sampson, *Black and Gold*, pp. 245–6.
5. Anthony Sampson, *Mandela: The Authorized Biography* (London: HarperCollins, 1999), p. 363.
6. *Sunday Tribune*, 15 June 1989.
7. Statement by M. M. Corbett, 23 June 1989.

Chapter 16: Mandela

1. R. W. Johnson is a journalist and author who consistently attacked the ANC in the *Sunday Times*.
2. *Guardian*, 25 April 1991.
3. Anthony Sampson, *Mandela: The Authorized Biography* (London: HarperCollins, 1999), p. 229.
4. Ibid., p. 495.

Chapter 17: The fire and the rose

1. Samuel Johnson, lines added to Oliver Goldsmith's *The Traveller* (1764).
2. J. B. Priestley, 'Growing Old', *New Statesman*, July 1966.

Bibliography: the works of Anthony Sampson

Drum: A Venture into the New Africa (London: Collins, 1956)

The Treason Cage: The Opposition on Trial in South Africa (London: Heinemann, 1958)

Common Sense about Africa (London: Victor Gollancz, 1960)

Anatomy of Britain (London: Hodder & Stoughton, 1962)

Anatomy of Britain Today (London: Hodder & Stoughton, 1965)

Macmillan: A Study in Ambiguity (London: Allen Lane, 1967)

The New Europeans: A Guide to the Workings, Institutions and Character of Contemporary Western Europe (London: Hodder & Stoughton, 1968)

The New Anatomy of Britain (London: Hodder & Stoughton, 1971)

The Sovereign State: The Secret History of ITT (London: Hodder & Stoughton, 1973)

The Seven Sisters: The Great Oil Companies and the World They Made (London: Hodder & Stoughton, 1975)

The Arms Bazaar: The Companies, the Dealers, the Bribes – from Vickers to Lockheed (London: Hodder & Stoughton, 1977)

The Money Lenders: Bankers in a Dangerous World (London: Hodder & Stoughton, 1981)

The Changing Anatomy of Britain (London: Hodder & Stoughton, 1982; rev. ed. 1983)

Drum: An African Adventure – and Afterwards (London: Hodder & Stoughton, 1983)

Empires of the Sky: The Politics, Contests and Cartels of World Airlines (London: Hodder & Stoughton, 1984)

The Oxford Book of Ages (co-edited with Sally Sampson) (Oxford: Oxford University Press, 1985)

Black and Gold: Tycoons, Revolutionaries and Apartheid (London: Hodder & Stoughton, 1987)

The Midas Touch: Money, People and Power from West to East (London: Hodder & Stoughton/BBC, 1989)

The Arms Bazaar in the Nineties: From Krupp to Saddam (Sevenoaks: Coronet, 1991)

The Essential Anatomy of Britain: Democracy in Crisis (London: Hodder & Stoughton, 1992; rev. ed., Sevenoaks: Coronet, 1993)

Company Man: The Rise and Fall of Corporate Life (London: HarperCollins, 1995)

The Scholar Gypsy: The Quest for a Family Secret (London: John Murray, 1997)

Mandela: The Authorised Biography (London: HarperCollins, 1999)

Who Runs This Place?: The Anatomy of Britain in the 21st Century (London: John Murray, 2004)

Drum: The Making of a Magazine (Johannesburg: Jonathan Ball, 2005)

Index

The abbreviation AS is used for
Anthony Sampson. The suffix *n* after
a page number denotes a note. Books
are by Anthony Sampson unless
otherwise stated.

9/11 168–9, 191, 255

Africa
    armed conflict 180
    independence 106–7, 235–6
    mining companies 135
    'wind of change' speech 94–5
Africa Bureau 89
African National Congress (ANC)
    Christian roots 38–9
    election campaign 243–5, 246
    exile in Zambia 223
    in government 247
    negotiations to end apartheid 226
    resistance campaign 33–4, 91,
        97–8, 99, 222–4
    Sharpeville crisis 97
    treason trials 90–92, 103–5
    unbanned 236–7
Agnelli, Gianni 122, 132, 134
Agnew, Vice-President Spiro 155
aid 191, 216–17
Aldrich, Richard 77
Allende, President Salvador 136,
        142, 145

Alvarez, Al 84
Amin, Idi 103
Amouzegar, Jamshid 165
Anatomy of Britain
    decision to write 69–70
    further editions 204, 257
    and Haile Selassie 99, 101
    and Nelson Mandela 239
    research for 70–83
    success of 83–4, 99, 121
Anderson, Andy 29, 35
Anderson, Bruce 242
Anderson, Robert O. 64–5
Andrews, Eamonn 82
Angola 180
Animal Farm (Orwell) 15
Anna (AS's granddaughter) 257, 259
Arab–Israeli War (1973) 159
Aramco 165
Araskog, Rand 144
The Arms Bazaar 171, 174, 179
arms dealers 172–4, 177–80
arms trade 170–81
Armstrong, Robert 15
Armstrong-Jones, Anthony 61
Arnold, Mary (AS's aunt) 4, 259
Ascherson, Neil 60
Aspin, Les 152
Aspinall, John 241–2
Astor, David
    Africa Bureau 89

and AS 42–3, 46, 70
committees 54
family background 44–5, 50–53
and Nelson Mandela 239
Observer editor 45–50, 54–8,
    59–60, 63–4
and South Africa 224, 228, 231,
    232
Astor, John Jacob 55
Astor, Michael 52–3, 55
Astor, Nancy 51
Auden, W. H. 80
Avramović, Dragoslav 185
Ayer, A. J. 59

Bagehot, Walter 73
Bailey, Jim 15, 17, 20–21, 31–2
Balkans, arms trade 179
Ball, Chris 228
Bank of England 78
banks 78, 79, 211–12
Barber, Lord 228
Barclays Bank 211–12
Baring, Nicholas 72
Barings 211
Barker, Dr Anthony 36–7
Bateman, H. M. 72
Bayley, John 15
Beard, Dita 136
Behan, Brendan 49
Behn, Sosthenes 141
Belgian Congo 95, 108
Belgium 124
Beloff, Nora 47
Benn, Tony 7, 208
Benson, Mary 51, 224, 239
Bentlif, Sally *see* Sampson, Sally
Bernhard, Prince 171
Berridge, Norman 44
Berry, Pamela 83

Betjeman, John 79
Bevan, Sir Timothy 228
Biko, Steve 220
bin Laden, Osama 169
Birley, Robert 85
Bizos, George 104, 235, 246
Black, Conrad 241
Bligh, Tim 75, 93
Bloom, Tony 228
Boateng, Paul 247
Boothby, Robert 74
Botero, Rodrigo 184
Botha, President P. W. 221–2, 224,
    225, 227–8, 232, 233
Boumédienne, President Houari
    182–3
Boyle, Sir Edward 14–15
BP 160, 166
Brademas, John 152
Bradlee, Ben 152–3, 190
Bradshaw, Thornton 65
Brahimi, Lakhdar 245
Brandt, Willy 166, 183–4, 185,
    186–8, 189–90
Brandt commission 183–90
Bridges, Lord 75
Briggs, Asa 71, 81
Britain
    Alliance (SDP–Liberal) 201, 202,
        203–4
    arms trade 175–6, 180–81
    Black Wednesday 217
    civil service 75–7
    class divisions 77, 79–80, 195
    energy crisis 166
    'establishment' 72–3, 79–80,
        81–2, 195
    and Europe 118–19, 120, 121,
        125, 196–7, 215
    financial institutions 78–9, 208–12

and France 264*n*
and Germany 10–12, 117
industry 77, 195–6
Liberal Democrat Party 205
and money 207–8
nuclear war, government plans for 76–7
oil supplies 165–6
science and engineering 80
SDP (Social Democratic Party) 199–206
and South Africa 98–9, 238
South African exiles 86–8
and student rebellions 129
Suez crisis 54–6
under Thatcher 193–6
unemployment 194
and United States 148, 151
British Aerospace 177
Brittan, Sir Samuel 47, 181
Brocklebank-Fowler, Christopher 199
Broe, William 142
Brook, Sir Norman 76, 80
Brooke-Rose, Christine 130
Brown, Leslie 78
Browne, Sir Thomas 109
Bruce, David 152
Buchan, Alistair 48
Buffett, Warren 152
Bush, George 154–5
Bush, George W. 146, 168
business
    Mammon business column 47, 57
    and South Africa 103–4, 216, 225–6, 227–8, 244
    under Thatcher 195, 196
Buthelezi, Chief Mangosuthu 238, 241–2, 243, 244

Butler, Richard Austen (Rab) 54, 75
by-elections 201, 202, 203, 205, 206

Cameron, James 110
Campbell, Duncan 67
Carter, President Jimmy 190
Cassen, Bernard 129–30
Cassen, Robert 186
Cassirer, Reinhold 28, 40, 88
Castro, Fidel 189
Cataclysm (Clark) 192
Cecil, Lord David 15
Central African Federation 94
Central Intelligence Agency (CIA) 142–3, 176
Chamberlain, Neville 90
Chambers, Paul 77
The Changing Anatomy of Britain 204
Chapple, Frank 199
Charles Johnson Memorial Hospital 36–7
Chaskalson, Arthur 104
Chayefsky, Paddy 146
Cherwell, Lord 14
Chile 136–7, 141–3, 145–6
China 177
Church, Frank 141–3, 161
Churchill, Winston 13, 38
CIA (Central Intelligence Agency) 142–3, 176
City of London 208–12
Cixous, Hélène 130
Clark, Alan 181
Clark, Kenneth 15
Clark, William 17, 43, 46–7, 54, 192
Clore, Charles 71
Cobbold, Lord 78
Cockburn, Claude 51
Coetzee, J. M. 252
Coghill, Nevill 15

Cohn-Bendit, Daniel 127–8, 129, 132
Cold War, in Africa 107–8
Cole, John 198
Collins, Norman 81
commodities 182–3, 191
Conference on International Economic Co-operation (CIEC) 183
Congo *see* Belgian Congo
Conservative Party 115, 193–4, 202
Conundrum (Morris) 111
Corbett, M. M. 232
Corcoran, Thomas 156
Crawley, Aidan 61
Crisp, Bob 20
Crosland, Anthony 148
Csaky, Mick 212
Cummings, Sam 177–80
Curwen Press 16

Dadoo, Dr Yusuf 92
Dankworth, Johnny 88
Davie, Michael 21, 49, 58–9
Davison, Ian Hay 210
Dawson, Geoffrey 90
Day, Robin 15, 198
Deighton, Len 81
Delmer, Sefton 110
Denniston, Robin 7, 70, 72, 83, 89
Desta, Alex 101
developing countries *see* Africa; North–South divide
development aid 191, 216–17
Devlin, Lord 72
Dinkins, David 247
Dommergues, Pierre 130
Drake, Sir Eric 166
Drayton, Harley 78–9

Drum
    AS appointed 17, 19–20, 21
    AS leaves 40–41
    censorship 221
    news stories 23–5, 33–4, 35–6, 37
    origins 19–21
    talented black contributors 21–4, 30, 31–2
Dubai 167–8
Dulany, Peggy 231
Duncan, Patrick (Pat) 34, 51, 90
Dutschke, Rudi 126
Dworkin, Ronald 67, 216–17, 232

eastern Europe 216–17
Eden, Sir Anthony 54–5
EEC 118–20, 123–5, 133
Ehrlichman, John 154
elections
    South Africa 243–7
    UK by-elections 201, 202, 203, 205, 206
    UK general elections 203–4, 205, 215
energy crisis 159–60, 186, 190–91
Ethiopia 99, 100–101
Europe
    AS researches *The New Europeans* 121–5
    EEC 118–20, 123–5, 133
    and multinationals 133–4
    oil crisis 166
    student rebellions 126–9, 132–3
European Commission 123–4
European Parliament 124, 133
Evans, Sir Ifor 55

Faber, Michael 183
Fairlie, Henry 72, 83
Falklands War 202

Faure, Edgar 129–30
Feltrinelli, Giangiacomo 122, 132
Fenby, Jonathan 261–2*n*
Fiat 132
financial institutions
British 78–9, 208–12
US 212–13
First, Ruth 38, 92
Fischer, Bram 104, 237
Fleck, Sir Alexander 77
Fleming, Ann 83
Foot, Sir Dingle 54
Foot, Michael 197, 202
Forbes, Malcolm 212–13
Forbes, Steve 213–14
Ford, President Gerald 155, 156
Frame, Sir Alistair 226
France 122, 127–9, 129–31, 189
Frayn, Michael 60
Freud, Clement 5–6
Freud, Lucian 6
Friedman, Milton 165
Frost, David 82
Fukuyama, Francis 218

Gaddafi, Colonel Muammar 164,
254
Gaitskell, Dora 70
Gaitskell, Hugh 71
Galbraith, John Kenneth 257
Gale, John 48–9, 59
Gaulle, Charles de 118, 119, 120,
123, 125, 128
Geneen, Harold 136, 137–8, 142–3,
144, 145, 146
Germany
arms bribes 171
AS researches *The New Europeans*
121
Baader-Meinhof gang 132

and Brandt report 189
post-WWII 9–14, 117–18
slave labour in WWII 135
student rebellions 126–7
Gerrity, Ned 143
Ghana 93, 99–100, 110
Ginwala, Frene 230
Gold Fields 230
Goldsmith, Sir James 214–15, 241
Goodman, Lord 63, 64, 65, 208
Gordimer, Nadine
and apartheid 89, 220, 221,
237
friend of AS 28–9, 40–41, 88
and South African elections 244,
245
as writer 28–9, 88–9
Gosani, Bob 22, 23, 30, 105
Gosling, Nigel 45
Gowrie, Grey 60
Graham, Katharine (Kay) 152–3,
185–6, 190
Graham, Sheila 140
Green, O. M. 55
Greider, William 213
Gulf War 177
Gwigwi, Ben 40

Haffner, Sebastian 45–6
Haile Selassie, Emperor 99, 101
Hailsham, Lord 49, 80
Haldeman, H. R. 154
Hall, Richard 60
Hall School 5–6
Hallstein, Walter 123
Halton, Kathleen (later Tynan) 60
al-Hamad, Abdlatif 67, 162–3, 184,
187
Hamburger, Michael 6
Hamilton, Lyman 144

Hamlyn, Paul 6, 79
Harriman, Averell 152
Harris, Kenneth 49, 64–5
Harrod, Roy 14
Havers, M. R. O. (Lord Chancellor)
  7
Healey, Denis 200, 201, 205
Heath, Edward
  and Brandt commission 185–6,
    187, 188, 189
  and Europe 118–19
  as Prime Minister 166, 193
Heilpern, John 49, 60
Heligoland 12–13
Helman, Ellen 34
Helms, Dick 142
Hennessy, Peter 76–7
Heyns, Professor Johan 242
Hitler, Adolf 6
Hodgson, Godfrey 60
Hodson, Haro 55
Holmes, Sir Peter 230, 231
Holroyd, Michael 109
Home, Earl of 73
Hope, Christopher 252
Horak, John 242–3
Hornby, Dick 72
Howard, Anthony 60, 204
Howard, Sir Michael 264n
Howe, Geoffrey 208, 231–2
Huddleston, Father Trevor
  in England 87–8
  and Nelson Mandela 240, 244
  in South Africa 22, 29–30, 34–5
  in Tanzania 95–6
Hughes, Bob 247
Hughes, Langston 147
Hume, Brit 140
Hurd, Douglas 240
Huxley, Elspeth 89

industry *see* business
Ingrams, Richard 67
Institute of Race Relations 89
insurance sector 78, 209–11
International Energy Agency 163
Iran 162, 175–6, 180, 186
Iran–Iraq War 167, 176, 180, 190
Iraq War 169, 255
Islam
  and fundamentalism 168–9, 191
  in Iran 176
Israel 159, 255
Italy 121–2, 132, 171
ITT 137–46
  bribery of Nixon administration
    139, 143
  and Chile 136–7, 141–3, 145, 146
  management 137–40, 144–5
  reaction to *The Sovereign State*
    143–4
  and WWII 141–2

Jamal, Amir 184
Japan, arms bribes 172
Jay, Antony 75
Jenkins, Peter 151
Jenkins, Roy 53, 197–8, 199–201,
  202–6
Joffe, Joel 104
Johnson, Frank 203
Johnson, Paul 230
Johnson, R. W. 239, 266n
Jones, John 59
Jones, Tristan 44, 56

Kahn, Herman 164
Kathrada, Ahmed 104, 237, 251
Keeler, Christine 51–2, 84–5
Keith, Sir Kenneth 163
Kemsley, Viscount 55, 56

Kennedy, Charles 204
Kennedy, Ludovic 198
Kenya 41, 102–3
Kenyatta, President Jomo 103–4
Khashoggi, Adnan 173–4
Khène, Abderrahman 164
Khomeini, Ayatollah Ruhollah 176
Khrushchev, Nikita 50
Kiesinger, Kurt Georg 126
Kilmartin, Terence (Terry) 45, 50,
    63–4
King of Wartnaby, Lord 244
Kissinger, Henry 142, 145, 152, 153,
    164–5
Klaasen, Thandi 40, 249
Klerk, President F. W. de 233, 236,
    241, 243–4
Knox, Julian 150
Kock, Gerhard de 225
Kodama, Yoshio 172
Kotchian, Carl 172–3
Kraft, Joe 152
Kretzmer, Herbert 21
Kundera, Milan 246
Kuwait 162–3
Kynaston, David 208

Labour Party 196–7, 205–6
Lacouture, Jean 128
Lazard Frères 139
le Carré, John 109, 179
Lebanon 162
Legum, Colin 46
Lekota, Patrick 'Terror' 242–3
Lessing, Doris 88–9
Letelier, Orlando 145
Levin, Bernard 83, 210
Levinson, Jerome (Jerry) 141, 161,
    170
Lewis, C. S. 16

Lewis, Michael 211
Libya 254
Liebling, Joe 147
Limehouse declaration 197
Lloyd's of London 209–11
Lockheed Corporation (Lockheed-
    Martin) 171–2, 173–4, 177
Loder, Robert 67
London, City of London 208–12
Longford, Lord 78
Loudon, John 160
Lowenthal, Richard (Rix) 46
Luthuli, Albert 38, 90, 92, 93, 95, 97
Lynn, Jonathan 75

MacColl, René 110
McCone, John 142
McFadzean, Sir Frank 162, 166
Maclean, Stuart 43
Macleod, Iain 73, 74
Macmillan, Harold
    Africa tour 92–5
    on Americans 151
    and *Anatomy* 71
    and Europe 118
    on power 81
    as prime minister 73–4, 80
    resignation 115
    'wind of change' speech 94–5
McNamara, Robert 183, 192
McWhirter, Norris 59
Magubane, Peter 224, 238
Maharaj, Mac 232
Maimane, Arthur 22, 91
Makins, Virginia 60, 72
Malan, Rian 252
Mandela, Nelson
    ANC government 245, 246,
        247–8, 251–4
    AS biography of 248, 257

and Britain 239–41, 249
early years 248–9
election campaign 243–7
empathy with opponents 250–51
and Israel 255
Macmillan's 'wind of change'
  speech 94
and Margaret Thatcher 240
in prison 249–50
release from prison 237–9
separates from Winnie 241
treason trials 90, 92, 104–5
and UN 254, 255
violent resistance 35–6, 39, 40, 97,
  99
world influence 254–5
Mandela, Winnie 231, 238–9, 241
Masemola, Nat 230
Mason, Philip 89
mass media 82–3
Massingham, Hugh 54, 59–60
Matshikiza, Todd 22, 31, 32, 41, 86,
  91, 105
Mattei, Enrico 160
Mattera, Don 26, 40
Matthews, Joe 91
Maud, Sir John 99
Maund, Commodore 11
Maxwell, Robert 83, 208
Mayanja, Abu 88
Mbeki, Govan 92, 247
Mbeki, Thabo 226, 229, 231, 233–4,
  255
Meade, James 199
Meinhof, Ulrike 126, 132
Mengistu Haile Mariam 101
merchant banks 78, 79, 211–12
Meyer, André 139
The Midas Touch (TV) 212, 213,
  214–18, 256

Middle East, arms trade 170, 180
Milner, Lady 90
Milner, Lord 90
Mintz, Morton 140, 152
Mitford, Nancy 80
Modisane, Bloke 23, 28, 86, 91
Modise, Joe 247
Mohammad Reza Pahlavi, Shah of
  Iran 162, 164, 165, 167, 175–6,
  183
Mohammed, Ismail 232
Molefe, Popo 228
Le Monde 125
money *see* financial institutions;
  wealth
The Money Lenders 215
Monnet, Jean 119–20, 133, 134
Morgan, John 199
Morris, James/Jan 110–11
Moseneke, Dikgang 232
Mothopeng, Zeph 98
Motjuwadi, Stanley 224, 227
Motlana, Nthato (Harrison) 221
Motsisi, Casey 23, 28, 105
Mpahlele, Ezekiel (Zeke) 23, 27,
  30, 86, 237
Mugabe, Robert 246
Muggeridge, Malcolm 73
multinational corporations 133–4,
  135–6, 141–3, 146
Murphy, Sir Leslie 199
Musi, Obed 224
Muslims
  fundamentalism 168–9, 191
  in Iran 176
Mutloatse, Mothobi 224

Naicker, Dr Monty 92
Nakasa, Nat 86, 105
Napoleonic Wars 264*n*

Naught for Your Comfort (Huddleston) 87
Nawiasky, Mechthild 49–50
Netherlands 171, 189
Neville, Jill 117
The New Europeans 121, 125, 129
new international economic order 182–3
Nigeria 93
The Night Manager (le Carré) 179
9/11 168–9, 191, 255
Nixon, President Richard 153–6
Nkosi, Alpheus 40
Nkrumah, President Kwame 93, 99–100
Nokwe, Duma 97
North–South: A Programme for Survival 188, 189–90
North–South divide 183, 190–92
  Brandt commission 183–90
Nthite, Peter 92
Nxumalo, Henry 21, 22, 23, 91
Nyerere, Julius 102, 190

Obank, Kenneth 46, 50
Obote, Milton 103
O'Brien, Conor Cruise 65
O'Brien, Edna 130
Observer
  AS career with 43–4, 46–7, 60, 85
  AS edits the magazine 62–3
  AS leaves 66, 204
  AS's overseas assignments 55, 147, 148–57
  AS's Pendennis column 61–2
  competitors 56–7, 62–3
  journalists 45–6, 47–50, 58–60, 67
  Suez crisis 54–6
  weekly routine 46–7
O'Donovan, Patrick 45, 48

Ohlin, Göran 185
oil
  as commodity 182, 185
  oil companies 159–62, 165–7
  oil crisis 164–6, 167–8
  as political weapon 190
  producers 159, 161–5, 167–9
  supplies 168–9
  see also OPEC
Okello, John 102
On the Natural History of Destruction (Sebald) 10
O'Neill, Sir Con 61
OPEC (Organization of the Petroleum Exporting Countries) 159, 162, 163–5, 183
Oppenheimer, Harry 34, 91, 220–21, 225–6
Orwell, George 15
Oubaas (teacher) 30
Owen, David
  and SDP 197–8, 200–201, 202–3, 204–5
  and South Africa 220
The Oxford Book of Ages 259

Page, Bruce 66
Pahad, Aziz 247
Pakendorf, Harald 228
Pakenham, Thomas 60
Palme, Olof 166, 184, 187
Pan Africanist Congress 34, 97
Parsons, Sir Anthony 175–6, 233
Paton, Alan 20, 27, 93
Peterson, Pete 187
Pfaff, William 146
Phillips, James 86
Pinochet, President Augusto 145–6
The Pirate (Robbins) 174
Pitt, Harry 149

Powell, Charles 194–5, 233, 240
Pringle, John 46
Pritchett, Victor 109
Private Eye 67
Profumo, John 51–2, 84
Proops, Marjorie 199

Qoboza, Percy 227
Quinton, Tony 15

Raisaka (AS's friend) 246
Ramaphosa, Cyril 227–8
Ramphal, Sonny 185, 187
Rathebe, Dolly 40, 249
raw materials 182–3, 191
Raynes, Father Raymond 87–8
Reagan, President Ronald 190, 222
Rees-Mogg, William 15, 198
religious fundamentalism 168–9, 191
Relly, Gavin 226
Renwick, Robin 232–3, 237–8, 240
Rey, Jean 124
Rhodesia 93–4
Richard Clay printing works 16
Robbins, Harold 174
Robinson, John 7
Robson, Wallace 15
Rockefeller Brothers Fund 231
Rodgers, William (Bill) 197–8, 201,
    204, 205
Rohatyn, Felix 139
Rosholt, Mike 225
Rothschild, Evelyn de 228
Rothschild, Jacob 72
Rowland, Tiny 65–6, 68, 107
Russell, Sir John 100–101
Russia 179, 216, 218
Rwanda 103

S. G. Warburg 79, 211

Sachs, Albie 232
Saddam Hussein 176, 180–81, 183
Sainsbury, David 199, 226
Salomons 218
Sampson, Anthony
    CAREER
    Brandt commission 183–4, 186,
        187, 189
    Daily Mail 43
    Drum 17, 19–20, 20–25, 40–41
    Lloyd's name 209–10, 211
    Mammon business column 47, 57
    Le Monde 125
    New Statesman 66–7, 199
    Observer see Observer
    printer 16
    Royal Navy 8–14
    'Sampson Letter' 67–8
    Scott Trust 68
    Die Zeit 118
    CHARACTERISTICS
    desire to write 4, 256–7
    enjoys leisure in retirement 258
    favourite childhood authors 5
    sense of alienation 15, 109–10,
        111
    and social class 80
    EDUCATION
    Oxford University 14–16
    schooling 5–8
    studies African history 89–90
    FAMILY
    childhood 1–4
    children 115
    family life 115, 121
    grandfather 3–4, 259
    meets and marries Sally 115
    see also names of family members
    HEALTH
    depression 15, 116

heart attack 256
LSD treatment 112–15
POLITICS
and Labour 196–7
and SDP 197–9, 203
and Thatcher's Britain 196
and United States 157–8
PUBLICATIONS
Anatomy of Britain 83–4
see also Anatomy of Britain
The Arms Bazaar 171, 174, 179
The Changing Anatomy of Britain 204
Company Man 257
Drum see Drum
The Essential Anatomy of Britain 257
Mandela 248–51, 257
The Money Lenders 215
The New Europeans 121–5, 129
The Oxford Book of Ages 259
The Scholar Gypsy 259
The Seven Sisters 161–3, 166–7
The Sovereign State 137–44
The Treason Cage 38, 92
SOUTH AFRICA
ANC preparations for power 243
and apartheid 89, 221, 224,
    225–6, 236–40
banned from South Africa 228,
    236
Charles Johnson Memorial
    Hospital 36–7
elections 244–7
leaves South Africa 40–42
moves to Johannesburg 20
nationalism 38–9
and Nelson Mandela 35–6,
    236–9, 248, 257
sails to South Africa 17–19
Sharpeville crisis 97–8
township life 26–8, 30–31, 35

treason trials 90–92, 103–5
see also Drum
TRAVEL ABROAD
Africa 92–5, 99–103
Ethiopia 99, 100–101
Ghana 99–100
Suez crisis 55
visits Trevor Huddleston in
    Tanzania 95–6
Europe 121–5, 129
Germany 9–14, 121
IBM lecture in Paris 134
university in Vincennes 129–31
United States
holidays 155–6, 157
New York 147–8, 212–13
Washington 149–56
TV SERIES
The Midas Touch 212, 213, 214–18,
    256
Sampson, Dorothy (sister) 3, 259
Sampson, John (brother) 3
Sampson, John (grandfather) 3–4, 25
Sampson, Katie (daughter) 115, 121,
    235, 240
Sampson, Michael (father) 2–3, 17
Sampson, Paul (son) 115
Sampson, Phyllis (mother) 1, 2, 17
Sampson, Sally (née Bentlif, AS's
    wife)
and AS's heart attack 256
and Barbara Wootton 70
children 115
in Europe 121, 122
holidays in United States 155–6,
    157
meets and marries AS 115
The Oxford Book of Ages 259
and South Africa 228–9, 236–7,
    244–7, 248

UK politics 197, 205
in Wales 259
in Washington 148–9, 153
Sarbanes, Paul 152
Saudi Arabia 163, 165, 169, 173–5, 177
Sauer, Paul 98
Savile, Jimmy 82
Schadeberg, Jürgen 21–2
Schmidt, Helmut 189
The Scholar Gypsy 259
Scott, Michael 89
Scott Trust 68, 261–2*n*
SDP (Social Democratic Party) 199–206
Sebald, W. G. 10
Sekoto, Gerard 86
September 11 2001 atrocity 168–9, 191, 255
'Seven Sisters' 160
The Seven Sisters 166–7
see also oil
Seward, Sir Albert (grandfather) 1
Shah of Iran (Mohammad Reza Pahlavi) 162, 164, 165, 167, 175–6, 183
Shanahan, Eileen 140, 154
Sharpeville 97–8, 222
Shell 132–3, 160, 166, 230
Shonfield, Andrew 47
Sibeko, David 91–2
Silverlight, John 49
Simon, William 164–5
Simon, Youtta 181
Sirica, Judge John 153
Sissons, Michael 60, 70, 110, 200
Sisulu, Walter 36, 98, 104, 237, 247
Skinner, Dennis 202
Slabbert, Frederik van Zyl 229
Slovo, Joe 38, 229, 247

Smith, Colin 59
Smith, Solly 229
Snow, C. P. 76
Sobel, Robert 144
Social Democratic Party (SDP) 199–206
Sommer, Dr (German teacher) 9–10
Sommer, Ted 117
Sophiatown 26–7, 39–40, 244
Soros, George 81, 215–18, 228, 234
Soros, Susan 215
South Africa
apartheid
discredited 242
negotiations to end 223–6, 228–34, 243
repression 30–33, 103–6, 220, 221, 222, 243
resistance to 98, 99, 220–24
state of emergency 224, 227
arms trade 179
Black Consciousness 220, 223
and Britain 37–8
business and 103–4, 216, 225–6, 227–8, 244
and communism 38–9, 106, 229
Defiance Campaign 33–4, 38
elections 243–7
exiles in London 86–9
history 89–90
Sharpeville crisis 97–8, 222
Sophiatown 26–7, 39–40, 244
Soweto 21, 220, 224
townships 21, 26–30, 39–40, 220, 221, 244
transition 251–4
treason trials 90–92, 103–5
Truth and Reconciliation Commission 246

United Democratic Front (UDF)
222

white population 25–6, 34–5, 91,
251–2

Zulu nationalism 241–2, 244

see also African National Congress
(ANC); Mandela, Nelson

The Sovereign State 143–4

Soweto 21, 220, 224

Sparrow, John 59

Spender, Stephen 53

Spengler, Major 40

Spock, Dr Benjamin 49

Spooner, Sir James 72, 226

Steer, Philip Wilson 2

Stengel, Richard 251

Stephens, Bob 47

Stephenson, Hugh 67

Stern, Larry 140, 152

Stewart, Jim 15

Stockman, David 213

Stone, Izzy 141

Strachey, John 58

Strange, Susan 47, 49

Strauss, Franz Josef 171

student rebellions 126–9

Suez crisis 54–6

Sunday Times 55, 56, 57

Surtee, Yusuf 239

Suzman, Helen 34, 240–41

Suzman, Janet 199

Sweden 129, 132

Sylvester, David 59

Taiwan 177

Tambo, Adelaide 240, 241, 247

Tambo, Oliver
AS opinion of 36, 222
campaign against apartheid
222–4, 226, 228–9, 231–4

Christian belief 38–9

Tanzania 96–7, 102

Taylor, Bob 196–7

television
commercial 78–9, 81
The Midas Touch 212, 213, 214–18,
256

terrorism 168–9, 191, 192

Thatcher, Margaret
British institutions 193–5
and Falklands War 202
and foreign aid 189, 190, 216
and Nelson Mandela 240
and South Africa 222, 232–3
and unemployment 194

Themba, Can
disillusionment and death 32, 98,
105
Drum journalist 22–3, 26, 30, 39,
40
unbanned 237

Thomas, Franklin 232

Thompson, Francis 111

Thompson, John 60

Thomson, Roy 57

Thorpe, Jeremy 15

Thurber, James 147

Tickell, C. C. C. (Sir Crispin) 7

Tolkien, Professor J. R. R. 15, 16

Toynbee, Philip 45, 47–8, 147

Toynbee, Polly 151, 199, 205

The Treason Cage 38, 92

Trelford, Donald 63, 66

Trevor-Roper, Hugh 14, 55, 83,
154

Trilling, Lionel and Diana 149

Truman, President Harry 13

Tutu, Archbishop Desmond 39, 227,
247

Tynan, Kenneth 59, 60

Uganda 103
Unilever 135
United Kingdom *see* Britain
United Nations (UN)
  arms register 177
  Conference on Trade and
    Development (UNCTAD) 182,
    186
  Mandela's view of 254–5
United States
  aerospace industry 170, 171–2
  arms trade 171–2, 176–7
  AS compares with Europe 157–8
  and Brandt report 189–90
  and Britain 151
  business influence on government
    policy 146
  and Chile 145
  financial institutions 212–13
  Foreign Corrupt Practices Act
    (1977) 177
  foreign policy 158, 161, 175
  ITT and Nixon administration
    139, 143
  and Libya 254
  and Middle East 175
  New York 147–8, 212–13
  and oil 164–5, 168–9
  Senate investigations 141–3, 161,
    170
  and South Africa 220
  Washington 149–56
  Washington Post 152–3
  Watergate 152–6
Urquhart, Clara 228

van der Post, Laurens 241
Venables, Dr 111–14, 116
Verwoerd, Dr Hendrik 92, 93,
  98

Vidler, Charles 44
Vietnam War 152, 156
Voice 221
Vorster, John 221

Wain, John 130
Waite, Terry 227
Warburg, Siegmund 79
wars *see* Cold War; Falklands War;
    Arab–Israeli War; Gulf War;
    Iran–Iraq War; Napoleonic
    Wars; Vietnam War; World
    War II
Washington Post 152–3
Watergate 152–6
Wathen, G. A. 5
Waugh, Evelyn 97
wealth 207–8, 212–18
Weinstock, Lord 244
Welensky, Sir Roy 94
Westminster School 6–8
Wheen, Francis 67
Whitehorn, Katharine 49
Williams, Shirley 72, 197–8, 200,
    201–2, 204
Wilson, Harold 82, 121, 125
Wolff, Karl-Dietrich 126
Woodward, Bob 152
Woody (AS's friend) 91
Woolfson, Isaac 71
Wootton, Barbara (Baroness
    Wootton of Abinger) 70, 75
A World of Strangers (Gordimer) 29
World War II 6–8, 135, 141–2
Worsthorne, Peregrine 108, 246
Wriston, Walter 213
Wyndham, John 94

Yaker, Layachi 184
Yamani, Sheikh Ahmed 163, 169

Yates, Anne 231
Yates, Ivan 71
Yeltsin, Boris 216–17
Yes, Minister 75
Young, Gavin 59
Young, Hugo 68
Young, Michael (Gold Fields adviser) 226, 230
Young, Michael (sociologist) 79, 84
Young, Pierre 7

Zaharoff, Basil 174
Zahedi, Ardeshir 150
Zaire 95
    see also Belgian Congo
Zambia 223
Zanzibar 101–2
Die Zeit 118
Zhou Enlai 99
Zimbabwe 246
Zuma, Jacob 232